*Hybrid Organizations and the*

Global Organizations and the Third Sector

# Hybrid Organizations and the Third Sector

## Challenges for Practice, Theory and Policy

Edited by
David Billis

First published 2010 by
PALGRAVE MACMILLAN

Palgrave Macmillan in the UK is an imprint of Macmillan Publishers Limited,
registered in England, company number 785998, of Houndmills, Basingstoke,
Hampshire RG21 6XS.

Palgrave Macmillan in the US is a division of St Martin's Press LLC,
175 Fifth Avenue, New York, NY 10010.

Palgrave Macmillan is the global academic imprint of the above companies
and has companies and representatives throughout the world.

Palgrave® and Macmillan® are registered trademarks in the United States,
the United Kingdom, Europe and other countries.

ISBN-13: 978–0–230–23463–5 hardback
ISBN-13: 978–0–230–23464–2 paperback

This book is printed on paper suitable for recycling and made from fully
managed and sustained forest sources. Logging, pulping and manufacturing
processes are expected to conform to the environmental regulations of the
country of origin.

A catalogue record for this book is available from the British Library.

A catalog record for this book is available from the Library of Congress.

10   9   8   7   6   5   4   3   2   1
19   18   17   16   15   14   13   12   11   10

Printed in China

*For Jacquie*

# Contents

# List of Figure and Tables

**Figure**

**Tables**

# Acknowledgements

The idea for this book came about for two reasons. The first was to mark 30 years of uninterrupted history of the first research and teaching university-based initiative devoted to what is now called the 'third sector'. Originally called 'PORTVAC' (Programme of Research and Training in Voluntary Action) at Brunel University, it transferred to the London School of Economics (LSE) as the Centre for Voluntary Organisation (CVO) and most recently renamed again as the Centre for Civil Society.

The second impetus arose from my long-standing research interest in hybrid organizations. Previous books, celebrating the 15th and 20th anniversaries of the Centre, had focused on voluntary organizations. Since then the greatly increased role of hybrids in the third sector (and elsewhere) led me to believe that they would provide an appropriate topic for a 30th anniversary book.

I was delighted to find many others in the field who shared this belief. My first and most important thanks therefore are to those colleagues who have joined me in this venture. They have collaborated with enthusiasm and professionalism and I have benefited greatly from their comments and experience.

From this group, I would like to single out the contribution of Colin Rochester. He has provided magnificent support not only in providing assistance in the editing of the book, but also as a colleague and friend offering wise counsel on numerous occasions.

Warm thanks are also due to David Lewis, another colleague and friend from the CVO period who, despite heavy pressure of work, was always prepared to offer unstinting help.

Beyond this, having being in the business a long time, I have accrued innumerable debts to colleagues, former students and many thousands working in the third sector, and indeed the public and private sectors, with whom I have collaborated in research and consultancy during this period. From all these individuals and groups I have learnt much, and offer my gratitude. Special thanks also to Catherine Gray from Palgrave Macmillan for her help and support in this project and to the anonymous reviewers for their valuable comments and suggestions.

Finally, my most important debt is to my dear wife Jacquie who continues to support my academic endeavours, and tolerates in the house a lifelong fan of the local football team.

**David Billis**

# List of Abbreviations

| | |
|---|---|
| ACVAR | Aston Centre for Voluntary Action Research |
| ARNOVA | Association for Research on Nonprofit Organization and Voluntary Action |
| ARVAC | Association for Research in the Voluntary and Community Sector |
| AVAS | Association of Voluntary Action Scholars |
| BERR | Department for Business, Enterprise and Regulatory Reform |
| BME | Black and Minority Ethnic |
| CEO | Chief Executive Officer |
| CIC | Community Interest Company |
| CLG | Company Limited by Guarantee |
| CVO | Centre for Voluntary Organisation |
| DCLG | Department for Communities and Local Government |
| DFID | Department for International Development |
| DoE | Department of the Environment |
| DTI | Department of Trade and Industry |
| DWP | Department for Work and Pensions |
| FTE | Full-Time Equivalent |
| HA | Housing Association |
| HLC | Healthy Living Centre |
| HMT | Her Majesty's Treasury |
| ICA | International Co-operative Alliance |
| I&DeA | Improvement and Development Agency for Local Government |
| IVAR | Institute for Voluntary Action Research |
| IVR | Institute for Volunteering Research |
| JVAR | *Journal of Voluntary Action Research* |
| LSE | London School of Economics |
| LT | Leisure Trust |

| | |
|---|---|
| NCVO | National Council for Voluntary Organisations |
| NED | Non-Executive Director |
| NGO | Non-Governmental Organization |
| NHF | National Housing Federation |
| NHS | National Health Service |
| NOF | New Opportunities Fund |
| NPM | New Public Management |
| OTS | Office of the Third Sector |
| PCS | Public and Commercial Services Union |
| PCT | Primary Care Trust |
| PONPO | Program on NonProfit Organizations |
| PORTVAC | Programme of Research and Training in Voluntary Action |
| SEC | Social Enterprise Coalition |
| TP | Tomorrow's People |
| TSO | Third Sector Organization |
| UWE | University of the West of England |

# Notes on the Contributors

## The Editor

**David Billis** is Reader Emeritus at the London School of Economics (LSE). In 1978, he founded PORTVAC, the first university-based programme working with voluntary organizations. In 1987, he became Director of the LSE Centre for Voluntary Organisation which extended the work of PORT-VAC. The Centre was later renamed the Centre for Civil Society. He co-founded the journal *Nonprofit Management and Leadership*. He is the only non-American to receive the Distinguished Lifetime Achievement Award from Association for Research on Nonprofit Organization and Voluntary Action (ARNOVA), the leading international third sector research association. Recent posts include Visiting Professor at Imperial College. He has extensive research and consultancy experience in the public, private and third sector and has published widely in these areas. His books include *Organisational Design*, *Welfare Bureaucracies* and *Organising Public and Voluntary Agencies*.

## Contributors

**Mike Aiken** is Head of Research at the Institute for Voluntary Action Research (IVAR) in London where his recent work included an evidence review on the community control of assets and the advocacy and representation roles of multipurpose community organizations. As a Visiting Research Fellow at the Open University, he researched European social enterprises, work integration projects and the reproduction of organizational values. He previously worked for 20 years in the third sector and remains active in Latin American issues.

NOTES ON THE CONTRIBUTORS

**Ben Cairns** is the Director and co-founder of the IVAR and a Visiting Fellow of Birkbeck College, University of London. He has almost 25 years' experience of working in and around the third sector: as a volunteer, manager, trustee, student and researcher. Ben has published widely with colleagues in national and international academic journals. His recent research work at IVAR has focused on organizational development and change, inter-organizational relationships and high engagement funding.

**Chris Cornforth** is Professor of Organisational Governance and Management at the Open University. His research focuses on the governance of third sector organizations (TSOs). He was part of a team commissioned by government to develop a strategy for improving the quality of governance in the third sector, and served on a steering group overseeing the development of national occupational standards for board members. His publications include *The Governance of Public and Nonprofit Organizations: What Do Boards Do?* (Ed.), London: Routledge, 2003.

**Angela Ellis Paine** is Director of the Institute for Volunteering Research (IVR). With over 10 years of research experience into volunteering and participation, Angela has undertaken numerous research projects on different aspects of volunteering and been involved in evaluations of national and international volunteering initiatives. Along with Colin Rochester and Steven Howlett, she is co-author of *Volunteering and Society in the 21st Century*, (2009). She is co-author of *Helping Out: A National Survey of Volunteering and Charitable Giving* (2007).

**Margaret Harris** is Emeritus Professor, Aston University; Visiting Professor at Birkbeck College, University of London; and Academic Adviser to the IVAR. She was formerly Assistant Director of the LSE's Centre for Voluntary Organisation and also worked in local government and the voluntary sector. She is the author of *Organising God's Work: Challenges for Churches and Synagogues* (1998) and has published widely on voluntary sector management and governance, faith-based organizations, grass-roots bridge-building and the public policy context of third sector action.

**Joanna Howard** is a research fellow at Cities Research Centre at the University of the West of England (UWE). Her work focuses on the third sector, local governance and citizen participation. She has carried out research in Central America and Europe as well as within the UK. Currently she is involved in research into building the capacity of the third sector. She has published journal articles and book chapters on citizen participation, neighbourhood and urban governance.

**Romayne Hutchison** is a Senior Research Associate at the Institute for Voluntary Action Research. She has worked as a freelance researcher, trainer and consultant since 1993, having previously held posts in the third sector and in a local authority. She has an MSc in Voluntary Sector Organisation from the LSE. She has worked on numerous IVAR research projects relating to organizational mergers, partnerships and collaborations, and is particularly interested in inter-organizational relationships, governance and volunteering.

**David Lewis** is Professor of Social Policy and Development at the London School of Economics and Political Science. A social anthropologist by background, he has specialised in research on development issues with a particular focus on South Asia. His most recent book is *Non-Governmental Organisations and Development* (2009, co-written with Nazneen Kanji. He has worked as a consultant for a range of agencies, including the Department for International Development, Oxfam and the Bangladesh Rural Advancement Committee.

**David Mullins** is Professor of Housing Policy in the Centre for Urban and Regional Studies and the Third Sector Research Centre at the University of Birmingham. He is co-author of *Housing Policy in the UK* with Alan Murie (2006) and *After Council Housing* with Hal Pawson (2010, May). In 2007, he was Visiting Professor at Delft University of Technology and is involved in comparative research on third sector housing organizations, network governance and urban regeneration in the Netherlands and England.

**Nick Ockenden** has worked at IVR since 2005 and is Head of Research. He has led a wide variety of research projects but has a particular interest in volunteering within smaller organizations; he led on IVR's work exploring the impact of public policy on volunteering within community-based organizations and a further piece examining leadership in groups with no paid staff. Nick's most recent areas of work include a project exploring volunteering and employability, and an evaluation investigating the impact of volunteering on young offenders.

**Hal Pawson** is a Professorial Fellow at the School of the Built Environment, Heriot-Watt University, Edinburgh. Hal's special interests are in housing and urban policy, especially homelessness, social housing management and area regeneration. As well as leading numerous national research studies for central government departments and other bodies, Hal has published widely in academic journals. He is also a member of expert panels for both the Westminster government and the Australian Housing & Urban Research Institute.

**Colin Rochester** has recently retired as Director of the Centre for the Study of Voluntary and Community Action at Roehampton University. He has more than 40 years' experience of working in and with TSOs. His publications include *Juggling on a Unicycle: A Handbook for Small Voluntary Organizations* (1999); (with Margaret Harris) *Voluntary Organisations and Social Policy in Britain* (2001); and (with Angela Ellis Paine and Steven Howlett) *Volunteering and Society in the 21st Century* (2009, October).

**Roger Spear** is Chair of the Co-operatives Research Unit, Member of the Ciriec Scientific Committee and founder member and vice-president of EMES research network on social enterprise. He teaches organizational systems and research methods at the Open University. His most recent projects are as follows: Governance and Social Enterprise; an EC Peer Review of the social economy in Belgium; and an OECD project on the social economy in Korea. He is visiting professor at Roskilde University, Copenhagen, Denmark, teaching on a Masters in Social Entrepreneurship.

**Joanna Stuart** is Head of Research at IVR. She has carried out a wide range of research projects and evaluations focused on volunteering, participation and community action. Her recent research includes studies exploring volunteer management issues and the impact of volunteering on individuals, organizations and communities. She works closely with voluntary and community groups in their work to evaluate their volunteering programmes. Joanna is also an editorial reviewer of the *International Journal of Volunteer Administration* (IJOVA).

**Marilyn Taylor** is Professor Emeritus at the University of the West of England (UWE). Formerly a researcher and policy analyst in the third sector, she joined academia in 1990 and has worked at the universities of Bristol and Brighton as well as UWE. She has written widely for policy practice and academic audiences over many years, with research interests spanning state–third sector relations, citizen participation, service user involvement and neighbourhood renewal. She is the author of Public Policy in the Community (Palgrave Macmillan, 2003).

**Malcolm Torry** has worked in the Church of England's full-time ministry for nearly 30 years and is currently Team Rector of the Parish of East Greenwich and co-ordinating chaplain for the Greenwich Peninsula Chaplaincy. He is the author of *Managing God's Business: Religious and Faith-based Organizations and their Management* (Ashgate, 2005) and, with Margaret Harris, of *Managing Religious and Faith-based Organisations: A Guide to the Literature* (Aston Business School, 2000).

# PART I

## Introduction

# 1 From welfare bureaucracies to welfare hybrids

## David Billis

This book is about the growing and increasingly significant role of 'hybrid organizations' in the 'third sector'. Both these terms will be explored in detail later in the book, but they demand some immediate working definitions in order to clarify the main focus and themes of the book.

First, hybrid organizations. What has often been called the 'blurring' of the boundaries of the public, private and third sector has long been recognized in the literature. This chapter argues that we need to move beyond that vague description and that practice, policy and theory now have an urgent need for a tougher conceptual approach to the phenomenon. In response to that need a tentative theory of hybrid organizations is offered in Chapter 3 which discusses in detail the nature of their accountability and ownership. However, without pre-empting that discussion, a few preliminary words may help set the scene.

A first step might be to consider them as organizations that possess 'significant' characteristics of more than one sector (public, private and third). We might think of 'partially nationalised banks', 'social enterprises' and Fannie Mae and Freddie Mac as examples of the genre. Taking one step beyond this and again for purposes of early clarification, I shall argue that organizations have 'roots' and have primary adherence to the distinctive principles – the 'rules of the game' – of just one sector. Hybridity is not therefore just any mixture of features from different sectors, but according to this view, is about fundamental and distinctly different governance and operational principles in each sector.

Next, the third sector. Again, by way of an initial entry point into an area, we shall adopt a relaxed attitude to the boundary of a sector tellingly described as a 'loose and baggy monster' (Kendall and Knapp, 1995). The task of understanding the voluntary, nonprofit, NGO sector, and possibly taming the monster, will be an important underlying theme of the book. However, in order to manage what is clearly a vast territory, we have focused on third sector organizations (TSOs), mainly in the UK, which are primarily concerned with 'welfare' as generally understood in the social policy literature.

Even in the comparatively short period between the original idea for the book and its submission, its subject matter has become uncomfortably topical. 'Welfare' was always important but in the Western democracies it has for several decades been at a comfortable distance from the main concerns of the majority. The global recession has changed all that.

In the UK, the same economic disaster has led the government to emphasise even more the potential role of TSOs in the economy (Cabinet Office, 2009). A significant number of these TSOs will be 'hybrids': And, for the same economic reasons, hybrid organizations in the other sectors have also risen to prominence but for very different, and negative, reasons.

Hybrids have moved from being a minority scholarly interest to centre stage in mainstream political discourse. They are complex organizations and one of the underlying themes of the book is the challenge to increase our understanding in the belief that this will diminish the widespread phenomenon of stumbling into change.

The task of this opening chapter is to provide an introductory background, to set out the main themes of the book, to raise some initial issues and challenges and to provide a brief guide to the other chapters. It consists of four sections.

The chapter opens with a brief and selective gaze over a period of about 40 years, from the dominance in UK public policy of the traditional welfare bureaucracy to the rise of what we might call the 'welfare hybrid'. Our focus is on the third sector and the message is that 'blurring' is an inadequate way to describe the current complex institutional environment. The second section notes the way in which what are regarded as the distinctive features of the third sector are held in high regard by government and highlights the debate within the sector about its future. This is followed by a discussion which suggests that hybrids are ubiquitous and makes a link between them and current events. The chapter concludes with a more detailed explanation of the territory and issues to be explored in the book and a brief introduction to the chapters that follow.

## Beyond blurring in social policy

Forty years ago the study of UK social policy was more straightforward. It was an era when social services were mainly both funded and delivered by large public sector organizations. These governmental welfare bureaucracies (Billis, 1984) were the dominant organizational form and the Seebohm Report reflected the pinnacle of the policy zeitgeist. It proposed new social services departments whose aim was no less than 'to meet all the social needs of the family or individuals together and as a whole' (Seebohm, 1968, p. 160). Today, it is difficult to comprehend such optimism.

What was generally called the 'voluntary sector' had a modest place in welfare provision, public policy and academic study. Whilst innumerable numbers of people benefited from its presence, it played a minor role in the formal political and academic arenas. The private sector was scarcely visible in the UK social policy debates. In the US, with its different welfare structure and its large educational system, what is generally referred to there as the nonprofit sector, had begun to develop a more prominent academic role. The Association of Voluntary Action Scholars (AVAS) was founded in 1971, and David Horton Smith founded the *Journal of Voluntary Action Research* (JVAR) in 1972. The following year Etzioni (1973) advocated the identification of a 'third sector' as an alternative to the public and private sectors 'to serve our needs' and which 'may well be the most important alternative for the next few decades' (p. 315).

Reel forward some 10 years and the old straightforward world had begun to disappear. Resources became increasingly scarce. Public bureaucracies were heavily criticised. In the UK the Seebohm approach was in decline and was being replaced by the 'mixed economy' (Webb and Wistow, 1982) of statutory, voluntary, private and informal provision. One of the key writers of the time, Adrian Webb, had already begun to analyse what he called the collapse of 'the pure doctrine of state welfare' (Webb, 1979).

1978 turned out to be a busy year for the voluntary and nonprofit sectors. The Wolfenden Report on 'the future of voluntary organisations' appeared and the voluntary sector moved closer to centre stage (Wolfenden, 1978). The Association for Research in the Voluntary and Community Sector (ARVAC) was established and the world's first postgraduate research and teaching initiative the Programme of Research and Training in Voluntary Action (PORTVAC) was launched at Brunel University. Shortly after, the popular Open University voluntary sector management programme was established and it slowly became respectable for the voluntary sector to be discussed in academic circles. The year 1978 also saw the establishment in the US of the Program on NonProfit Organizations (PONPO) at Yale University to foster interdisciplinary research aimed at developing an understanding of nonprofit organizations and their role in economic and political life.

Since then we have grown familiar with the increasing adoption of the norm and methods of the market by both the public and third sectors. A bundle of approaches collectively known as 'The New Public Management' (NPM) became influential in the 1980s and 1990s in the provision of public services (see the following chapter by Margaret Harris). Contracting and payment for services has long been a familiar part of the welfare scene in the US (Kramer and Terrell, 1984; Demone and Gibelman, 1989; Smith and Lipsky, 1993) and in Europe (Kramer, 1993; Lewis, 1999; Alcock et al., 2004).

There were also changes in the study of the third sector. PORTVAC moved to the London School of Economics (LSE) in 1988, changed its name to the Centre for Voluntary Organization (CVO) and yet again to the Centre for Civil Society. A series of seminars held at the CVO between 1993 and 1995 led to the establishment of the Voluntary Sector Studies Network (VSSN) which was to play an increasingly important research role. At the time of writing, a new journal (*The Voluntary Sector Review*) is due to be published.

Around the world, other universities had established their own centres. The Mandel Center for nonprofit organizations in Case Western Reserve University was founded in 1983. It provided a home and also the founding editor (Dennis Young) for *Nonprofit Management and Leadership*, which started publication in 1990 and was co-sponsored with the CVO. In 1991, there were sufficient academic research and education centres to establish the Nonprofit Academic Centers Council and by 2009, it listed 45 member centres.

In 1992, the International Society for Third-Sector Research and its associated journal *Voluntas* further strengthened the field of study. By now a stream of books was leaving the printing presses and a new generation of third sector scholars emerged. The private sector spotted the developments and an army of consultants and trainers offered their services to the sector. For better or worse, third sector staff – in common with their colleagues in the public sector – became increasingly subjected to the virtues of concepts originally developed for the private sector.

With the advent of New Labour, the pace of policy initiatives and institutional experimentation dramatically increased (see Chapter 2). In part this might, as Alcock (2003) argues, have resulted from a combination of the Labour embrace of a third way located between the state and the market (Blair, 1998; Giddens, 1998), and a more pragmatic approach to policy-making and service delivery.

But whatever the precise nature of the Third Way and its linkage with New Labour policies and whether policies such as partnership actually work (Glendinning et al., 2002), we now appear to have reached a new pinnacle of complexity with a bewildering array of policy initiatives and apparently new organizational forms. The list is lengthy and includes compacts, partnerships, social enterprises, quasi-markets, networks, transfer associations, community interest companies, foundation trusts, city academies and others. Many of these can be found, in somewhat different shapes, both in Europe and in the US. Thus, as Defourney and Nyssens point out, the 'concept' of social enterprise (an important group of organizations for this study) made its breakthrough both in the US and in Italy in the early 1990s. In 2002, the debate accelerated in the UK when 'the Blair government launched the Social Enterprise Coalition and created a "Social Enterprise Unit" ' (Nyssens et al., 2006, pp. 3–4).

This dramatic growth of increasingly complex organizations with opaque accountability structures which apparently straddled several sectors has reinforced a long-standing concern about sector identity in the UK and US. For example, as Lan and Rainey (1992) point out in a helpful review of some of the early literature, social scientists have been exploring blurring and the boundaries between public and private organizations 'for decades' (p. 7). Academics, particularly those working in and with the third sector, have been particularly prone to worry about sector boundaries. It is probably no accident since, in the past, they have often been made acutely aware of its modest place in the economy compared with the public and private sectors. Indeed, one well-known American third sector writer (O'Neill, 1989) was compelled to complain that: 'We often talk of government and business, the "public" and "private" sectors, as if there were no other' (p. 1). This agonising over the boundary of the third sector has often led to it being described as 'messy' and 'blurred' (Powell, 1987; Van Til, 1988; James, 1990; Simon, 1990; Billis, 1991; Lohmann, 1992; Powell and Clemens, 1998; Weisbrod, 1998; Ott, 2001).

However, organizations in all three sectors (public, private and third) are now so influenced by adjacent sectors that 'blurring' scarcely does justice to what is happening. Yet we are faced with a paradox. Despite blurring and the apparent diminution of boundaries, sector identity remains powerful and important. It still provides a deep-rooted and fundamentally different way of responding to problems. The sector title is readily understood by citizens, since it appears to have reasonable clarity of ownership and accountability, and can consequently form the basis of public debate and policy. Sector characteristics and alleged advantages, although they may deviate from the ideal model, still provide a benchmark for what things ought to be like and for how they should work. And, if there were indeed any doubt about the continued power of the sector concept, it is only necessary to open a daily paper and engage with the discussion as to why taxpayers should bail out the banks.

If we return to the area of our own concern, the entire landscape has changed. Even the sector walls of the bastion of governmental provision have been breached. The National Health Service (NHS), the institution above all others which epitomised the very fundamentals of the UK welfare state, is undergoing what a *Times* leader describes as a 'quiet revolution'. In reality, the influences from the private and third sector have been nibbling away at the walls for some time. Those who seek evidence of the astonishing growth of complexity need do no more than spend a few minutes looking at the organizational structure and accountabilities of a Hospital NHS Trust. Some began as charity hospitals and then moved into the NHS. They can in addition receive support from their own charitable foundations; earn income from overseas patients; have a complicated structure of governance of Trust Boards (with heavy staff membership) and Special Trustees; involve hundreds of volunteers; and in at least one case (Great Ormond Street) have 4500 'members'. But the action that led *The Times* to realise that a 'revolution' is taking place throughout the NHS was the government's decision to introduce patient contributions to care ('co-payments'). It has taken this sort of controversial decision to bring the 'quiet revolution' into the public arena.

## The Debate: A Faustian Pact?

At the centre of the current maelstrom of institutional change is the sector which is most ill-defined, which has no generally agreed name, but it is most frequently known as the 'non-profit', 'voluntary', 'community', 'non-governmental' or – what we shall prefer here – 'the third' sector. Notwithstanding its fragmented and contested boundaries, it is this sector that has risen to prominence as a central player in the policy arena. Although it is a process that has been evident for some time, the sector's appeal for New Labour should hardly be surprising. After all, Anthony Giddens, one of the architects of the 'third way', argued that 'there are no permanent boundaries between government and civil society' (Giddens, 1998, pp. 79–80).

In spite of the absence of a generally agreed name or boundary for the sector as a whole, TSOs are seen to possess attributes that have become increasingly attractive to public policy makers. These have been identified in various policy statements as, among other features, providing services and care, mobilising communities, helping to identify and solve new needs as well as old ones, campaigning for social change, focusing on the needs of service users, tackling complex needs and difficult social issues, being flexible and offering joined up services, capable of earning users' trust, promoting volunteering and mentoring, building stronger and connected communities and helping to transform public services (Home Office, 1998; Cabinet Office Strategy Unit, 2002; HM Treasury, 2002, 2006).

For obvious reasons, the role of the sector is seen to be even more critical:

> As a vital part of the economy, a key deliverer of public and community services, and the glue which hold our communities together, the third sector is playing a vital role in delivering real help and support to people from all walks of life who are affected by the recession. (Cabinet Office, 2009, p. 6)

This positive image is widely held, and future generations of third sector commentators might look back and reflect on this period as a golden age of widespread political consensus and public support.

Nonetheless, there are those working in and with the sector who question whether these traditional distinctive attributes are being eroded in the new welfare landscape. Certainly, the extensive academic and practitioner literature continually points to the dangers of the increasing influence of adjacent sectors, and the potential loss of independence and possible mission creep. (For a recent critique, see Haugh and Kitson, 2007.) The tenor of the critique is that these pressures will lead, or have already led, to voluntary/nonprofit organizations losing their soul. They have entered into a Faustian pact in which the sector gains resources, possible influence and the opportunity to deliver more services at the cost of those fundamental attributes which made it an attractive proposition in the first place: its mission, values and voluntary contribution.

The alternative approach is more optimistic. The core values and ethos of the sector will survive. Substantial increases in government contracts and market-driven sources of income will enable the sector to meet the needs of even more people. Campaigning for unpopular and unfashionable causes will continue. The growth of large paid-staff hierarchies will not affect the ability to innovate and to respond rapidly and sensitively to the needs of users. Enthusiastic advocates of this approach make a strong case. Stephen Bubb, the Chief Executive Officer (CEO) of the professional association of the most senior paid staff in the sector, is sensitive to the traditional argument. He responds that becoming 'large and professional' does not mean that the sector loses its soul. Large organizations can 'remain closely in touch with clients and communities' (Bubb, 2007). Furthermore, 'to compromise on certain issues in order to deliver on other objectives is not evidence of a loss of independence. It is evidence of pragmatism and, often achievement of gain for beneficiaries'. (p. 16)

Stuart Etherington, the Chief Executive of the National Council for Voluntary Organisations (NCVO), steers a more cautious course. After noting that voluntary organizations 'can and do bite the hand that feeds us on a regular basis', he introduces several critical preconditions if they are to deliver services and also campaign. This he suggests can be done 'with good governance, with good management and with good contracts' (Etherington, 2004).

Both optimistic and pessimistic approaches deserve serious attention. The debate is about the allocation of resources and who is best positioned to respond to what sort of social problems. In this new era, systems of governance and accountability have become increasingly obscure. The public, staff and users have probably given up attempting to understand these new initiatives. All too often, polemic fills the vacuum.

## The ubiquitous hybrid

One thing is sure. We are not going to return – at least in the near future – to an (apparently) benign era of more straightforward organizational boundaries. Even the notion of 'the mixed

economy of welfare', itself a concept that 'remains problematic' (Powell, 2007, p. 2), does not entirely capture what is
happening. What we are now facing are fundamental changes
in the nature of the organizations that are financing, planning and delivering welfare. It is not just the economy, but
also the organizations themselves that have become 'mixed'!
This has been a slow process which has taken place during several decades but has accelerated dramatically during the period
of New Labour with the growing influence of the hybrid
organization.

A comprehensive report to the US Congress makes a similar
case: 'in recent years both Congress and the President have
increasingly used hybrid organizations for the implementation
of public policy functions' (Kosar, 2008, p. 1). As is often the
situation, both the US and the UK seem to be marching to the
same drumbeat.

The pace and noise of the hybrid drumbeat have intensified
on both sides of the Atlantic. Kosar's report was concerned
with hybrids as part of 'quasi government'. It contained mini-
case studies of two organizations that would then have been
largely unknown to UK readers. Today, those organizations,
Fannie Mae and Freddie Mac, have achieved international
notoriety. Indeed, in a telling phrase, (at least) one UK com-
mentator blames them for the global financial collapse and
refers to them as 'the abominable hybrid' (Baker, 2008, p. 23).
This is but the latest and most dramatic example of the dis-
quiet that is often generated by institutions that do not have
explicit clarity of accountability either to the state or the market. Take for example the unloved quango. As Hirst notes, they
'have been an issue of public concern in Britain since roughly
the mid 1970s'. He suggests that this is because of the clash
between the 'principles of democratic and transparent accountability and the placing of public money and government
functions in the hands of unelected persons' (Hirst, 1995,
p. 341).

Yet, whilst they may have been sometimes vilified, they are
widespread and growing. They have been around for a long
while and can be uncovered in most areas of social activity. In
the more limited field of enquiry of this book it is evident that
hybrid TSOs are not just an Anglo-Saxon phenomenon. They

are widespread in Europe (Evers and Laville, 2004; Osborne, 2008) and well beyond (Lewis, 1998).

They might perhaps also be seen as a constructive and creative organizational solution. This therefore presents an intriguing agenda of challenges for practice, theory and policy. The third sector provides a ready-made laboratory to study a creative variety of hybrid since it is here that many volunteer-driven associations have slowly adopted entrepreneurial and market-driven initiatives. A prominent example of welfare hybridity is the rise to prominence of social enterprises – organizations that illustrate in their title the fusion of third/public and private sector values.

Although hybrids are playing an increasingly important role in social policy, we appear almost to have stumbled into a new era of welfare hybridity. Bearing all this in mind, the authors believe that the study of hybrid TSOs is critical for an understanding of social policy and that they also provide a rich territory for the development of ideas about hybrid organizations in general. There are indications that this is, at the very least, a prudent moment to begin the process of seeking some answers. The publication of the cross-party Public Administration Select Committee Report with its vigorous, almost withering, critique of the sector's claim to distinctiveness represents a warning shot over the bow (Public Administration Select Committee, 2008). There are increasing demands in UK public policy statements for more evidence of distinctiveness and value-added contribution.

From across the Atlantic – often a good barometer for what might happen here – come warnings from the editor of *The Nonprofit Quarterly* that the UK should not look to the US for good practice (Jump, 2008, p. 1). 'The government-funded third sector in the US', she claimed, 'had stagnated, with many service-delivering charities losing touch with their beneficiaries'. Perhaps more worrying is evidence from within the UK sector. Practically every issue of its main trade journal (*Third Sector*) reports problems that echo our own agenda of questions. Even a superficial reading demonstrates that most of the examples surround the role and activities of third sector hybrids substantially dependent on resources originating from the public and private sectors.

Even in a period of economic stability there would therefore be a compelling case for the study of hybrid organizations. But it seems we are no longer in such a desirable state. It would be naive to imagine that it will be business as usual for the third sector whose functioning is now so intimately linked to numerous resource streams, few of which are likely to escape unscathed.

## Territory, issues and structure of the book

The *territory* of the book can now be laid out in more detail. Clearly, by definition, organizational hybridity is not restricted to one particular sector or one country. It is a huge area and in various chapters of the book we have attempted to acknowledge this broader institutional arena. Many of our authors have substantial overseas experience in several sectors and where relevant this has been drawn upon. Nevertheless, the study of hybridity is in its infancy and inevitably our aims must be more limited. Consequently, our focus is hybrid TSOs. But even here a word of warning is in order.

The very nature of hybridity demands a flexible approach to organizational boundaries. In this area of study, all is not necessarily what it seems to be on the surface. Organizational titles and policy categories, such as social enterprises, community interest companies (CIC), partnerships and so on, can obscure the real nature of organizations and accountability. So, in order not to constrain the analysis, most of the usual culprits have been included in our broad third sector boundary. They comprise voluntary and community organizations, nonprofits, charities, non-governmental organizations, social movements, grassroots associations, self-help groups, social enterprises and numerous other organizations that do not fall obviously into the public and private sectors (Kendall, 2003). For those who are perhaps not yet battle-scarred in the intricacies of the definitional debate about these types of organizations, some helpful texts in this area are referenced in Chapter 3 and elsewhere in the book.[1] Since Chapter 3 and other chapters will be discussing sectors and their boundaries, we might feel more relaxed than usual in adopting this standard approach of third sector researchers.

In order to understand better the nature of hybridity in TSOs, the majority of the case studies in Part II of the book have been chosen not only in order to provide a reasonable cross-section of the UK third sector, but also because they appear to provide particularly challenging boundary issues for the study of hybridity.

This book is focused on TSOs primarily operating in the field of what is generally regarded as welfare in social policy programmes. However, despite the unquantifiable substantial place of the third sector in all its myriad varieties to the well-being of the vast majority of citizens, commentators, particularly in the Western democracies, have emphasised other fundamental aspects of its role.

There is a long and distinguished history of writers who have emphasised these other (non-welfare) aspects. In practice the third sector's role in welfare and its broader societal contribution are often difficult to disentangle. For example, the important Wolfenden committee had two central concerns. These were 'the strengthening of collective action in meeting important social needs and the maintenance of a pluralistic pattern of institutions' (Wolfenden, 1978, p. 21). In the United States, Warren (2001) points to the 'remarkable consensus [that] is emerging around Tocqueville's view that the virtues and viability of a democracy depend on the robustness of its associational life' (p. 3). Although focused on the contribution to democracy, Warren makes an elegant argument for the wider role of associations.

The Wolfenden Committee, reflecting on the 'voluntary movement', declared that they have 'all the time...been conscious of one over-riding fact...There is nothing static about the scene' (p. 13). Indeed there is not: a fact that needs to be remembered when exploring the nature of change in the sector.

Finally, I hope that all this succeeds in delineating the territory and main focus of the book, and in the following section I move on to consider some of the challenges to be considered. But before then I would like to conclude this section with a few words about our potential readership. Clearly, we hope that these studies will interest and prove useful for academics and students, practitioners and policy makers concerned with the third sector within the UK and internationally, which is the main research focus of the contributors. The study of the third sector has now become genuinely international, with academics, practitioners and policy makers in different countries increasingly interacting in the main sector journals and conferences and we hope to make a contribution to that international endeavour. Increasingly, also, the growing degree of hybridity on the public/third sector boundaries has led to greater theoretical interchange in the public administration journals. The private sector literature is also paying greater attention to the third sector.

Beyond that, I hope that those in the business and management field will find the concept of hybrid organizations of relevance. The extent and scale of these hybrids deserves attention from the widest possible disciplinary approaches.

### Challenges for practice, theory and policy

In keeping with an investigatory approach we are primarily concerned to open up 'hybrid organizations' as an important new area of study. In order to do that, a number of questions need to be addressed. They can be grouped together in four main areas:

1. What is the nature of change in the third sector?

Because of the sector's perceived role not only in the provision of welfare services, but also in advocacy and the development of what is generally regarded as a healthy and flourishing democratic society, change with respect to its core attributes requires serious consideration. For example, is the choice only between the optimistic or pessimistic scenarios; or can a somewhat more sophisticated model be developed?

2. What are hybrid TSOs and how can the issues of accountability and transparency be addressed?

Why has hybridity grown so rapidly in the past decade? Is it possible at least to begin the process of theory building in this area? How can we approach the vexed problem of clarity of accountability amidst a sea of hybridity? What are some of the unresolved issues?

3. Stumbling into hybridity: can theory help?

The organizations described in this book represent different types of hybrid TSOs, coping with a variety of different pressures and responding in different ways. What light can an emerging theory throw on the problems faced by the case study hybrid TSOs, in particular the dangers of stumbling into hybridity? Might different sorts of hybrids present distinctive challengers?

4. What are the wider questions and implications for practice and policy?

Do the concepts and approaches raise helpful questions for those responsible for the governance and operations of TSOs? Can a better understanding of the third sector and its hybrid organizational forms improve consistency of public policy towards the sector and improve the coherence and effectiveness of support from sector? And, looking beyond the third sector, does the theory at least raise useful questions particularly with respect to hybridity in the public sector?

Many of these questions, and others raised by the contributing authors, will serve as a possible research agenda.

## Organization of the book

The remaining chapters of Part I of the book comprise three further contextual studies covering the following: social policy influences; a theory of hybrid organizations; and reflections on the nature of governance in hybrid sector organizations.

The public and social policy context, which is briefly touched upon in this chapter, is dealt with more extensively in the following chapter by Margaret Harris who looks at the policy environment within which TSOs have been operating, especially during the period of New Labour governments since 1997. Many elements in the environment in this period are considered to have been particularly conducive to the trends outlined in this chapter – towards greater TSO hybridity and to the formation of new complex hybrid structures. The chapter argues that there are other, often contradictory, influences in the TSO policy environment that may be not only simultaneously pushing TSOs in different directions – towards greater TSO hybridity, but also exerting pressures on them to preserve their organizational autonomy.

In Chapter 3, I lay out an emerging theory of hybrid organizations. I begin by developing ideal models of the public and private sectors, provide a definition of 'principal ownership' and lay out their distinctive 'rules of the game'. A comparable archetype is then built for the third sector. Having built the foundations, a model of the three sectors and their hybrid zones is presented. The analysis is completed by offering the concepts of (a) 'shallow' compared with 'entrenched' hybrids (those with deeply embedded characteristics of neighbouring sectors) and (b) 'organic' compared with 'enacted' (those instigated by other organizations) hybrids. The ideas in this chapter are picked up where appropriate in later chapters.

The final contextual chapter by Chris Cornforth and Roger Spear (Chapter 4) focuses on the governance of hybrid organizations and in particular the challenges posed by the growth of the more complex structures. It identifies the main governance arrangements adopted by unitary TSOs with single boards and highlights the current failure of governance research to keep pace with the growth of multi-level structures with main and subsidiary boards. The authors suggest that many important challenges that face hybrid TSOs are shaped by their different origins (legal structures, regulatory requirements and development paths).

Part II of the book contains seven studies of important areas of hybridity, relates these to the main themes of the book and provides a foundation for the concluding chapter. The general rationale and direction of the studies is to move from the 'shallow' types of hybridity to the more 'entrenched' examples.

The opening chapter by Angela Ellis Paine, Nick Ockenden and Joanna Stuart discusses the involvement of volunteers, both at board and at service level. Underlying themes are the impact of changes on the experience of the volunteers, the diversity of their involvement and practical implications for the sector. The authors discuss the impact of the relatively rapid professionalisation of the sector and the displacement of volunteers by paid staff. The conclusion of their analysis is that the nature of volunteering is changing significantly in hybrid TSOs and particularly so in entrenched hybrids.

In Chapter 6, Colin Rochester and Malcolm Torry present the first of the studies that focus on a particular set of organizations, those that are faith-based and are, at most, at the 'shallow' end of hybridity. They suggest that while the commitment of religious congregations to serving their local communities and the government's interest in seeing them delivering public policy may overlap to some extent, they are not rooted in the same values and operating principles. The apparent slowness of faith-based organizations to embrace the public service delivery agenda, they argue, is not the product of lack of capacity (as is generally believed to be the case) but a kind of passive resistance rooted in non-negotiable theological values which are different from those which underpin government policy.

The book enters more firmly into the territory of 'shallow' hybridity with the study by Romayne Hutchison and Ben Cairns (Chapter 7) of 'community anchor organizations' many of which the authors analyse as shallow hybrids. They identify a chronic tension within these organizations between their traditional commitment to the potential of community development and organizational change arising from policy and funding pressures. Hybridity, they conclude, is not necessarily to be avoided; but community anchor organizations need to be aware of its implications, particularly for their distinctive history and potential problems of managing accountability.

In Chapter 8, Mike Aiken presents three organizational case studies of social enterprises in the work integration field. The particular challenges and tensions faced by each organization are discussed by utilising ideas about hybridity. Using the idea of 'principal ownership' as a dominating logic, Aiken reaches the preliminary possibility that each of the organizations had a primary affiliation to different sectors. He concludes that understanding how social enterprises manage their internal tensions is important for policy and practice, and will require analysis of their depth of hybridity, the nature of their moves across sectors and the possibility of reconciling competing sector logics within one agency.

We move even further into hybrid territory in the following chapter by Joanna Howard and Marilyn Taylor who examine the opportunities and challenges that arise in two 'partnership hybrids'. Both began life as state-sponsored partnerships, but reconstituted themselves as non-statutory entities. They suggest that hybridity can offer space for innovation but that this depends on commitment to a clear vision for the organization and a clear overall structure. They conclude that while it is too early to make a judgement on success or failure of these forms of hybridity, conflicting expectations and commitments led to the collapse in one organization, whereas the other is an organization in transition.

In Chapter 10, David Mullins and Hal Pawson examine the rise of housing associations, analyse their changing position on the public–private spectrum and discuss the extent to which it remains accurate to portray associations as part of the voluntary sector. This is followed by an exploration of the changing forms of hybridity and the shifting public/private boundary, growing pains associated with the emergence of very large organizations and the impact of the post-2007 economic downturn on the hybrid model. In conclusion they consider the relevance of the two faces of hybridity: 'for-profits in disguise' and 'agents of policy' in understanding English and Dutch housing associations.

In the last of these seven chapters, David Lewis introduces an essential counterbalance to the emphasis so far by appropriately bringing us back to the individual in organizations and their experience of working across the sector boundaries. Drawing on ethnographic research on the life-work histories of individuals who have crossed between the third and the public sector, he argues that they embody at the individual level elements of the bigger picture of sector hybridity discussed in the book. The author examines the tensions that exist between the ideal model of the sector and real life in organizations. He concludes that despite increased hybridization, the model continues to play an important role for individuals in managing sector realities.

In the final chapter, I return to key questions posed in this opening chapter. A typology of hybrid organizations is constructed utilising concepts presented in Chapter 3 and tested in the light of the material presented by my colleagues in earlier chapters. The typology first examines the nature of hybridity, mission and identity and a second section speculates about the possible implications for ownership and accountability. Both these sections discuss challenges presented by change in hybrid TSOs, but the earlier case studies lead to the conclusion that a broader analysis of change is required, and a number of different processes are discussed in relation to the sector as a whole.

The chapter and the book conclude with reflections on the implications of this study of third sector hybrid organizations for those who lead and work in the sector, those who develop and implement public and social policy and those who research and study in this and neighbouring areas. I believe that policy expectations – both at the public and the individual organizational level – cannot be divorced from an understanding of organizations that are expected to deliver those policies. Failure to close that gap is at the expense of those who receive the end products of our organizations.

## Note

1. A good entry point is Powell, W. W. and R. Steinberg (eds) (2006) *The Non-Profit Sector: A Research Handbook*, Newhaven and London: Yale University Press.

## References

Alcock, P. (2003) *Social Policy in Britain: Themes and Issues*, Basingstoke: Palgrave Macmillan.

Alcock, P., T. Brannelly and L. Ross (2004) *Formality or Flexibility? Voluntary Sector Contracting in Social Care and Health*, London: Countryside Agency and NCVO.

Baker, G. (2008) *That Rubbish They Talk About the Credit Crunch*, London: *The Times*. 3rd October 2008.

Billis, D. (1984) *Welfare Bureaucracies: Their Design and Change in Response to Social Problems*, London: Heinemann.

Billis, D. (1991) 'The roots of voluntary agencies: A question of choice'. *Nonprofit and Voluntary Sector Quarterly*, 20 (1) pp. 57–70.

Blair, T. (1998) *The Third Way*, Fabian Society.

Bubb, S. (2007) *Transforming Our Public Services Through the Third Sector*, London: ACEVO.

Cabinet Office (2009) *Real Help for Communities: Volunteers, Charities and Social Enterprises*, London: HM Government.

Cabinet Office Strategy Unit (2002) *Private Action, Public Benefit. A Review of Charities and the Wider Not-For-Profit Sectors*, London: HM Government.

Demone, H. W. and M. Gibelman (1989) *Services for Sale: Purchasing Health and Human Services*, New Jersey: Rutgers University Press.

Etherington, S. (2004) *Keynote Speech to the 2004 Annual Conference of NCVO* at http://www.ncvo-vol.org.uk/press/speeches/?id= 2461 accessed September, 2009.

Etzioni, A. (1973) 'The third sector and domestic missions.' *Public Administration Review*, 33 (4) pp. 314–323.

Evers, A. and J.-L. Laville (2004) *The Third Sector in Europe*, Cheltenham: Edward Elgar Publishing.

Giddens, A. (1998) *The Third Way: The Renewal of Social Democracy*, Oxford: Polity Press.

Glendinning, C., M. Powell and K. Rummery (2002) *Partnerships, New Labour and the Governance of Welfare*, Bristol: Policy Press.

HM Treasury (2002) *The Role of the Voluntary and Community Sector in Service Delivery: A Cross Cutting Review*, London: The Public Enquiry Unit HM Treasury.

HM Treasury (2006) *The Future Role of the Third Sector in Social and Economic Regeneration: Interim Report*, London: HMSO.

Haugh, H. and M. Kitson (2007) 'The third way and the third sector: New Labour's economic policy and the social economy.' *Cambridge Journal of Economics*, 31 pp. 973–994.

Hirst, P. (1995) 'Quangos and democratic government.' *Parliamentary Affairs*, 48 (2) pp. 341–359.

Home Office (1998) *Compact on Relations Between Government and the Voluntary and Community Sector in England*, London: Home Office.

James, E. (1990) 'Economic theories of the nonprofit sector: A comparative perspective' in H. K. Anheier and W. Seibel (eds) *The Third Sector: Comparative Studies of Nonprofit Organizations*, Berlin and New York: De Gruyter.

Jump, P. (2008) 'Don't follow the Americans, charity editor warns.' *Third Sector*. 3rd October 2008.

Kendall, J. (2003) *The Voluntary Sector*, London: Routledge.

Kendall, J. and M. Knapp (1995) 'A loose and baggy monster: boundaries, definitions and typologies' in J. Davis Smith, C. Rochester and R.Hedley (eds) *An Introduction to the Voluntary Sector*, London: Routledge.

Kosar, K. R. (2008) *The Quasi Government: Hybrid Organization with both Government and Private Sector Legal Characteristics*, CRS Report for Congress, Congressional Research Service.

Kramer, R. and P. Terrell (1984) *Social Services Contracting in the Bay Area*, Berkeley, Calif.: Institute of Governmental Studies, University of California.

Kramer, R. M. (1993) *Privatization in Four European Countries: Comparative Studies in Government–Third Sector Relationships*, Armonk, N.Y.: M.E. Sharpe.

Lan, Z. and H. G. Rainey (1992) 'Goals, roles, and effectiveness in public, private, and hybrid organizations: More evidence on frequent assertions about differences.' *Journal of Public Administration Research and Theory*, 2 (1) pp. 5–28.

Lewis, D. (1998) 'Nongovernmental organizations, business and the management of ambiguity.' *Nonprofit Management and Leadership*, 7 (2) pp. 135–151.

Lewis, J. (1999) 'Reviewing the relationship between the voluntary sector and the state in Britain in the 1990s.' *Voluntas*, 10 (3) pp. 255–270.

Lohmann, R. A. (1992) *The Commons: New Perspectives on Nonprofit Organizations and Voluntary Action*, San Francisco: Jossey-Bass.

Nyssens, M., S. Adam and T. Johnson (2006) *Social Enterprise: At the Crossroads of Market, Public Policies and Civil Society*, London: Routledge.

O'Neill, M. (1989) *The Third America: The Emergence of the Nonprofit Sector in the United States*, San Francisco: Jossey-Bass.

Osborne, S. P. (2008) *The Third Sector in Europe: Prospects and Challenges*, London and New York: Routledge.

Ott, J. S. (2001) *The Nature of the Nonprofit Sector*, Boulder, Colo.: Westview Press.

Powell, M. A. (2007) *Understanding the Mixed Economy of Welfare*, Bristol: Policy Press.

Powell, W. W. (1987) 'Hybrid organizational arrangements: New form or transitional development?' *California Management Review*, 30 (1) pp. 67–87.

Powell, W. W. and E. S. Clemens (1998) *Private Action and the Public Good*, New Haven and London: Yale University Press.

Powell, W. W. and R. Steinberg (eds) (2006) *The Non-Profit Sector: A Research Handbook*, Newhaven and London: Yale University Press.

Public Administration Select Committee (2008) *Public Services and the Third Sector: Rhetoric and Reality volume 1*, London: House of Commons: 97.

Seebohm, F. (1968) *Report of the Committee on Local Authority and Allied Personal Social Services*, London: HMSO.

Simon, J. G. (1990) 'Modern welfare state policy toward the non-profit sector: Some research considerations' in H. K. Anheier and W. Siebel (eds) *The Third Sector: Comparative Studies of Nonprofit Organizations*, Berlin and New York: De Gruyter.

Smith, S., Rathgeb and M. Lipsky (1993) *Nonprofits for Hire: The Welfare State in the Age of Contracting*, Cambridge, Mass. and London: Harvard University Press.

Van Til, J. (1988) *Mapping the Third Sector: Voluntarism in a Changing Social Economy*, New York: The Foundation Center.

Warren, M. (2001) *Democracy and Association*, Princeton N.J.: Princeton University Press.

Webb, A. (1979) 'Voluntary social action: In search of a policy.' *Journal of Voluntary Action Research*, 8 pp. 8–16.

Webb, A. L. and G. Wistow (1982) *Whither State Welfare? Policy and Implementation in the Personal Social Services, 1979–80*, London: Royal Institute of Public Administration.

Weisbrod, B. A. (1998) *To Profit or Not to Profit: The Commercial Transformation of the Nonprofit Sector*, Cambridge: Cambridge University Press.

Wolfenden, J. (1978) *The Future of Voluntary Organisations: Report of the Wolfenden Committee on Voluntary Organisations*, London: Croom Helm.

# 2 Third sector organizations in a contradictory policy environment

## Margaret Harris

This chapter looks at the public and social policy environment within which third sector organizations (TSOs) in the UK have been operating in recent years, especially during the period of New Labour governments since 1997. It shows that many elements in the policy environment in the period have been particularly conducive to the trends outlined in Chapter 1 – towards greater TSO hybridity and to the formation of new complex hybrid structures. It also shows that there are other influences in the TSO policy environment that may be simultaneously pushing TSOs in a different direction – towards preserving their organizational autonomy and protecting their organizational boundaries.

The chapter starts by identifying four broad streams in public and social policy which, particularly under New Labour, have provided fertile ground for the development of hybridity: the emphasis on partnerships and other forms of organizational collaboration; the public services agenda; the dominance of market principles in policy making; and rising expectations on local communities. In this changing environment, moving from being a stand-alone organization towards participation in more complex hybrid organizational structures can be seen as a common sense TSO response to the policy trends.

As well as using a range of published material, the chapter draws on research conducted by the author and colleagues at the Aston Centre for Voluntary Action Research (ACVAR) and its successor, the Institute for Voluntary Action Research (IVAR).

## Partnerships and collaboration

Public and social policy in the New Labour period has laid heavy emphasis on partnership working. The idea has been reflected in numerous policy documents focused on the delivery of welfare and other public services (see, for example, Cabinet Office, 2002; HM Treasury, 2007) and has gradually achieved 'best practice' status (Glendinning et al., 2002). What is understood by 'partnership' varies, but users of the term have in common an assumption that public services delivered through organizational collaborations (not only partnerships but also consortia, networks, alliances and full mergers) will be more efficient and have more effective outcomes than actions taken by a single organization acting independently.

The ideal of efficient and effective collaborative working has been reflected in the funding criteria for participation in a range of EU, national and local governmental programmes; in relation, for example, to urban regeneration, crime reduction, poverty reduction and community cohesion. Obtaining funding often requires collaboration between service-providing organizations both in the application process and in the implementation of plans once funding is obtained. (Similar requirements for cross-sectoral collaborations in order to draw down public funding have been observed in the US (Poole, 2007) so the partnership idea is not one confined to the UK or European policy arenas.) As the implementation of Local Strategic Partnerships in English local authorities illustrates (Maguire and Truscott, 2006), the need to maintain long-term co-operative efforts between several organizations from the public, private and third sectors while programme funding is being spent can result in meta-organizations with organizational lives of their own. This kind of hybrid organization is discussed in more detail in Chapter 9 of this volume.

Although the policy pressures for organizational collaboration are not sector-specific, the trend has impacted on TSOs in distinctive ways. It has encouraged them to consider seriously alliances with other TSOs, to engage with third sector infrastructure organizations and to participate in third sector networks. Since September 2007, special support to facilitate third sector collaborations has been available through the government's Capacitybuilders programme whose aim is to 'create a more effective third sector' (Cabinet Office, 2008).

Research undertaken by the author and colleagues since 2000 suggests that many collaborative developments have been driven by governmental funders' growing assumption that it is inefficient and therefore inappropriate for TSOs in similar or adjacent fields to be working independently of one another. Since the underpinning rationale for organizational collaboration relates to efficiency and effectiveness, the pressure on TSOs to work together has increased as the economic environment has worsened.

Sometimes collaborative behaviour holds out the promise of immediate financial benefits for TSOs, such as when Government specified that its capacity building funds for local TSOs or its Grassroots Grants were to be distributed via third sector intermediary organizations (Harris and Schlappa, 2007). In other cases, the perceived advantages were less clear but TSOs felt that if they did not show positive interest, they would lose the opportunity to obtain resources at a future date. Thus English TSOs invested in regional third sector networks, even though the potential benefits of such participation was not clear to them (Harris et al., 2004).

Another impact on TSOs of the policy discourse about partnership is to encourage them to consider seriously organizational collaborations across sectoral boundaries, that is, with organizations in the private or public sectors. Third sector organizations have become less cautious, for example, about collaborating with business to obtain donations in kind; to recruit volunteers; to obtain ITC, human resource management, public relations and other support services at low or no cost; and to benefit from event sponsorships and cause-related marketing. Furthermore, it is no longer unusual to find TSOs collaborating with for-profit agencies to deliver services to vulnerable people. There is continuing debate as to whether it is ethical for businesses to achieve their own social responsibility goals via TSOs (Parkes and Harris, 2008) and about what the implications are for a healthy civil society of a close link between the third and private sectors (Edwards, 2008). All the same, the work of Business in the Community (2009) and the pages of the magazine *Third Sector* attest to the growing trend in the UK for alliances across the business-third sector boundary (which are also found in the US; see Austin, 2000). While collaborations across the private-third sector boundary have increased in the last decade, collaborations across the public-third sector boundary have been a notable part of the public policy landscape for much longer and were given added impetus by the policy initiatives of New Labour governments (Lewis, 1999). The drive for closer collaboration between TSOs and governmental organizations was reflected in the publication of the Compact soon after New Labour first attained power (Home Office, 1998) and the subsequent development of local and specialist compacts. The compacts were underpinned by the idea of encouraging organizations in both sectors to become more trusting of each other's motives and more knowledgeable about each other's cultures and norms (HM Treasury, 2002). The hope was that compacts could smooth the path to much closer collaboration across sectoral boundaries which had been marked formerly by indifference, disputes, competition, unequal power relations and fears on the third sector side about threats to autonomy (McDonald, 2005).

The overall impact on TSOs of the partnership stream in public policy can be seen then as encouragement to be less concerned about preserving their own organizational boundaries and autonomy and to be more willing to collaborate with other TSOs, governmental agencies and for-profit businesses. The emphasis is on meeting needs in whatever way seems to work best, while not being too concerned about which organizations, or combination of organizations, provide the services or which sector they are located in. This comparatively relaxed approach to possible organizational hybridization reflects broader post modern or late modern thinking which points towards the increasing importance of networks and alliances (Rodger, 2000) and the growing irrelevance of modernist concerns with the policing of national, organizational or sectoral boundaries.

Collaborations among TSOs and between TSOs and organizations in other sectors may be short-term and fairly informal, or they may be longer-lived and structured. In the latter case, the need for new or additional organizational structures may become apparent to the partners themselves. Action research focused on improving relationships between local authorities and third sector infrastructure bodies (I&DEA, 2006) found that the need for a shared governance structure to ensure accountability for jointly organized initiatives emerged as partnerships deepened. Longer-lived partnerships can, then, segue into hybrids new; organizational forms of varying complexity which have an organizational life of their own.

## Public services provision

Another key policy stream has been the trend to redefine the idea of 'public services'. Under New Labour the use of the term has been extended to cover not only those services directly provided by governmental agencies but also all services, irrespective of sectoral base, which receive governmental funding or whose provision is a governmental goal. One policy document, for example, describes public services simply as 'services that are wholly or partly funded, or could be funded, from the public purse, including national, regional and local government and statutory agencies at all levels' (HM Treasury, 2003, section 1.10).

This extended usage of public services reflects a particular conceptualisation of the public good and how it can be assured. It shifts the focus of thinking about service provision in response to need from the provider institutions and their sectoral location (in the public, private or third sectors) to the needs and services themselves: in this way, the importance of the concepts of 'sector' or 'sectoral distinctiveness' is minimised. Instead, 'what matters is what works' and what can be done to meet need efficiently and effectively in line with national policy goals (Brandsen and Pestoff, 2006). This message was clear, for example, in the development of the government's capacity building programme (Home Office, 2004) which was intended to encourage TSOs to become more organizationally capable of delivering services. Third sector organizations were funded to adopt specific business-derived quality systems; to set up and then achieve performance targets; to replace volunteers with paid staff; and to ensure that both staff and board members were trained to standards acceptable to government and other funders (Cairns et al., 2005). This clear pressure for organizational hybridization, as described in Chapter 1 of this volume, led to TSOs taking on characteristics formerly associated with the private and public sectors.

In the pragmatic New Labour era with its much expanded conceptualisation of public services, TSOs may hesitate to express reservations about the pressure on them to work according to principles traditionally associated with other sectors. All the same, recent research (Pharoah, 2007) has revealed that many TSOs do have concerns about the implications for their organizational autonomy of the public services agenda and the pressure it exerts on them to deliver services as participants in complex new structures.

The expanded conceptualisation of public services provides an intellectual justification for hybridization. It also discourages critical discussion within TSOs about the implications of that hybridization for TSOs themselves. It tends to minimise, for example, possible concerns about government encouragement for TSOs to become business-like social enterprises (Evers, 2005); about the incorporation of the third sector into the government sector through contracting and scrutiny (Taylor et al., 2002); or about the implications for democracy of a less independent third sector whose advocacy role is restricted by fears about future funding (Kelly, 2007). The general message from the public services policy stream is all hands to the pump to deliver services. By implication, those who question the complex organizational arrangements required to achieve this can be seen as not really having the public good at heart.

## Market principles

Although the pressures for partnership and other kinds of collaborative behaviour by TSOs have been increasing under New Labour, there have also been parallel policy pressures for TSOs to compete with one another and with organizations in other sectors (Le Grand, 1999). These pressures are an extension of the growing influence of economic theory on public policy formulation since the Thatcher governments of the 1980s. Neo-liberal economic theories have led to policy makers arguing that welfare and public services provision required the discipline of 'the market' (Clarke, 2004). Although often portrayed as no more than common sense, this view of public services provision marked a fundamental ideological shift away from the egalitarian needs-based and rights-based philosophies which underpinned the original Welfare State (Rodger, 2000).

The New Public Management (NPM) movement of the 1980s and 1990s helped to embed the shift towards a market-like approach to the provision of public services as it eclipsed the older Public Administration paradigm with its focus on serving the public good (Bourgon, 2007). A key principle of NPM was that management of governmental organizations was not essentially different from management of for-profit organizations; that there were generally applicable principles of management and governance which applied equally to the public sector (Pollitt, 1995). NPM also argued for a replacement of hierarchical command and control forms of government with market-driven incentives. In due course, this argument was extended to the third sector and was disseminated through vocational and educational courses, including MBA programmes, which were opened to managers irrespective of their sector.

The Third Way ideas (Giddens, 1998), which were an important influence in the early years of New Labour government, were much more measured and cautious about the workings of markets. Yet they did not lead to any reversal of the general trend to see market-like mechanisms as appropriate means through which to deliver welfare and other public services. The focus on economic aspects of public policy implementation has been reinforced in many ways. For example, since the EU has its roots in a drive for economic benefits for members, many of the programmes in which the UK participates, and from which it has benefited hugely in recent years (such as regional regeneration initiatives), have overtly economic goals. This approach has inevitably encouraged thinking about the UK's social problems within an economic frame, with social benefits regarded as subsidiary to economic development. The conflation of economic and social purposes in policy thinking has also been reflected in the enthusiasm under New Labour for the formation of hybrids in the form of social enterprises; organizations which intentionally combine features traditionally associated with the business and third sectors (HM Treasury, 2007; Spear et al., 2007).

Reflecting and driving the marketisation of policy thinking have been two related trends for TSOs. One has been the move of TSOs into mainstream services, as one of a number of possible providers in a 'market place' of service provision (alongside for-profit businesses, social enterprises and governmental agencies themselves). The Welfare State era assumption that key human services would be provided by governmental agencies with TSOs taking a complementary, supplementary or innovative role (Thane, 1982) became invalid during the 1980s and early 1990s, while Third Way thinking later in the 1990s also envisaged a society in which 'Expenditure on welfare ... will be generated and distributed not wholly through the state, but by the state working in combination with other agencies including business' (Giddens, 1998, p. 127). Governmental agencies have retained their responsibility for ensuring that the needs of the public are met but now they increasingly commission services they consider necessary from private and third sector providers in the 'market place' who might be expected to be cheaper, more effective or more responsive to need.

This constitutes yet another encouragement for TSO hybridity since moving to mainstream provision of, for example, health, education and welfare services requires TSOs to think in ways which are closer to those of governmental agencies: a form of normative isomorphism. Third sector organizations moving into mainstream provision need to think strategically about national welfare needs and how to respond to them rather than to focus on the needs of particular or local groups or on the provision of specialist services. This was a point made in the course of a project in which the author and colleagues examined the welfare-providing role of local churches (Cairns et al., 2007). Whereas the church volunteers we interviewed were mainly motivated by the idea of 'sharing God's love' by providing informal social care on a small scale, they often found themselves under pressure to scale up their services provision, to compete for governmental funding or to adapt their goals to respond to the governmental regeneration policy agenda.

Third sector organizations which move into mainstream services provision also need to ensure economies of scale; be focused on costs and prices; conform to public accountability principles such as regular external monitoring and reporting; and be seen to meet quantitative performance targets (measurable outputs) of a kind familiar in industry and governmental agencies. So while the organizational and governance structures of TSOs of this kind may appear in public documents such as returns to the Charity Commission to be relatively unchanging, major shifts may in fact be taking place in their strategic management, monitoring procedures, internal accountability systems and even their goals. For example, a study of multi-purpose community-based organizations (IVAR, 2006; and see also Chapter 7 of this volume) found that their ability to work in accordance with their founding goals was restricted by governmental funding regimes which were pulling them away from community development work to service provision. It was also found that they were developing for-profit ventures such as cafes and nurseries to try to secure funding less closely tied to the goals of external funders. In short, TSOs may acquire some of the organizational characteristics associated with governmental agencies and for-profit businesses as they learn to be efficient players in the services market place.

A second trend which drives and reflects market assumptions in public policy formulation has been changes in funding relationships between TSOs and governmental and quasi-governmental agencies. Arms' length funding, in which grants were offered to TSOs against generalised commitments to provide services for those in need, has now largely been replaced by funding relationships which are subject to 'competitive procurement'; are tightly specified; and are regulated and monitored through contracts. The underpinning assumption here is that TSOs compete in a market in which governmental agencies select the services they will buy from the providers (irrespective of sector) who offer the best value for money or who promise to conform most closely with the requirements of the purchaser. This, too, constitutes a pressure for

TSO hybridization, in this case pressure to take on patterns of behaviour associated with the private sector where profit is the prime purpose and management's focus is on external operations including competition and responsiveness to prospective customers (Wei-Skillern and Marciano, 2008).

Adopting this kind of business-like behaviour will have an impact on more traditional philanthropic and needs-focused strategic priorities. In a market-like environment, board members can drift away from their traditional stewardship role (Harrow and Palmer, 2003) and start to think in a more business-like fashion, questioning, for example, the use of charitable funds to subsidise the prices charged for services – not only the prices charged to purchasing governmental agencies but also those charged directly to individual clients. Recent research conducted by IVAR has found numerous examples of smaller TSOs imposing charges for services formerly provided to clients at little or no charge. Certainly, philanthropic approaches to the provision of care can take a knock in TSOs as they give priority to matters of economy, efficiency and effectiveness and embrace market values such as full cost recovery. Volunteers, too, can start to question why they are offering the gift of their time to organizations which appear to be operating as businesses (Milligan and Fyfe, 2005; and see also Chapter 5 of this volume).

### Expectations on local communities

Whereas the public services agenda and the drive to embrace market principles in public policy are particularly likely to impact on the organizational features of medium and larger TSOs, the fourth policy stream conducive to TSO hybridization is particularly likely to impact on smaller TSOs such as community associations and neighbourhood groups. This is the drive to 'new localism' to devolve power and responsibility for the solution of social problems to the local area level (DCLG, 2006).

The high expectations on local communities have been evident for at least the last two decades, although they have been expressed in different programmes and using different terminologies over the years (Sullivan, 2002). The Green Paper published by the Conservative Party (2008) emphasises the importance that they, as well as New Labour, attach to local and community action to meet need. The key point about the community expectations policy stream is that it reinforces the same message as other policy streams discussed above – 'what matters is what works' – rather than the preservation of TSO autonomy or distinctiveness. Concern about the latter is cast as trivial in comparison with the evident need to find solutions to complex social problems (HM Treasury, 2007).

The more serious and complex the social problems whose solution is devolved (at least partially) to the very local level (including poverty; social exclusion; ill-health; ethnic and faith-based social divisions; child neglect; political extremism; street crime; and environmental degradation), the more churlish it seems if community associations and neighbourhood groups express concern about being pulled into taking responsibility for local manifestations of national and global problems. Small local TSOs can feel that they have no choice but to participate with good grace in partnerships and consortia involving large TSOs, local businesses and local authorities. However, they inevitably have a very junior status within such arrangements and can find themselves under pressure to change their operating systems and structures so that they complement those of more powerful partners (Taylor et al., 2002).

For example, research with small and informal community groups working at the local level to build bridges across faith and ethnic divides (Harris and Young, 2009) found that in order to obtain any kind of external funding from governmental sources, they had to be able to demonstrate that they had formal constitutions, regular committee meetings, audited accounts and 'representatives' who could speak authoritatively on their behalf at meetings of local partnerships and consortia. And in order to remain a player in decision-making at the local level, they often needed to surrender to third sector infrastructure bodies their right to speak on their own behalf, either because they did not have the resources to attend multiple meetings or because powerful members of consortia insisted that the third sector spoke with one voice in the same way that a local authority could do (Cairns et al., 2006). Despite apparent acceptance by New Labour governments that the third sector contains many voices (HM Treasury, 2005), there are in practice pressures for smaller TSOs to speak with a single voice and to avoid advocating on behalf of particular groups or specialist agendas (IVAR, 2008).

In short, the impact of the community expectations policy stream on small local community organizations can be to erode the boundaries between themselves and other local organizations, both those in the third sector and those in the public and private sectors (Milbourne, 2009). As boundaries are eroded, the way is opened for the development of complex hybrid structures at the local level.

## The impact of the four policy streams

So far this chapter has pointed to four policy streams which together and separately have provided a policy environment conducive to the development of TSO hybrids in the New Labour period. Although they have been distinguished from each other and discussed separately here, in practice they can reinforce each other as they have common elements. Each stream in its own way exerts pressure on TSOs to be pragmatic in addressing social problems and social need, rather than to be concerned about preserving distinctive third sector features and defending organizational boundaries. And each exerts pressure on TSOs to collaborate with whichever other organizations, that in whichever sector, are able to contribute to meeting public needs; and to accept funding for service provision irrespective of the conditions attached or the fit with their organizational mission (McKinney and Kahn, 2004).

Thus, from the perspective of an individual TSO, the pressure to deliver mainstream public services, to tender for service-providing contracts and to collaborate with other TSOs may be seen by, for example, a harassed board of trustees concerned about the long-term survival of its TSO, as a single pressure requiring a single rapid organizational response. This kind of perception may increase the attractiveness of moving to hybrid organizational forms by, say, forming a strategic alliance with a local business; permitting a local authority funder to control the TSO's activities through very tight monitoring mechanisms; or collaborating with other TSOs on a project which, although well-funded, has unclear lines of accountability or is not in keeping with the TSO's own strategic goals. Third sector organizations are also experiencing other pressures towards hybridization. These include the impact of paid staff and board members who move into the third sector from the business and governmental worlds and bring with them organizational norms and policy assumptions (see Chapter 11 for further discussion of this process) and the concerns of senior staff and board members to secure the survival of their agency in hard economic times, irrespective of the price paid in organizational autonomy. Pressures of this kind can reinforce the impact of the four policy streams identified earlier and make hybrid organizational forms appear to be an appropriate pragmatic response to them.

The major impact of the four identified policy streams in creating an environment conducive to TSO hybridization is explained by their deep roots in enduring social and public policy concerns. Much of the thinking behind is rooted in a search for an alternative to a state monopoly in responding to public needs, a search which gathered pace during the 1980s and 1990s as the idea of welfare pluralism or welfare mix took hold (Powell, 2007). Likewise, the argument about the need to be pragmatic and 'realistic' about effective delivery of services fitted well with a changing approach to social, economic and environmental problems during the 1990s. There was a growing acknowledgement by policy analysts of the complexity and inter-related nature of intractable issues (so-called 'wicked problems') such as urban degradation, environmental pollution and family poverty. Alongside this new kind of analysis came a recognition that tackling complex problems really required 'joined up working'; that is, co-ordination, collaboration and co-production across organizations and sectors (Brandsen and Pestoff, 2006; Denhardt and Denhardt, 2007). These continuities between the policy streams developed under New Labour and earlier social and public policy concerns have helped to give the policy streams legitimacy and to make hybrid organizational structures appear to be a natural response to them.

## Contradictory policy pressures

The policy pressures for TSO hybridization have increased and deepened as New Labour governments' social and public policies have evolved since 1997. Yet there have also been strong pressures for TSOs *not* to take on the characteristics of other sectors and to safeguard the features that, traditionally, have been regarded as distinctive to TSOs and part of their special contribution to the public good. These have included: an explicit values base; closeness to beneficiaries; user and community involvement; innovation and flexibility in responding to needs; multiplicity of stakeholders; involvement of volunteers; independent governance; and a commitment to advocacy activities. It has also been suggested that TSO's are particularly well suited to fulfilling societal roles such as identifying new welfare needs; building and defending civil society; facilitating and enabling citizen participation; providing an independent voice on public policy; and building social capital. The argument has not been that such features and capabilities are unique to the sector, nor that any one TSO is likely to exhibit all of them, but simply that, taken together, these features tend to distinguish TSO's from organizations in the business and governmental sectors (Harris et al., 2001; Rothschild and Milofsky, 2006).

During the New Labour period, politicians and policy makers have continued to praise these features as ones to be respected and nurtured. Indeed, there have been assumptions that the sector has not only retained such features but will continue to do so in the future. Policy expectations on the sector to be involved at a local level in encouraging civic participation (Milligan and Fyfe, 2005; HM Treasury, 2007) suggest that TSOs need to retain not only their capacity to involve citizens in independent action and problem-solving but also their capacity to advocate on behalf of those who are vulnerable and to involve the users of their services in the design of those services. The raft of policies intended to encourage community and social cohesion (Cantle, 2001; DCLG, 2008) assumes the existence of innovative grassroots organizations which are able to respond flexibly to changing local demographics and emergent potential conflicts. Again, government policies which encourage socially responsible behaviour by businesses (DBERR, 2008) assume the existence of a third sector which is open to receiving philanthropic donations of money and volunteer time and which is doing demonstrably 'good works' with needy and vulnerable people who might otherwise be ignored. And the numerous consultations by policy makers with third sector infrastructure bodies, along with the many references in official policy documents to an independent sector and to the special values espoused by the sector (e.g. HM Treasury, 2005; OTS, 2006), seem to assume the existence of a group of organizations whose perspectives are different from those of business and governmental organizations because they work in different ways. Finally, the refusal of successive governments to allow payment to be made to charitable trustees suggests that there is a deeply held view by politicians that TSO's should be driven by values of philanthropy and voluntarism.

In short, policy makers seem to assume the existence of the distinctive characteristics of TSOs listed above yet they do not seem to have a sense that retaining those characteristics may be problematic for TSOs in the face of strong contradictory pressures towards hybridization in their policy environment. On the one hand, there are strong pressures on TSOs to take on patterns of behaviour which move them towards hybridization; towards taking on characteristics associated with the public and private sectors. Yet, on the other hand, there are also strong pressures on TSOs to retain distinctive features and roles; in effect, pressures to defend their organizational boundaries.

The Third Way ideas which contributed to the development of New Labour policies during the late 1990s showed little awareness of the possibility of these kinds of contradictory pressures on TSOs. Indeed Giddens (1998, pp. 117–118) explicitly argued that a greater role for third sector agencies in the provision of welfare services should go hand in hand with 'programmes for the active development of civil society' (a pressure to retain distinctive features). More recent policy analysts have also not expressed much interest in the implications of contradictory policy pressures for TSOs. A few academics have expressed concern about the implications of new collaborative and network organizational arrangements, but not so much for TSOs as for public accountability and democracy (Newman, 2004; Edwards, 2008). Others have mostly confined themselves to describing what they see as a general move from 'government' (in which organizational and sectoral boundaries and accountabilities were relatively clear) to 'new governance' in which government 'acts, in concert with private and nonprofit groups and organizations, to seek solutions to the problems communities face' (Denhardt and Denhardt, 2007, p. 84; also Evers, 2005).

All the same, the contradictory pressures do raise important questions about the overall policy environment for TSOs in the future. For example, what will happen to TSOs' ability to recruit and retain volunteers if the latter come to see TSOs as less distinctive in their approach to social problems; less obviously altruistic and caring; and more focused on achieving a profit or responding to the demands of governmental funders? What will happen to TSOs' ability to advocate to government on behalf of specialist groups if TSOs are incorporated into complex cross-sectoral structures in which they sit alongside governmental funders and are focused on collaborative service-delivery mechanisms? What will happen to the funding contributed to TSOs by charitable foundations and individual donors if the latter come to see TSOs as just one relatively junior participant in the provision of general public services? And how much involvement will local people want to have in community organizations if they no longer see the latter as focused on users and local issues but rather as jostling for power in consortia which include representatives of local authorities and businesses? The way in which these questions about the competing policy pressures on TSOs are eventually answered has implications not only for the accountability of public services but also for the sustainability of a strong civil society which is independent of both state and market.

## References

Austin, J. (2000) *The Collaboration Challenge: How Nonprofits and Businesses Succeed Through Strategic Alliances*, San Francisco: Jossey-Bass.

Backman, E. and S.R. Smith (2000) 'Healthy Organizations, Unhealthy Communities?' *Nonprofit Management and Leadership*, vol. 10, 4 pp. 355–374.

Bourgon, J. (2007) 'Responsive, Responsible and Respected Government: Towards a New Public Administration Theory', *International Review of Administrative Sciences*, vol. 73, 1 pp. 7–26.

Brandsen, T. and V. Pestoff (2006) 'Co-Production, the Third Sector and the Delivery of Public Services', *Public Management Review*, vol. 8, 4 pp. 493–501.

Business in the Community (2009) *About Business in the Community*, www.bitc.org.uk (accessed 17 February 2009).

Cabinet Office (2002) *Private Action, Public Benefit: A Review of Charities and the Wider Non-Profit Sector*, London: Strategy Unit, Cabinet Office.

Cabinet Office (2008) *Capacitybuilders* http://www.cabinetoffice. gov.uk / third_sector / funding_finance_support / changeup_and_ capacitybuilders.aspx (accessed 17 February 2009).

Cairns, B., M. Harris, R. Hutchison and M. Tricker (2005) 'Improving Performance? The Adoption and Implementation of Quality Systems in UK Nonprofits', *Nonprofit Management and Leadership*, vol. 16, 2 pp. 135–151.

Cairns, B., S. Brier, J. Harris, M. Harris and H. Hughes (2006) *Making it Real: A Report of the Partnership Improvement Programme with Voluntary and Community Organizations and Local Authorities*, London: Improvement and Development Agency.

Cairns, B., M. Harris and R. Hutchison (2007) 'Sharing God's Love or Meeting Government Goals? Local Churches and Public Policy Implementation', *Policy and Politics*, vol. 35, 3 pp. 413–432.

Cantle, T. (2001) *Community Cohesion: A Report of the Independent Review Team*, London: Home Office.

Clarke, J. (2004) 'Dissolving the Public Realm? The Logics and Limits of Neo-Liberalism', *Journal of Social Policy*, vol. 33, 1 pp. 27–48.

Conservative Party (2008) *A Stronger Society: Voluntary Action in the 21st Century*, London: Conservative Central Office.

DBERR (2008) *Corporate Social Responsibility: A Government Update*, London: Department for Business Enterprise and Regulatory Reform.

DCLG (2006) *Strong and Prosperous Communities: The Local Government White Paper*, London: Department for Communities and Local Government.

DCLG (2008) *Guidance for Local Authorities on Community Cohesion Contingency Planning and Tension Monitoring*, London: Department for Communities and Local Government.

Denhardt, J. and R. Denhardt (2007) *The New Public Service: Serving Not Steering*, London: M.E. Sharpe.

Edwards, M. (2008) *Just Another Emperor? The Myths and Realities of Philanthrocapitalism*, London: Young Foundation and Demos.

Evers, A. (2005) 'Mixed Welfare Systems and Hybrid Organizations: Changes in the Governance and Provision of Social Services', *International Journal of Public Administration*, vol. 28, pp. 737–748.

Giddens, A. (1998) *The Third Way: The Renewal of Social Democracy*, Cambridge: Polity.

Glendinning. C., M. Powell and K. Rummery (2002) *Partnerships, New Labour and the Governance of Welfare*, Bristol: Policy Press.

Harris, M., C. Rochester and P. Halfpenny (2001) 'Voluntary Organisations and Social Policy: Twenty Years of Change' in Harris, M. and C. Rochester (eds) *Voluntary Organisations and Social Policy in Britain: Perspectives on Change and Choice*, Basingstoke: Palgrave, pp. 1–20.

Harris, M., B. Cairns and R. Hutchison (2004) 'So Many Tiers, So Many Agendas, So Many Pots of Money: The Challenge of Regionalisation for Voluntary and Community Organisations', *Social Policy and Administration*, vol. 38, 5 pp. 525–540.

Harris, M. and H. Schlappa (2007) 'Hoovering Up the Money? Delivering Government-Funded Capacity-Building Programmes to Voluntary and Community Organisations', *Social Policy and Society*, vol. 7, 2 pp. 1–12.

Harris, M. and P. Young (2009) *Bridging Community Divides: Impact of Grassroots Bridge Building Activities*, London: Institute for Voluntary Action Research.

Harrow, J. and P. Palmer (2003) 'The Financial Role of Charity Boards' in Cornforth, C. (ed.) *The Governance of Public and Non-Profit Organisations: What do Boards Do?* London: Routledge, pp. 97–114.

HM Treasury (2002) *The Role of the Voluntary and Community Sector in Service Delivery: A Cross Cutting Review*, London: HM Treasury.

HM Treasury (2003) *Futurebuilders: An Investment Fund for Voluntary and Community Sector Public Service Delivery*, London: HM Treasury.

HM Treasury (2005) *Exploring the Role of the Third Sector in Public Service Delivery and Reform: A Discussion Document*, London: HM Treasury.

HM Treasury (2007) *The Future Role of the Third Sector in Social and Economic Regeneration – Final Report*, London: HM Treasury and Cabinet Office.

Home Office (1998) *Compact: Getting it Right Together*, London: Home Office.

Home Office (2004) *ChangeUp: Capacity Building and Infrastructure Framework for the Voluntary and Community Sector*, London: Home Office.

I&DEA (2006) *Making it Real: A Report of the Pilot Partnership Improvement Programme with Voluntary and Community Organisations and Local Authorities*, London: Improvement and Development Agency for Local Government.

IVAR (2006) *Servants of the Community or Agents of Government? The Role of Community Based Organisations and their Contribution to Public Services Delivery and Civil Renewal*, London: bassac.

IVAR (2008) *Exploring the Advocacy Function of Multi-Purpose Community-Based Organisations*, London: bassac.

Kelly, J. (2007) 'Reforming Public Services in the UK: Bringing in the Third Sector', *Public Administration*, vol. 85, 4 pp. 1003–1022.

Le Grand, J. (1999) 'Competition, Cooperation or Control? Tales from the British National Health Service', *Health Affairs*, vol. 18, 3 pp. 27–40.

Lewis, J. (1999) 'Reviewing the Relationship between the Voluntary Sector and the State in Britain in the 1990s', *Voluntas*, vol. 10, 3 pp. 255–270.

McDonald, I. (2005) 'Theorising Partnerships: Governance, Communicative Action and Sport Policy', *Journal of Social Policy*, vol. 34, 4 pp. 579–600.

McKinney, R. and H. Kahn (2004) 'Lottery Funding and Organizational Identity in the UK Voluntary Sector', *Voluntas*, vol. 15, 1 pp. 1–19.

Maguire, K. and F. Truscott (2006) *Active Governance: The Value Added by Community Involvement in Governance Through Local Strategic Partnerships*, York: Joseph Rowntree Foundation.

Milbourne, L. (2009) Remodelling the Third Sector: Advancing Collaboration or Competition in Community-Based Initiatives?' *Journal of Social Policy*, vol. 38, 2 pp. 277–298.

Milligan, C. and N. Fyfe (2005) 'Preserving Space for Volunteers: Exploring the Links between Voluntary Welfare Organizations, Volunteering and Citizenship', *Urban Studies* vol. 42, 3 pp. 417–433.

Newman, J. (2004) 'Constructing Accountability: Network Governance and Managerial Agency', *Public Policy and Administration*, vol. 19, 4 pp. 17–33.

OTS (2006) *Partnership in Public Services: An Action Plan for Third Sector Involvement*, London: Office of the Third Sector.

Parkes, C. and M. Harris (2008) 'Corporate Responsibility, Ethics and Strategic HRM in Aston Centre for Human Resources' in *Strategic Human Resource Management: Building Research-Based Practice*, London: Chartered Institute of Personnel and Development, pp. 296–326.

Pharoah, C. (2007) *Sources of Strength: An Analysis of Applications to the Baring Foundation's Strengthen the Voluntary Sector – Independence Grants Programme*, London: The Baring Foundation.

Pollitt, C. (1995) 'Justification by Works or by Faith', *Evaluation*, vol. 1, 2 pp. 133–154.

Poole, D. (2007) 'Organizational Networks of Collaboration for Community-Based Living', *Nonprofit Management and Leadership*, vol. 18, 3 pp. 275–293.

Powell, M. (2007) 'The Mixed Economy of Welfare and the Social Division of Welfare' in Powell, M. (ed.) *Understanding the Mixed Economy of Welfare*, Bristol: The Policy Press, pp. 1–22.

Rodger, J. (2000) *From a Welfare State to a Welfare Society: The Changing Context of Social Policy in a Postmodern Era*, London: Macmillan.

Rothschild, J. and C. Milofsky (2006) 'The Centrality of Values, Passions and Ethics in the Nonprofit Sector', *Nonprofit Management and Leadership*, vol. 17, 2 pp. 137–143.

Spear, R., C. Cornforth and M. Aiken (2007) *For Love and Money: Governance and Social Enterprise*, London: NCVO for the Governance Hub.

Sullivan, H. (2002) 'Modernization, Neighbourhood Management and Social Inclusion', *Public Management Review*, vol. 4, 2 pp. 505–528.

Taylor, M., G. Craig and M. Wilkinson (2002) 'Co-option or Empowerment? The Changing Relationship between the State and the Voluntary and Community Sectors', *Local Governance*, vol. 28, pp. 1–11.

Thane, P. (1982) *The Foundations of the Welfare State*, London: Longman.

Wei-Skillern, J. and S. Marciano (2008) 'The Networked Nonprofit', *Stanford Social Innovation Review*, vol. 6, 2 pp. 38–43.

# 3 Towards a theory of hybrid organizations

*David Billis*

## Introduction

Hybrid organizations are ubiquitous. They are international, multi-sector phenomena and their unclear sector accountability often engenders unease and distrust. And in our area of concern we appear to have stumbled into a period of intense organizational hybridity in which we appear to be drifting up the (welfare hybrid) creek not only without a paddle, but also without a reliable map. Expressed in a somewhat more scholarly fashion the first priority in the preliminary agenda of issues laid out in Chapter 1 is the need to develop 'tentative theories' (Popper, 1972) of hybrid organizations.

The objective of this chapter is therefore to begin to get to grips with the agenda of questions. It is laid out as a 'building blocks' exercise and contains five parts.

1. Any study of hybridity must inevitably begin by establishing the nature of the 'non-hybrid' state of the phenomenon. This first part explores the position in the public and private sectors which are more readily understood and well established than the third sector. At the heart of the model is an approach to 'ownership' in terms of decision-making accountability that is intended to be applicable to all three main sectors.
2. This part develops a similar model for the third sector. Reflecting on previous research it is suggested that the

archetypal characteristics of the Third Sector Organization (TSO) are most closely found in the associational form of organization. A new approach to membership and ownership leads to a re-evaluation of the role of some paid staff in the association.

3. The third, pivotal level proposes a 'principal sector' hypothesis which is intended to resolve the paradox of strong sectors in the midst of the growth of hybrid types. The centrepiece of this part is a model of sectors and their hybrid zones.

4. The final level of analysis considers the nature of hybridity in the third sector. In order to do this, the concepts of 'shallow', 'entrenched', 'organic' and 'enacted' hybrids are introduced.

5. The chapter concludes with a summary and a few thoughts as to how this approach to hybridity might prove helpful in thinking about the agenda of issues from Chapter 1.

## Part one: Building an ideal model: The public and private sectors

This part constructs an ideal type model of the public and private sectors. It opens by explaining how both 'sector' and 'ideal type' will be employed and follows this with a brief review of some of the previous research and a reconsideration of the nature of ownership. It concludes with a table which compares what are called the elements and principles of both sectors.

### Sectors and ideal types

Sectors, in this chapter, are treated as collections of (non-hybrid) organizations. It is suggested that (a) all organizations have broad generic structural features or *elements* (such as the need for resources) but that (b) their nature and logic or *principles* are distinctly different in *each sector*. These principles have a logical interdependence and provide a coherent explanation for meeting objectives and solving problems. Together they represent the 'rules of the game' of the ideal model for each sector.

For my purposes the model or 'type' must draw sufficiently from empirical reality so that it can be used in both practice and in policy-making. Following this broad (Weberian) approach, the 'pure' ideal type very rarely exists (Weber and Parsons, 1964). But, notwithstanding the wide variations in structures, organizations within each sector appear to derive their strength and legitimacy (Suchman, 1995) from the characteristics and rules of the game of their own distinctive ideal type. In reality, organizations within any sector, whilst adhering to the core principles, will vary in the degree to which they fully match the ideal model (Chapter 4). And individuals, particularly those in powerful roles or organizational positions, who can contribute to shaping hybridity, will encounter the tensions between the ideal type and organizational reality (Chapter 11).

## Core structural elements in the public and private sector

My choice is selective and based on the search for the pre-dominant structural features of organizations. Of particular importance is 'the political economy' approach of Wamsley and Zald (1976) who emphasise the role of ownership and funding in a comparative analysis of the public and private sectors. More than a decade later Bozeman reviewed the literature and concluded that studies comparing the structures in the two sectors 'are uncommon' (Bozeman, 1987, p. 24). In the same period, however, an extensive critique of the distinction between the sectors (Perry and Rainey, 1988) concluded by developing a typology of organizations based on (a) ownership, (b) funding and (c) mode of social control. The pioneering work of Perry and Rainey was extended by Koppell (Koppell, 2003) who in his exploration of quasi-government hybrid organizations produces a 'simplified typology of institutions' which leaves only 'ownership' and 'funding' as the key variables (p. 11). A succinct but comprehensive review and analysis of management in the public and private sectors can be found in Rainey and Chun (2005).

Summarising this selective dip into the literature and my own research (Billis, 1991), it can be seen that the following five core *elements* persistently appear:

(1) ownership
(2) governance
(3) operational priorities
(4) human resources
(5) other resources

Clarifying the nature of ownership is essential if any model building that includes the third sector is not to be scuppered at the onset. The reason for this is, as Grønbjerg points out in her summary of the literature, that the third sector is usually regarded as not possessing 'owners' as usually defined (Grønbjerg, 2001). This is discussed in the following section.

### Revisiting the definition of ownership

Economists have been energetic in defining ownership. An extensive study by Milgrom and Roberts claims that 'Economic analyses of ownership have concentrated on two issues: the possession of a residual decision rights and the allocation of residual returns' (Milgrom and Roberts, 1992, p. 289). Their analysis is overwhelmingly focused – as are much of the other economic writings – on the for-profit firm. Consequently, it has been helpful to look at authors who have also taken a rather wider perspective including consideration of the third sector.

Prominent amongst these authors is Hansmann who has approached the issue of ownership in nonprofits by raising the question of 'ultimate control', defined as 'the power to elect the board of directors' (Hansmann, 1987, p. 28). In a later work he suggests that because of the 'nondistribution constraint, a nonprofit firm, by definition, has no owners – that is, no persons who have a share in both control and residual earnings' (Hansmann, 1996, p. 228). An important distinction is made between 'formal control' which is different from 'effective control' (p. 11).

When faced by this distinctive problem of ownership in nonprofits Speckbacher introduces the idea of 'key stakeholders who play the role of the "firm's owners" [and]...should have the right to interpret the mission in controversial situations' (Speckbacher, 2003, pp. 275–276). Ben-Ner and Jones link ownership and control more closely and extensively with organizational features which range from 'determination of the objectives of the organization' through to how people 'are induced to carry out their functions' (Ben-Ner and Jones, 1995, pp. 532–534). Chew and Osborne, in their analysis of strategic positioning in charities, also emphasise the influential role of stakeholders, particularly key organizational decision makers (Chew and Osborne, 2009, pp. 42–43).

The following analysis picks up these threads of different layers of ownership, organizational decisions and stakeholders/members. The approach abandons residual returns as an essential feature of ownership that in any case does not seem persuasive for the public sector (Wamsley and Zald, 1976). Consequently, in this chapter, ownership is defined according to different levels of decision-making accountability (formal, active and principal) *within* the broad category of ownership. For the moment, the discussion is confined to the private and the public sectors. Here can be identified groups of people who have the 'formal rights' to elect the board of directors and political representatives respectively known as shareholders and the electorate. Nevertheless a sizeable percentage of this *formal/legal ownership* can be inactive. In reality they may have little interest or motivation to participate in any of the decision-making activities of business or government.

In both sectors people can be found within the formal ownership who (at least) *do* exercise their votes at the annual board meeting and who *do* vote in government elections. These can be regarded as *active owners* even if their influence on Hansmann's small set of fundamental issues is slight.

The third group are the *principal owners*: those who *in effect* can close the organization down and transfer it to another sector – what Weisbrod (1998) refers to as 'conversion' – or change the fundamental boundary and mission of the organization through mergers or other actions (Gray, 1997). In the private sector it may be large pension funds or other major investors. In the public sector it likely to be the elected representatives or a caucus of those representatives.

With these definitions in mind, it is now possible to return to the main objective of this part: building an ideal type of the public and private sectors.

### Building the foundations: A model of the public and private sectors

So far, five *elements* which might serve as a basis for building a model of the public and private sectors have been identified. *Each element comes with a distinctive set of principles for each sector.* In summarising these principles I can draw attention only to a few particularly relevant studies, for example, the works of Stewart and Ranson (Ranson and Stewart, 1994; Stewart and Ranson, 1988) which compare the rationale for management in the public domain to that in the private domain. They both discuss the elements and principles in the two sectors and contrast collective choice in the polity with individual choice in the market.

What emerge are tentative models of

- A *private sector* which is (a) owned by shareholders and (b) governed according to the principle of size of share ownership, working according to (c) operational priorities driven by principles of market forces in individual choice, with typical (d) human resources consisting of paid employees in a managerially controlled *firm* and (e) other resources primarily from sales and fees.
- A *public sector* which is (a) owned by the citizens and (b) governed according to principles of public elections with work driven (c) by principles of public services and collective choice and as its typical (d) human resources consisting of paid public servants in legally backed bureaux and (f) resourced by taxation.

The following part of the chapter will explore how the complexities of the third sector could be similarly developed into an ideal type.

**Part two: Developing a model for the third sector**

The objective of this part is to utilise the same five structural elements, discussed above, and to identify *principles* which are distinctly applicable to the third sector.

## The search for distinctive principles

There is an impressive list of authors who have sought to uncover the sector's general distinctive features (for example, Kramer, 1981; Young, 1983; Mason, 1984; Van Til, 1988; O'Neill, 1989; Lohmann, 1992; Smith, 2000). (For an important comparative discussion of the public, private and what is called the 'commons' see Lohmann, 1992 Chapter 2). Much of this literature has been summarised and analysed by Grønbjerg who identified five major attributes (1) private auspices (2) absence of formal ownership rights (3) volunteerism (4) particular missions and substantive goals and (5) the challenge of changing people (Grønbjerg, 2001). The extensive international mapping exercise undertaken by Johns Hopkins University (Salamon and Anheier, 1992) identified the key 'common features' as self-governing, nonprofit distribution, private and nongovernmental in basic structure and voluntary to 'some meaningful extent' (Salamon et al., 2000).

Interestingly, a European analysis of social enterprises, despite the attempt to distance these 'new entrepreneurial forms' from the 'more traditional' third sector, is also compelled to rely on a similar set of characteristics (Bacchiega and Borzaga, 2001, pp. 273–274).

In sum, the literature highlights a number of principles which are seen to be distinctive. These include independence, use of voluntary labour, sensitivity and closeness to users and being mission driven.

However, much of the research, as Smith (2000) points out, ignores the vast number of small grass roots organizations, a similar point made in a comprehensive review of community movements and local organizations (Cnaan and Milofsky, 2008). Also, rather neglected in current third sector research are social movements (Davis, 2005) and, at the other end of the scale, many huge membership organizations such as the National Trust (which has 3.5 million members and 52,000 volunteers) let alone political parties. It is likely therefore that a more balanced overview of the third sector would give increased emphasis to the role of volunteers and the distinctive type of resources of these organizations.

All this, in addition to the actual history of many organizations, indicates that an ideal type of the third sector is best typified by the association. In this model people establish a formal organization in order to resolve their own or other people's problems. These members, through a process of private elections, elect committees and officers to guide the work of the organization. The organization may need additional volunteer labour to forward its policies. Other resources may also be sought and these are typically membership dues, donations and legacies. Work is driven neither by the need to make a profit nor by public policies but primarily by the association's own agenda. This approach differs from most prevailing theoretical approaches to the sector. The association, rather than being a rather peripheral component (as in the Johns Hopkins research), is now seen as the 'ideal model' and source of the distinctive sector attributes (Rothschild-Whitt, 1979).

Nevertheless, in the development of a model comparable to the private and public sectors, one stumbling block still remains: the place of members and 'owners' in the third sector model.

## Ownership in membership associations

A recent analysis notes that previous indictments regarding the absence of a compelling theory (Gordon and Babchuk, 1959; Knoke, 1986) 'still hold today... empirical research on governance and structure of non-profit membership association is thin' (Tschirhart, 2006, pp. 534–535). Consequently, this section of the chapter explores whether the preceding analysis of different layers of owners helps in the model building of the sector.

In the association, the gap between *formal*, *active* and *principal* owners may be small. However, even in small, tightly knit groups, it is possible to differentiate between those (formal members) who stay in the shadows (see Putnam (2000) for a seminal study); those who play an active part in committee and other activities; and a core group of those (principal owners) 'who everybody knows' will really be the key players in the defining moments of the group's history.

The distinctive characteristics of associations are the linkage and logical flow between its ownership by members, principles of governance, reliance on volunteer resources for its operational work and principles of membership accountability which together enable it to function as a robust and effective organization. Critically, although there may be clear differentiation in the roles of governing body, committees and volunteer workers, all will usually be part of the active and membership/ownership groups as defined. In addition, those receiving services may be past or present members, or have close links through family, neighbourhood, friendship and other groups. Active members will be dedicated to the cause which may be expressed tangibly both through financial contributions and through a preparedness to take on unpopular and sometimes unpleasant work, readiness to recruit others into the organization and, if necessary, advocacy – the determination to persuade those outside the group of the rightness of the mission.

According to this approach, *formal, active* and *principal* member/owners can also be identified according to their different levels of accountability for decision-making.

### The model of the three sectors

Employing a decision-making approach to the issue of membership/ownership enables their core elements and principles to be laid out together with those of the private and public sectors in the form of a table (Table 3.1).

According to this model, the ideal type 'work doing' operational units of the sectors are the firm, bureau and association.[1]

Underpinning the model of sectors is the notion of accountability and the role of principal owners. By organizational accountability, I am referring to those individuals and groups (governing bodies of all sorts, and individuals) who have the

**Table 3.1**   Ideal type sectors and accountability

| Core elements ⬇ | Private sector principles | Public sector principles | Third sector principles |
|---|---|---|---|
| 1. Ownership | Shareholders | Citizens | Members |
| 2. Governance | Share ownership size | Public elections | Private elections |
| 3. Operational Priorities | Market forces and individual choice | Public service and collective choice | Commitment about distinctive mission |
| 4. Distinctive human resources | Paid employees in managerially controlled *Firm* | Paid public servants in legally backed *Bureau* | Members and volunteers in *Association* |
| 5. Distinctive other resources | Sales, fees | Taxes | Dues, donations and legacies |

*authority* to carry out their designated duties and can be held to account to higher level individuals and institutions if they fail to carry out those duties.

## Part three: Building a model of hybrid organizations

### Approaches to the study of hybridity

Despite recent increased interest in hybrid organizations, the literature remains sparsely spread across many academic disciplines over several decades. In the absence of a systematic body of research, I have restricted myself to outline a few of the broad approaches that are particularly germane for this chapter. Many of the numerous studies of hybridity defy easy classification (see or example, Langton, 1987; Powell, 1987; Hasenfeld and Gidron, 2005; Cooney, 2006). However, for ease of analysis, much of the disparate literature might be loosely grouped into three approaches.

1. A popular approach regards hybrid organizations as occupying points on a *continuum* between sectors (for example, Dahl and Lindblom, 1953; Demone and Gibelman, 1989).
2. Other writers have adopted what might be called a *single sector emphasis*. Here, their main concern is either with the public or private sector, and organizations on their boundary are usually studied from the perspective of the implications for one particular sector (Gray, 1990; Courpasson and Dany, 2003; Koppell, 2003; Skelcher et al., 2005).
3. A few writers, mainly from continental Europe, appear to have gone one step further in a *separate sector* approach. For them, hybridization and hybrid organizations have replaced the sector metaphor and are now *the* permanent features in the welfare system (Brandsen et al., 2005; Evers, 2005). In an earlier paper, James (1983), although focusing on US nonprofits, seems to be arguing an almost similar case.

Reflecting on this emerging body of literature reinforces the contention made in Chapter 1 and the introduction to this chapter: any theory will need to (a) handle the paradox of a strong sector concept in a period of increased hybridity (b) cover all three sectors and (c) address the issue of accountability.

The following section attempts to address these issues.

## The model of hybridity: The prime sector approach

In this chapter, I shall take a different approach to those outlined in the previous section drawing on research that goes back some 30 years. Initially using the work of Edmund Leach on ambiguity (Leach, 1976), this early work can be tracked in Billis (1979; 1984a; 1984b).

My working hypothesis is that organizations will have 'roots' and have primary adherence to the principles of one sector (Billis, 1991; 1993; 2003). This is based on the inherent contradictory distinctive and conflicting *principles* (rules of the game) for each sector outlined in Table 3.1.

According to a prime sector approach, stakeholders and public policy makers need to be clear whether the organiza-

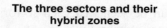

**The three sectors and their hybrid zones**

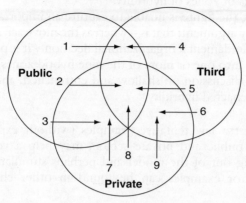

Key: The hybrid zones

1. Public/Third
2. Public/Private/Third
3. Public/Private

4. Third/Public
5. Third/Public/Private
6. Third/Private

7. Private/Public
8. Private/Public/Third
9. Private/Third

**Figure 3.1**   The three sectors and their hybrid zones

tions they are working with, and in, fundamentally adhere to the principles of accountability inherent in either the public, private or third sector. Thus, hybrids are not on a continuum but have a clear cut off point evident when principal owners take the boundary-shaping decisions (closures, conversions mergers etc.) according to the principles of the different sectors.

But neither are hybrids a separate sector since there is no evidence that they have distinctive and explicit *principles* of management and operation which set them apart from other sectors.

Figure 3.1 depicts the three sectors and their hybrid zones.

The model of the three sectors requires a few words of explanation.

Firstly, the circles which represent sectors are not intended to reflect the size of resources or impact of these sectors in different countries. These clearly vary from country to country.

Secondly, it can be seen that each sector may have three forms or zones of hybridity.

Thirdly, the figure is unable to capture an important aspect of my argument: that is – whereas the move across sectors is a fundamental organizational decision – it is possible to slide into one or more of the nine hybrid zones. (See the later discussion on shallow and entrenched, and organic and enacted hybridity).

Finally, just a few tentative examples (without explanation) from the public and private sectors may help a very modest fleshing out of the model and perhaps stimulate debate. Third sector examples can be found in other chapters of the book.

| | |
|---|---|
| Public/Third | NHS Foundation Trusts |
| Public/Private/Third | The BBC |
| Public/Private | Nationalised industries, Fannie Mae |
| Private/Public | Partnership UK (51 per cent private equity) |
| Private/Public/Third | The National Lottery |
| Private/Third | The John Lewis Partnership |

### Part four: The case of hybrid TSOs

Although the issues discussed in this part of the chapter are likely to have counterparts in other sectors, the following discussion is restricted to some key theoretical and practical issues for the third sector raised by the prime sector approach to hybridity. It opens by distinguishing firstly between 'shallow' and 'entrenched' hybridity and secondly between 'organic' and 'enacted' hybrids. These sections are followed by a consideration of one of the chronic dilemmas of third sector theory: the role of paid staff.

### Shallow hybridity

Hybridity in the third sector is not a new phenomenon. For many years, some organizations have moved into hybridity in a rather gentle fashion, causing minor disturbances, but not necessarily calling into question their basic third sector identity.

The introduction of a modest form of hybridity often arises from the desire to maintain or perhaps extend the range of activities. Board members with a business background might be keen for more commercial approaches. For example, in one case study, the appointment of an NHS consultant led to pressure to work more closely with the health service. Resources and grants from government or business might be received to support the general purposes of the organization.

Field work over several decades indicates that taking on the first paid staff (the typical human resources of the public and private sectors) can be felt as an important step into shallow hybridity for TSOs (Billis, 1984a). This can be uncomfortable but most TSOs appear to have survived this early discomfort and have preserved the integrity of their core missions. Initially, they may employ staff to handle their supporting non-operational activities.

At some point, the organization may decide that it needs one, or even a few, paid staff to undertake operational work to meet the needs of its users. A special grant might be sought, or an appeal launched, and workers are recruited. Often, the first paid staff may themselves have been committed members, perhaps founders of the organization. Even where tensions arise between volunteer workers and those who get paid for the same work, this may still be regarded as belonging to the shallow form of hybridity.

### Entrenched hybridity in the third sector

Whether planned at all or not, entrenched hybridity can arrive both at the (a) governance and (b) operational levels of organizations in all sectors.

At the governance level, the board or other form of governing body may find itself compelled to, or under pressure to, accept permanent government or private sector representatives in return for resources and influence.

More usually, entrenched hybridity in the third sector begins as a result of receiving private and public sector resources through grants, contracts and sales. These resources will increase and decrease according to political preferences and market forces but they may become sufficiently reliable that, together with third sector sources, they represent a flow of income adequate to maintain a structure of management. (But entrenched hybridity need not take this 'organic' route; it can arrive immediately through 'enactment' – see the following section).

At the operational level, entrenchment arises when paid staff become dominant in the delivery of the operational work of the organization and a management structure with several hierarchical levels is established. Then the organization can be considered to have embedded into its structure core features of the firm and bureau. The rules of the game begin to change and associational principles have to coexist with alien principles drawn from the private and public sectors (see Table 3.1). This is because maintaining a structure of staff leads to increased pressure towards considerations of individual and organizational survival. Significant resources have increasingly to be secured often through the political process (that they meet public policy needs), and/or through the market principles of cost and price.

Entrenched paid staff structures bring with them a different language and way of operation. People are then dependent on the organization for their livelihood and – quite naturally – hours and conditions of service, promotion and career development have to be accommodated. Formal job descriptions, managerial accountability, sanctions and reward systems all become daily features and replace the 'group' and 'committee' as the prime ways of organizing and solving problems. It becomes increasingly likely that such structures are influenced by political and commercial priorities and activities. There are other possible consequences. Volunteers might wonder why others should receive payment, whilst they give their labour freely on the basis of belief and commitment (see Chapter 5).

Although entrenched hybridity may increase the propensity for mission drift, I am far from arguing that this is inevitable. If third sector resources are themselves adequate, then entrenched hybrids can be established from within the sector itself. It seems reasonable to assume that despite the tensions that arrive with the introduction of employment hierarchies, this type of hybrid TSO will be less susceptible to mission drift. More importantly, paid staff may also be active or principal members/owners: an essential part of this analysis which is discussed shortly.

## Organic and enacted hybrids

Much of the third sector literature has been occupied with organizations where hybridity has resulted from the steady accumulation of external resources. Over many years, organizations may have moved from shallow to entrenched hybridity. However, in this new era of frenzied organizational experimentation, there are a growing number of hybrid organizations that are enacted, that are established from day one as hybrids, usually by other organizations.

A full analysis of enacted hybrids lies well beyond the scope of this chapter but we can note that – notwithstanding the recent upsurge – they have been around for many years. We need to think here only of the nationalised industries owned by government but operating in the market.

Enacted hybrids arise for different reasons, in different sectors and under different broad headings. Although they may be seen as part of the broader category of numerous collaborative mechanisms across sectors (including partnerships, networks, project groups, joint ventures and joint operating groups), they are distinguished by the fact that they have an *apparently* independent, often legal, structure. Thus governments can create or sponsor new organizational forms (see Chapters 8 and 9), oil companies can collaborate with national governments in separate legal forms and TSOs can establish trading companies (Chapter 4).

Enacted hybrids may present complex problems of accountability and later chapters will enter this territory. The only point that might be made in this chapter is to question the extent to which these arrangements are time-limited and the extent to which they affect the basic sector identity of individual organizations involved in the collaborations.

### Paid staff as members/owners?

Another problem remains unresolved. The theoretical quandary is as follows. Hybrid TSOs are usually and increasingly dependent on paid staff and may have few if any 'formal members', so how can these agencies be part of the third sector whose core principles, I have argued, are based on the association? In an attempt to resolve this apparent contradiction the nature of membership/ownership will be revisited.

My argument is that in hybrid TSOs paid staff may also be part of the *active* membership by similarly (to other active members) demonstrating their genuine commitment to organizational purposes through their freely given and un-coerced contributions to the operations and governance of the organization. Thus, additional to their normal work role, they may undertake voluntary work or provide other resources. They may participate in committees and other governance activities. They may have a more flexible approach to precise hours of work flowing from a belief in the purposes of the organization. 'Voluntary' must mean what it says. As Bacchiega and Borzaga put it in their analysis of social enterprises 'incentives for workers are not based exclusively on monetary rewards; rather, they derive mainly from workers' involvement in shaping and sharing the organization's goals and mission' (Bacchiega and Borzaga, 2001, p. 274).

Being part of the governance process is more than a consultation exercise in which staff opinions are solicited in order to help managers do *their* work. In contrast, in these meetings, the active TSO members combine their work role with a personal commitment to the cause to discuss broader organizational issues informally or perhaps in a more structured fashion. There is a degree of overlap and hybridity in their paid work and membership roles.

From this pool of paid staff of active members, there may be those who are sufficiently committed and influential to be considered a natural part of the ownership of the organization which makes the critical decisions discussed earlier.

**Part five: Discussion and conclusions**

This chapter presented a tentative theory of hybrid organizations in order to facilitate a later discussion of the list of issues laid out in the introductory chapter. This concluding part summarises that general approach to hybridity and offers just a few thoughts on its relationship to the opening catalogue of issues. I have not attempted to draw conclusions about the possible implications for research, policy and practice. That task seems more appropriately undertaken after taking into account the lessons that emerge from Part II of the book.

In view of the contested boundaries of the third sector, the chapter began the process of model building by drawing on research and literature from the private and particularly from the public sectors. The concepts of 'element' (present in all sectors) and 'principles' (distinctive sector rules of the game) were used in order to build a comparative model. It rapidly became clear that if a similar model were to be developed for the third sector, several intellectual challenges would need to be confronted. The first of these was the problem of *ownership*, a core component of these models. Applying the traditional economic definitions of ownership inevitably leads to the familiar conclusion that TSOs have no owners. Rather than abandon the concept in the model building, ownership was revisited and redefined in terms of its accountability for different levels of decision-making. Principal, active and formal owners were defined. Principal owners were seen to be those that take the major boundary shaping or strategic decisions. Approaching ownership in this way enabled the concept to be more realistically employed in the third sector model.

The second challenge was to uncover an 'ideal type' of the third sector which possessed an equally robust set of core distinctive principles. After reflecting on the policy and research literature, the conclusion was reached that the positive attributes most frequently claimed for the sector were found in their most pristine form in the archetypal association. This does not mean that such groups are unproblematic utopian communities, or that they are the most significant players in public policy. Placing the association and its claimed virtues at the heart of the third sector is comparable to the powerful ideal models of the public and private sectors under whose own general *principles* can be found equally diverse groups of institutions.

These two threads of argument (ownership and distinctive principles) and the proposition that organizations had *primary accountability* to the principles of one sector, led to the model presented in Table 3.1 and eventually to the depiction of hybrid organizations in Figure 3.1.

In an attempt to get to grips more closely with the nature of hybridity, *shallow* was differentiated from *entrenched states* of hybrid TSOs. It was hypothesised that entrenchment is likely to be associated with the development of hierarchical levels of paid staff and the associated resource demands, usually from public and private sector sources. In the belief that these may prove to have different problems, it was suggested that it might be worth while differentiating *organic* from *enacted types* of hybrid – those established by other organizations.

Finally, the chapter returned to what currently appears to be a central theme of the 'optimistic–pessimistic' debate, the position of large paid staff TSOs. I raised the possibility that based on the discussion about principal owners/members, paid staff may under certain circumstances be part of this group.

Where relevant, following chapters will reflect on these concepts and explore their utility in the light of their own specific areas of study. Although the notion of overlapping sectors and zones is based on a long history of personal research, many of the concepts ('the role of principal owners', 'shallow and entrenched hybridity' and 'organic and enacted hybridity') have had more limited testing. Those studies will also therefore present an opportunity to reflect on their potential usefulness in a wide range of third sector settings.

I hope, therefore, that the discussions of 'hybridity in action' in Part II of the book make it possible to respond to most of the questions raised in the introductory chapter. To take just one example: who are the accountable owners of hybrids?

This is one of the most pressing and puzzling questions for policy and practice. The decision-making approach to ownership – which was conceptualised in terms of principal, active and formal owners – was intended to help confront this question and assist in increasing transparency of accountability.

This chapter has primarily concentrated on the organic hybrids with a single accountable ownership body. I think that a strong case can be made that if we can ask more penetrating questions and get closer to an answer about ownership in these forms of hybrid TSOs, this would represent a major step forward. Nevertheless, as noted earlier, there is a growing body of more complex TSOs with interlocking layers of ownership and accountability that remains to be explored. To complicate matters even further, the tendency to enact hybrid organizations appears also to be increasing, with the possibility of another distinctive set of issues and challenges. Some of the following case studies enter this territory, and again this may provide the opportunity to test and possibly further develop the ideas presented in this chapter.

## Note

1. In earlier publications, I have referred to the third sector as the Association sector. However, this has caused some confusion between the definition of the 'sector' and its core organizational units. Other writers have met the same problem (Warren, M. (2001) *Democracy and Association*, Princeton, N.J.: Princeton University Press).

## References

Bacchiega, A. and C. Borzaga (2001) 'Social enterprises as incentive structures: an economic analysis' in C. Borzaga and J. Defourny (eds) *The Emergence of Social Enterprise*, London: Routledge.

Ben-Ner, A. and D. C. Jones (1995) 'Employee Participation, Ownership, and Productivity: A Theoretical Framework.' *Industrial Relations*, 34(4) pp. 532–554.

Billis, D. (1979) *Voluntary Organisations: Management Issues 1: Report from February 1979 Workshop*, Uxbridge: Brunel Institute of Organisation and Social Studies. Programme of Research and Training in Voluntary Action (PORTVAC).

Billis, D. (1984a) *Voluntary Sector Management: Research and Practice*, Uxbridge: Brunel University, Programme of Research and Training in Voluntary Action (PORTVAC).

Billis, D. (1984b) 'Self-Help and Service: An Action-Research Study with a Group of One-Parent Families.' *Working Paper/PORTVAC;* 2, London: Brunel University.

Billis, D. (1991) 'The Roots of Voluntary Agencies: A Question of Choice.' *Nonprofit and Voluntary Sector Quarterly,* 20(1) pp. 57–70.

Billis, D. (1993) 'Sector Blurring and Nonprofit Centres: The Case of the United Kingdom.' *Nonprofit and Voluntary Sector Quarterly,* 22(3) pp. 241–257.

Billis, D. (2003) *Sectors, Hybrids, and Public Policy: The Voluntary Sector in Context,* Paper Presented to the Annual Meeting of ARNOVA November, Denver.

Bozeman, B. (1987) *All Organizations are Public: Bridging Public and Private Organizational Theories,* San Francisco: Jossey-Bass.

Brandsen, T., W. van de Donk and K. Putters (2005) 'Griffins or Chameleons? Hybridity as a Permanent and Inevitable Characteristic of the Third Sector.' *International Journal of Public Administration,* 28 pp. 749–765.

Chew, C. and S. P. Osborne (2009) 'Identifying the Factors that Influence Positioning Strategy in UK Charitable Organisations that Provide Public Services: Towards an Integrating Model.' *Nonprofit and Voluntary Sector Quarterly,* 38(1) pp. 29–50.

Cnaan, R. A. and C. Milofsky (eds) (2008) *Handbook of Community Movements and Local Organizations,* Handbooks of Sociology and Social Research, New York: Springer.

Cooney, K. (2006) 'The Institutional and Technical Structuring of NonProfit Ventures: Case Study of a U.S. Hybrid Organization Caught Between Two Fields.' *Voluntas,* 17 pp. 143–161.

Courpasson, D. and F. Dany (2003) 'Indifference or Obedience? Business Firms as Democratic Hybrids.' *Organization Studies,* 24(8) pp. 1231–1260.

Dahl, R. A. and C. E. Lindblom (1953) *Politics, Economics and Welfare: Planning and Politico-Economic Systems Resolved into Basic Social Processes,* New York: Harper.

Davis, G. F. (2005) *Social Movements and Organization Theory,* Cambridge and New York: Cambridge University Press.

Demone, H. W. and M. Gibelman (1989) *Services for Sale: Purchasing Health and Human Services,* New Jersey: Rutgers University Press.

Evers, A. (2005) 'Mixed Welfare Systems and Hybrid Organizations: Changes in the Governance and Provision of Social Services.' *International Journal of Public Administration,* 28 pp. 737–748.

Gordon, C. W. and N. Babchuk (1959) 'A Typology of Voluntary Associations.' *American Sociological Review*, 24(2) pp. 22–29.

Gray, B. (1997) 'Conversion of HMOs and Hospitals: What's At Stake?' *Health Affairs*, 16(2) pp. 29–47.

Gray, B. H. (1990) 'Nonprofit Hospitals and the For-Profit Challenge.' *The Bulletin of the New York Academy of Medicine*, 66(4) pp. 366–375.

Grønbjerg, K. A. (2001) 'Foreword' in S. J. Ott (ed.) *The Nature of the Nonprofit Sector*, Colorado: Westview Press.

Hansmann, H. (1987) 'Economic Theories of Nonprofit Organization' in W. W. Powell (ed.) *The Nonprofit Sector*, New Haven and London: Yale University Press.

Hansmann, H. (1996) *The Ownership of Enterprise*, Cambridge, Mass.: The Belknap Press of Harvard University Press.

Hasenfeld, Y. and B. Gidron (2005) 'Understanding Multi-purpose Hybrid Voluntary Organizations: The Contributions of Theories on Civil Society, Social Movements and Non-profit Organizations.' *Journal of Civil Society*, 1(2) pp. 97–112.

James, E. (1983) 'How Nonprofits Grow: A Model.' *Journal of Policy Analysis and Management*, 2(3) pp. 350–366.

Knoke, D. (1986) 'Associations and Interest Groups', *Annual Review of Sociology*, 12 pp. 1–21.

Koppell, J. G. S. (2003) *The Politics of Quasi-Government: Hybrid Organizations and the Dynamics of Bureaucratic Control*, Cambridge: Cambridge University Press.

Kramer, R. (1981) *Voluntary Agencies in the Welfare State*, Berkeley and London: University of California Press.

Langton, S. (1987) 'Envoi: Developing Nonprofit Theory.' *Journal of Voluntary Action Research*, 16(1&2) pp. 134–148.

Leach, E. (1976) *Culture and Communication*, Cambridge: Cambridge University Press.

Lohmann, R. A. (1992) *The Commons: New Perspectives on Nonprofit Organizations and Voluntary Action*, San Francisco: Jossey-Bass.

Mason, D. E. (1984) *Voluntary Nonprofit Enterprise Management*, New York and London: Plenum.

Milgrom, P. R. and J. Roberts (1992) *Economics, Organization, and Management*, Englewood Cliffs, N.J.: Prentice-Hall.

O'Neill, M. (1989) *The Third America: The Emergence of the Nonprofit Sector in the United States*, San Francisco: Jossey-Bass.

Perry, J. L. and H. G. Rainey (1988) 'The Public-Private Distinction in Organization Theory: a Critique and Research Strategy.' *The Academy of Management Review*, 13(2) pp. 182–201.

Pieterse, J. N. (2001) 'Hybridity, So What? The Anti-hybridity back-lash and the Riddles of Recognition.' *Theory, Culture & Society*, 18(2–3) pp. 219–245.

Popper, K. R. (1972) *Objective Knowledge: An Evolutionary Approach*, Oxford: Clarendon Press.

Powell, W. W. (1987) 'Hybrid Organizational Arrangements: New Form or Transitional Development?' *California Management Review*, 30(1) pp. 67–87.

Putnam, R. D. (2000) *Bowling Alone: The Collapse and Revival of American Community*, New York and London: Simon & Schuster.

Rainey, H. G. and Y. H. Chun (2005) 'Public and Private Manage-ment Compared' in E. Ferlie, L. E. L. Jr and C. Pollitt (eds) *The Oxford Handbook of Public Management*, Oxford: Oxford University Press.

Ranson, S. and J. D. Stewart (1994) *Management for the Public Domain: Enabling the Learning Society*, Basingstoke: Macmillan.

Rothschild-Whitt, J. (1979) 'The Collectivist Organization: An Alter-native to Rational-Bureaucratic Models.' *American Sociological Review*, 44 pp. 509–527.

Salamon, L. M. and H. K. Anheier (1992) *In Search of the Nonprofit Sector 1: The Question of Definitions*, Baltimore: Johns Hopkins University Institute for Policy Studies.

Salamon, L. M., L. C. Hems and K. Chinnock (2000) 'The Nonprofit Sector: For What and For Whom?' *Working Papers, J.H.C.N.S. Project*, Baltimore: The John Hopkins Center for Civil Society Studies.

Schanze, E. (1993) 'Symbiotic Arrangements.' *Journal of Institu-tional and Theoretical Economics*, 149(4) pp. 691–697.

Skelcher, C., N. Mathur and M. Smith (2005) 'The Public Gover-nance of Collaborative Spaces: Discourse, Design and Democracy.' *Public Administration*, 83(3) pp. 573–596.

Smith, D. H. (2000) *Grassroots Associations*, Thousand Oaks, Calif.: Sage Publications.

Speckbacher, G. (2003) 'The Economics of Performance Manage-ment in Non-Profit Organizations.' *Nonprofit Management and Leadership*, 13(3) pp. 267–281.

Stewart, J. and S. Ranson (1988) 'Management in the Public Domain.' *Public Money and Management*, 8(2) pp. 13–19.

Suchman, M. C. (1995) 'Managing Legitimacy: Strategic and Insti-tutional Approaches.' *Academy of Management Review*, 20(3) pp. 571–610.

Tschirhart, M. (2006) 'Nonprofit Membership Associations' in Powell, W. W. and R. Steinberg (eds) *The Nonprofit Sector* (second edition), New Haven and London: Yale University Press.

Van Til, J. (1988) *Mapping the Third Sector: Voluntarism in a Changing Social Economy*, New York: The Foundation Center.

Wamsley, G. L. and M. N. Zald (1976) *The Political Economy of Public Organizations*, Bloomington: Indiana University Press.

Warren, M. (2001) *Democracy and Association*, Princeton, N.J.: Princeton University Press.

Weber, M. and T. Parsons (1964) *The Theory of Social and Economic Organization*, New York: Free Press.

Weisbrod, B. A. (1998) *To Profit or Not to Profit: The Commercial Transformation of the Nonprofit Sector*, Cambridge: Cambridge University Press.

Young, D. R. (1983) *If Not for Profit, for What?: A Behavioral Theory of the Nonprofit Sector Based on Entrepreneurship*, Lexington, Mass.: Lexington Books.

# 4 The governance of hybrid organizations

## Chris Cornforth and Roger Spear

### Introduction

The focus of this chapter is on the challenges that are raised by hybridity for the governance of third sector organizations (TSOs). In particular, it will explore how it affects governance structures and processes and the challenges it poses for governing bodies.

A number of factors are driving the growth of new hybrid forms of organizations in the third sector. Chapter 2 has discussed the ways in which government has sought to create a mixed economy of welfare by encouraging both private and TSOs to engage in public service delivery and the heavy investment it has made developing the third sector's capacity to take on this role. At the same time, many TSOs have been looking to diversify their income streams and have seen trading as an important way of achieving this. Figures from the 2006 Voluntary Sector Almanac showed that earned income of voluntary organizations had grown from 33 per cent in 1994/5 to 47 per cent in 2003/4, to become the largest single source of income (Wilding et al., 2006).

There has also been a growth in TSOs that identify themselves as social enterprises, hybrid businesses that trade in the market but pursue social or environmental goals (Nyssens, 2006 and for a fuller discussion of these organizations, see Chapter 8 of this volume). Government has responded to this development by creating a new legal form – the Community Interest Company (CIC) – and a new regulatory body.

Chapter 2 has also emphasised the drive by government to create new partnerships at a local level between organizations in the public, third and private sectors which has led to an evermore complex and varied organizational landscape which has implications for governance. At the inter-organizational level, there has been a growth of partnerships, federations, collaborations and alliances. At the organizational level, many organizations are adopting more complex structures with, for example, one or more trading subsidiaries.

Research on the governance of TSOs has not, however, kept pace with this growing complexity. A preponderance of research has taken place in the US and it has often focussed on the boards of medium and large-sized non-profit agencies that work in the field of human services (Ostrower and Stone, 2006). It has tended to ignore other aspects of the governance system such as membership; audit or regulatory requirements; or how other wider contextual factors influence governance. The focus has also been primarily on unitary organizations with single boards, rather than on the more complex governance structures that many hybrid organizations adopt, such as charities with trading subsidiaries.

This chapter starts to address this gap by exploring some of the implications of hybridity for organizational governance. It begins quite broadly by focusing on the different types of governance structures employed within TSOs. It suggests that the governance of TSOs varies quite widely from the ideal type of the membership association outlined in Chapter 3. Three broad types of governance structures are identified and their potential strengths and weaknesses are discussed. We then go on to explore the different governance challenges of organizations with few or no staff compared to those with an established professional staff structure (which Billis in Chapter 3 calls 'entrenched hybrids').

The chapter then goes on to examine governance in particular types of hybrid organization. The diversity and complexity of the sector mean that a selective approach has been taken. First, it will examine trading charities as an important example of third/private sector hybrids. It notes that one of the main ways of coping with the potentially different requirements of charitable and trading activities is by separating or 'decoupling' them from each other. Secondly, it will examine public/third sector hybrids that are created when services are spun-off out of the public sector.

Before looking at these different examples, however, we need to clarify what is meant by governance and to identify the key characteristics of organizational governance arrangements in the private and public sectors in order to explore whether and how governance practices in these sectors are influencing those of hybrid organizations.

## What do we mean by 'governance'?

The term 'governance' has become an important concept in a variety of different disciplinary and practice arenas. It has its roots in a Latin word meaning to steer or give direction. However, as Kooiman (1999) notes in a useful review article, the term is used in a number of different ways which can lead to confusion. He suggests one useful way of distinguishing between different usages is in terms of levels of analysis. The focus here is on the organizational level and how organizations are governed. At this level, what is often called 'corporate' or 'organizational' governance can be defined as the 'structures, systems and processes concerned with ensuring the overall direction, control and accountability of an organization' (Cornforth, 2004, p. 1). The body with the main responsibility in an organization for carrying out governance functions is the organization's board or governing body. The corporate governance system is, however, wider than this and includes the framework of broader responsibilities and accountabilities within which organizations operate, including regulatory and reporting requirements and relations with key stakeholders.

It is also important to distinguish organizational governance from political governance, at a higher level of analysis, where it is used to refer to new patterns of government and governing. In particular, it is used to describe the shift away from a unitary state to a more fragmented and arms-length system of government where a range of non-governmental bodies participate in the delivery of public services and policy formulation (Rhodes, 1994). Some of the issues arising from these forms of governance are explored in detail in Chapter 9 of the present volume.

The language used to refer to an organization's governing body and those that serve on it varies widely between and within the different sectors. In this chapter, for the sake of simplicity, the term 'board' will be used to refer to the governing body, and board members for those elected or appointed to it.

## The private sector

Modern systems of corporate governance in the private sector evolved with the increasing separation of ownership from control in companies (Learmount, 2002). As shareholders became separated from those that managed companies, they appointed boards to act on their behalf and systems of reporting, regulation, accounting and audit were developed to try to ensure corporations were run in their owners' interest and subject to constraints of the law. In the UK, public companies have 'unitary' boards, consisting of executives and independent or non-executive directors (NEDs) elected by shareholders, which are responsible for running the company and safeguarding shareholders' interests.

The requirements on quoted public companies are more demanding than for private companies and many of the recent corporate governance reforms in UK have been aimed at them. Prompted by concern over governance failures in a number of large corporations, these reforms started in earnest with the report of the Cadbury Committee in 1992 (Cadbury, 1992) and have been developed into a combined code of good practice in a series of subsequent reports. The main concern has been to strengthen the position of NEDs, so they are better able to hold executives to account. Important recommendations include separating the Chair and Chief Executive roles, ensuring that a majority of board members are NEDs and that audit and remuneration sub-committees are established consisting of NEDs. The code is not mandatory on listed companies, but if they deviate from the code they have to explain why. Critics of this system suggest that boards too often become self-perpetuating elites dominated by executives and that the majority of shareholders are too passive to hold boards effectively to account (Monks, 2005).

## The public sector

There are some parallels with the private sector in the development of governance arrangements in the governmental or public sector. As public institutions developed, it became necessary to put in place people who could oversee and control these institutions on behalf of the public. In a democracy these 'governors' are elected through a public vote of eligible citizens and are expected to be publicly accountable. The elected governors are expected to decide policy which is then carried out by public officials.

However, in practice, governance arrangements across the public sector are much more varied. Public services may be delivered by central government departments; by local authorities; by arms-length agencies; or through contracts with private and third sector providers (Europe Aid, 2009). Since the 1980s, central government has reformed the way many public services are delivered and governed. There has been an increase in the formation of public bodies that operate at arms-length from government with their own boards and a move away from elected to appointed board members, or some combination of elected and appointed posts. Steele and Parston (2003) estimated that just under a third of the governors of public bodies in areas such as health, police authorities, schools and housing associations were appointed. Although it is now more common for executives to have a place on governing bodies of public organizations, they are usually very much in the minority on the board.

These reforms also reflect a degree of hybridization. Many of these governance reforms were modelled at least in part on private sector practices and the language of corporate governance has become commonplace in many parts of the public sector. More recently, some changes have been influenced by practices from the third sector. For example, the new NHS Foundation Trusts are modelled in part on mutual and co-operative traditions found in the third sector, with local members of the community and staff electing the majority of members on a board of governors, who then appoint the NEDs onto the board of directors (Ham and Hunt, 2008).

There are also considerable differences in governance arrangements between public bodies in different fields. So for example a private sector model for boards of directors was adopted in health, with executive and non-executive directors on the board, whereas in schools a multi-stakeholder model prevailed, usually involving elected parent governors, local education authority appointees, staff governors and co-opted governors.

## Governance in the third sector

In Chapter 3, David Billis argued that the ideal typical TSO is the membership association run by its members and volunteers, reliant primarily for resources on membership fees and voluntary donations of time and money, and where the governing body is elected by the membership in 'private' elections. Third sector organizations are set up to serve a social mission, rather than being profit seeking or serving a statutory purpose, and it is the duty of the board to safeguard this mission.

It is important to note, however, that there are considerable variations in the governance arrangements of TSOs and many of them differ from this model of a pure membership association. There are also other important variations concerning the identity of the beneficiaries of TSOs that have implications for governance. It is useful to distinguish between those organizations set up to benefit the wider community or public and those set up primarily to benefit their members, such as many co-operatives and mutual societies. As mutual and co-operative societies are primarily trading organizations, they are perhaps better regarded as third/private sector hybrids. For reasons of space, they will not be considered in this chapter (although it should be noted that they face many similar governance challenges to other membership associations).

It is also important to recognise that governance arrangements and practices can change over time. In another important sign of growing hybridity, there has been considerable debate in the third sector about whether private sector practices, such as the payment of board members and allowing executives to serve on boards, should be adopted. Advocates have seen these practices as a way of improving the quality and commitment of board members, while their opponents have argued that they would undermine some of the key principles of TSOs. While in many parts of the third sector these changes have been rejected or resisted, they have become commonplace in some hybrid organizations, such as housing associations.

## Three models of third sector governance

While the membership association is an important ideal type for TSOs, there are in practice, we suggest, considerable variations in governance structures. At the level of the 'unitary' organization (i.e. an organization without subsidiaries), there are three main types of governance structures employed by TSOs: the 'pure' *membership association*, the *self-selecting board* and the *mixed* type, which combines feature of the two previous types.

In a *membership association* there is essentially a two-tier structure at the organizational level: the membership, which may consist of individuals or organizations (and is wider than the board), and a board, which is democratically elected by the members (In practice, the governance structures of many membership associations are more complex than this simple model: see Tschirhart (2006) for a review of the research on this topic.). The board is responsible for overseeing the day-to-day running of the organization and is expected to account to the membership at annual general meetings or extraordinary meetings that are called for special purposes. Some voluntary organizations may also have people associated with the organization that they call members, but do not have voting rights. Indeed there has been a growing trend to 'commoditise' membership and see it primarily as a source of funding and support rather than a mechanism for control and accountability. For our purposes, organizations that only have non-voting members are not regarded as membership associations. Unlike boards in the private sector – and some public sector organizations – membership does not include paid executives, although board members may also undertake operational roles as volunteers.

As a governance structure, the membership association has various potential advantages: it provides a mechanism for keeping the board accountable to the wider membership; the membership can act as a potential pool of volunteers, donors, campaigners and board members; and it can provide a source of feedback to the board on the needs of beneficiaries or users. However, it can also lead to potential governance problems. Research by the Charity Commission (2004) suggests that there is scope for governance disputes in membership associations if, for example, membership records are not kept up to date and so it is unclear who is entitled to vote; if member relations are not managed effectively; or if the membership lacks diversity or is dominated by particular interest groups.

In some organizations, the membership is restricted to board members; hence the governance structure is effectively reduced to a single tier with a *self-selecting board*. This has the advantage of being a very simple structure to operate. It gives the board greater control over who is selected to serve on it and offers the possibility that board members can be chosen for their experience and skills. This process may also help to reduce conflicts of interest between competing membership groups. However, it has a number of potential disadvantages: there is a danger the board may become self-serving or subject to group-think; there is a potentially important loss of accountability (although regulatory controls may provide some reassurances, the board is acting in the interest of its intended beneficiaries); and it may deprive the organization of a potential source of support and resources. As Billis notes in Chapter 3, the commitment of staff and volunteers to the values of an organization may 'compensate' for the absence of an active membership by placing demands for accountability on the board and helping to maintain the organization's mission and values.

The third type of governance structure, the *mixed type*, contains a mixture of the features of the previous two. There is a wider membership, but the membership elects only a proportion of board members, while the others are appointed; people may, for example, be co-opted to the board to fill skills gaps or nominated by particular stakeholder organizations. This mixed type of governance structure has the potential to harness the advantages of both the two previous types, ensuring a degree of democratic accountability to members and harnessing member support, but still allowing the board to ensure it has the necessary skills and experience. However, there are also potential disadvantages: the role of elected members can be marginalised if other board members are perceived to have greater expertise; involving board members from external stakeholder groups, such as funders, can lead to conflicts of interest and uncertainty over whether board members are acting in the best interests of the organization or their stakeholder group; and it may be more difficult to reach agreement on decisions in multi-stakeholder boards where a diverse range of interests are involved.

It is important to remember, though, that in practice the differences between governance structures that involve a wider membership and those where the board is self-selecting may not be quite as clear as at first appears. Over time, membership may decline or become inactive and in some organizations boards may control who is nominated for election. As a result, boards may still exercise a considerable degree of influence over who becomes a board member. Michels (1949) formulated the tendency of democratic associations to become dominated by elites as his 'iron law of oligarchy'. While many studies have confirmed the widespread nature of oligarchic tendencies, the inevitability of these processes has been challenged, and various factors have been identified that can help to safeguard member involvement and democracy (Knoke, 1990; Cornforth, 1995).

It is difficult to obtain accurate figures on the frequency of these different governance structures in the third sector. However, the Charity Commission (2004) estimated that about 80,000 charities, or roughly half those on in its register, have voting members (and a further 20 per cent of charities have non-voting members). This suggests that pure membership associations and those with mixed structures make up about half of all registered charities, and so presumably those with self-selecting boards also make up about half. These figures exclude, of course, the very many voluntary and community groups that are not registered as charities; by and large these are likely to be small organizations without paid staff, such as residents or sports associations, and are likely to be membership associations.

## Governance in organizations with and without staff hierarchies

In Chapter 3, Billis distinguished between associations that are run mainly by their members and employ relatively few or no paid staff and voluntary agencies that employ a larger number of paid staff and are managed by a professional managerial hierarchy. These differences have important implications for the practice of governance. Much of the research on the governance of TSOs has focused on these larger voluntary agencies and especially on US non-profit organizations providing human services. It has tended to concentrate on: governance functions and board roles, the determinants and consequences of board composition; the relationships between boards and management; and the determinants and consequences of board effectiveness (Ostrower and Stone, 2006). As Rochester (2003) notes, there has been a high degree of consensus on the different governance functions and board roles and how they are distinct from those of management or other paid staff.

In TSOs with few or no staff, however, the boundaries between governance, management and the operational work of the organization are much more blurred as there are few or no managers or staff for board members to delegate work to. As a result, board members are likely to get involved not only in governance but in management and operational matters as well. It is no accident that the governing bodies of these organizations are often called management committees rather than boards or governing bodies.

Once TSOs start to employ staff, a new dynamic occurs (Wood, 1992). Case study research by Cornforth and Edwards (1998) suggests that the transition to employing a paid staff hierarchy can lead to tensions and conflicts between boards and management as they struggle over redefining their respective roles and responsibilities. Based on a study of small voluntary agencies employing fewer than five staff, Rochester

(2003) suggests that these organizations face three distinctive problems with respect to governance compared to larger organizations with an established paid staff. First, they experience greater problems in recruiting and retaining board members, and those they do recruit are more likely to lack relevant experience and expertise. This finding is supported by results from a survey of charities in England and Wales which showed that difficulties in recruiting board members were inversely related to organizational size (Cornforth and Simpson, 2002). Second, the ability of these boards to carry out the commonly ascribed governance functions was limited. For example, Rochester observed that the boards were only involved fitfully in determining policies and that this was often done reactively in response to particular problems as they emerged. Third, senior staff found it difficult to find the time to properly service, support and help develop the boards of their organizations. He suggests these problems are not unique to small voluntary agencies but that they are felt in a particularly acute form.

Drawing on the work of Billis (1993), Rochester characterises these small voluntary agencies as hybrids combining elements of the pure membership association with that of a bureaucracy. This analysis does not, however, answer a key question: should the employment of a paid staff hierarchy be regarded as a sign of 'entrenched' hybridity in the sense of adopting private or public sector practices? While paid staff are more common in the public and private sectors, they also occur commonly in the third sector, and conversely it is not unusual for some public organizations to use volunteers. The motivation to employ paid staff in the third sector appears often to be one of needing to scale up and co-ordinate activities or draw on professional expertise, rather than an adoption of private or public sector approaches, so the degree to which this is an indicator of hybridity is open to question. It is, however, true that maintaining a staff structure can lead to greater pressures on voluntary organizations to seek government funding or grow commercial activities which can lead to greater hybridization, but this is not inevitable. This is an issue that is taken up next as we examine the growth of trading activities in charities and the implications for governance.

## The case of trading charities

Over more than a decade, there has been a growing trend for voluntary organizations to earn more of their income from trading activities. The UK Voluntary Sector Almanac in 2006 reporting on data from 2003/4 concluded that 'social enterprise activities are driving the sector's economy' (Wilding et al., 2006). Income from trading activities was estimated to increase from 33 per cent in 1994/5 to 47 per cent of total income in 2003/4 and surpassed voluntary income from donations and grants at 45 per cent of total income. The growth in earned income also reflected a shift in public sector funding from grants to contracts, with 53 per cent of public sector income into the sector coming from fees. This suggests that at the time, about 25 per cent of total income was coming from public sector contracts. In 2005/6, the earned income of general charities rose to over 50 per cent for the first time (Reichart et al., 2008).

This growth in commercial activity among charities raises important questions. Is trading leading to hybrid forms of organization and new governance structures? What challenges does this raise for charity trustees and how are they managing them? In order to consider these questions, it is important to examine first the different types of trading that charities may engage in and the legal requirements that exist to safeguard a charity's assets and mission.

Trading activities by charities may be divided into three types: *primary purpose trading*, which directly furthers the charity's objects or mission, like St Mungo's carrying out government contracts for the homeless; *ancillary trading*, which is indirectly related to the charity's mission, for example a café in a charitable museum; or *non-primary purpose trading*, which is not related to the charity's mission but designed purely to raise funds, such as many charity shops (Alter, 2006). These distinctions are important because, legally, charities can only carry out primary trading within the charity itself, apart from small-scale exemptions. If a charity wants to engage in significant trading that does not directly further its charitable objects, it is required by law to establish a trading subsidiary. Charities may also decide to set up trading subsidiaries as a way of protecting their charitable assets from commercial risks and for tax reasons (Sladden, 2008).

Interestingly, a number of social enterprises that were established to trade in the market have moved in the opposite direction towards the voluntary and community sector by establishing charitable subsidiaries where they have social goals that qualify as charitable. This has the advantage of helping to protect their social mission and means that their charitable activities are better able to attract grants and tax relief (Social Enterprise Coalition, 2007).

## Subsidiaries and governance

One of the main ways then for a charity to manage the risks from trading activities is to separate out or decouple trading from its other operations and manage it within a commercial subsidiary. Trading charities can be regarded as third/private sector hybrids, as the charity owns the subsidiary, with the charity fulfilling the social or charitable mission and the subsidiary being run as a commercial business to generate funds for the charity. This has important implications for how the organization is governed; leading to more complex, hybrid governance structures than in a unitary organization, as each subsidiary, as well as the charity as a whole, will need to have its own board.

This can lead to new challenges for trustees as Sladden (2008, p. 7) notes

> Charity trustees have a fair understanding of their responsibilities but may struggle with a full understanding of how trading subsidiaries fit into the governance picture. The problem lies in the fact that trading companies are established to generate a profit whereas charities are set up to serve the needs of beneficiaries.

An important governance challenge is that trustees of the charity and the directors of any trading subsidiary have separate and distinct responsibilities. Hence a trustee who becomes a director of the subsidiary needs to be aware of these separate duties.

This can of course lead to conflicts of interest. In order to mitigate these, the Charity Commission (2006) recommends that the board of any subsidiary should contain at least one director who is not a trustee or employee of the charity, and the charity should have at least one trustee who is not a director of the subsidiary. There also needs to be a complete separation of assets and resources, so if a subsidiary uses any of the charity's assets or resources it should be on a clear commercial and contractual basis. When establishing a subsidiary, trustees need to treat it as any other investment and consider whether the investment is justified and in the best interests of the charity, and set up arrangements for monitoring the subsidiary to evaluate its success, with contingency plans, should it not succeed.

Of course these legal safeguards cannot eliminate all problems and there can still be tensions between the social and business goals of the charity. Exploratory interviews with board members, staff and advisers of trading charities by Spear et al. (2007) revealed a number of perceived problems. In one children's charity, for example, there were regular discussions about putting fees for services up because of concerns about reserves. However, the charitable side of the organization resisted these proposals because of the likely negative impact on some of the charity's main beneficiaries. Another potential problem is that trustees may not be familiar with commercial operations and be ill-equipped to evaluate business propositions and risks. Some interviewees commented that their trustees were too risk averse or had established procedures and governance structures that were too cumbersome for commercial operations. There can also be problems recruiting directors with the necessary business skills. Again this problem is often felt most acutely in smaller organizations.

## Public sector spin-offs

As well as TSOs moving closer to the public sector through being contracted to provide public services, there are hybrid organizations being formed in a transition in the opposite direction from the public sector towards the third sector. That is when services that were once provided by public authorities are transferred or spun-off into independent charities or social enterprises. Common examples include housing associations formed by the transfer of council housing stock (discussed further in Chapter 10), leisure trusts (LTs) that have taken over the recreation and leisure services previously provided by local authorities and social enterprises formed to take over some social and health care services. Indeed the Department of Health has been actively promoting the establishment of social enterprises as a way of encouraging innovation in the health sector and bringing services closer to patients and the community (Walsham et al., 2007). The governance challenges of these new organizations are still emerging as these health quasi-markets are being constructed, with varying practices of service commissioners and considerable variety in the configurations of provision: including single organizations, partnerships, consortia and looser networks.

As a result, there is very little research on the governance structures and challenges faced by these particular hybrid organizations. However, exploratory interviews carried out with people involved in public sector spin-offs (Spear et al., 2007) revealed a number of different governance challenges associated with multi-stakeholder boards and the culture change necessary in order to enable boards and staff to face market challenges and move away from the bureaucratic processes and structures common in the public sector.

Many public sector spin-offs have multi-stakeholder boards embodying a variety of sectional interests, often including staff, users and trade union and local authority-nominated members. As one interviewee in an LT noted, this can lead to 'delegate syndrome', where board members act as if they are delegates for the particular stakeholder group they come from rather than act as a team in the best interests of the organization as a whole.

In some cases, staff members are the largest group on the board. The need to gain staff and trade union commitment to any transfer out of the public sector may be an important reason for their representation on boards. As another interviewee commented, this can lead to a particular type of delegate syndrome where staff initially get involved to protect their own interests:

> When we transferred from being council employees . . . the people that put their names forward were the ones that were cynical, suspicious of the organization. One of them was making sure that their rights were being protected so they're actually going in it for the wrong reasons, so they're not putting the best interests of the company forward but I was quite happy with that because it's better to have them on the inside rather than causing problems on the outside. Within a year they realised that there was no hidden agenda and that this was about doing things much, much better.

In health services the picture is often more complex because some categories of staff, like clinicians, can be particularly powerful and may be sensitive about the involvement of other groups on the board. Negotiating a balance between clinical governance and enterprise governance concerns has been a perennial challenge. One interviewee noted that 'clinical people don't think in a business way . . . marketing is on another planet'. There may also be problems in small health social enterprises of having access to the necessary expertise to manage clinical risks.

Tensions may also occur with other stakeholders such as users. Developing a range of mechanisms to involve users at board and other levels is often specified as a priority in public service delivery but can be difficult to achieve effectively. Users may find it difficult to move beyond representing narrow sectional interests or feel they do not have the expertise and skills to influence many board decisions, particularly with respect to commercial or financial matters.

The research also revealed contrasting views on the value of having someone from the main funding body on the board, for example local councillors on the boards of LTs. On the one hand, some interviewees pointed to difficulties with councillors wearing their local government hat and being unable to fully appreciate the different interests of the trust. However, other interviewees felt that having a local authority nominee on the board could be an advantage:

> . . . it works much better when you've actually got somebody who is interested in leisure and running leisure from a political point of view in a district that is also one of our stakeholders because you get to know exactly the priorities of the council and in which direction they are going . . .

Some LTs have grown and operate in a number of localities so that they are no longer so dependent on their parent local authority but others still operate only in one locality. This dependence can create tensions that may threaten the sustainability of LTs. As one interviewee noted

> ...some local authorities are now wanting a cut of the surplus...or they threaten to cut the grant the next year – this is not good for investment and future planning...in some cases these grants are on a one year basis and decisions are made very late...the impact on governance is massive.

Ensuring the independence and sustainability of relatively small social enterprises in public sector markets continues to be a key challenge both for board members and management.

## Conclusions

The growth of trading activities by TSOs, often stimulated by the contracting out of public services, and the growing involvement of TSOs in partnerships with organizations in the public and private sectors have led to more complex governance arrangements at both inter-organizational and organizational levels. To date, research on the governance of TSOs has focussed primarily on the boards of unitary organizations and has not kept pace with this growing complexity and the emergence of hybrid forms of organization.

In addressing the considerable complexity of governance arrangements in the third sector and the impact of hybridity, this chapter has attempted to clarify the main governance structures used by TSOs and how they differ from governance structures in the public and private sectors. Three main types of governance structures were identified for unitary organizations: the pure *membership association*; the *self-selecting board*; and the *mixed type*. It also examined some of the distinctive governance challenges of TSOs as they move from being entirely voluntary associations to taking on paid staff, including the potential for conflict in differentiating board and staff roles, the difficulty of recruiting and retaining suitable board members and lack of staff time for adequately servicing the board.

At the organizational level, an important strategy for dealing with hybridity is to decouple trading activities from those related to the organization's social mission through the creation of subsidiaries. This has led organizations to adopt more complex, multi-level governance structures, with main and subsidiary boards. Interestingly some social enterprises, established as businesses, have subsequently set up charities separate from their trading activities to further their social missions and to improve their tax efficiency and eligibility to seek grant funding. However, little is known about how these more complex governance arrangements work in practice. This raises a range of important questions that deserve more in-depth research. How do main and subsidiary boards divide up their responsibilities and manage relationships between themselves? How are board members recruited to the different boards and how do their different backgrounds and identities affect the way they interpret and perform their roles? How are differences and conflicts between subsidiary and main boards and between social and commercial goals managed?

Hybrid organizations have different origins or roots (see Chapter 3) and have to make different transitions. Some hybrids are formed when charities undertake trading activities to raise funds and others may be spun out of the public sector. Yet others may be started from scratch as social enterprises. These different transitions can raise particular challenges for organizations and their boards. Public sector spin-offs, such as LTs, often have to deal with staff and trade union fears that the change will impact adversely on terms and conditions of employment and their dependence on one key funder that may also be represented on the board. Charities that wish to engage in secondary trading to raise funds need to find a way of protecting their charitable assets and managing the risks associated with trading. Social enterprises started from scratch have to face all the challenges of establishing any new business, while at the same time furthering their social mission, and establishing the legitimacy of what is still a relatively poorly understood form of business.

This suggests that many of the important challenges that face hybrid organizations and their boards are shaped by their different origins, the legal structures they adopt, the different regulatory requirements they face and the paths they take as they develop. It also highlights the fact that hybridity is not a fixed characteristic of organizations, but evolves over time in response to changing pressures and demands. Another important direction for further research is to examine in more depth what drives organizations to adopt characteristics from other sectors and how the different origins and paths hybrids take influence the governance structures they adopt and the challenges they face.

## References

Alter, S. K. (2006) 'Social Enterprise Models and Their Mission and Money Relationships', in A. Nicholls (ed.) *Social Entrepreneurship: New Models of Sustainable Social Change*, Oxford: Oxford University Press.
Billis, D. (1993) *Organising Public and Voluntary Agencies*, London: Routledge.
Cadbury, A. (1992) *Report of the Committee on the Financial Aspects of Corporate Governance*, London: Gee and Co.
Charity Commission (2004) *Membership Charities* (RS7), London: Charity Commission.
Charity Commission (2006) *Charities and Trading* (CC35), London: Charity Commission.
Charity Commission (2007) *Stand and Deliver: The Future for Charities Providing Public Services*, London: Charity Commission.
Cornforth, C. (1995) 'Patterns of Co-operative Management: Beyond the Degeneration Thesis', *Economic and Industrial Democracy*, 16, pp. 487–523.
Cornforth, C. (2004) *Governance & Participation Development Toolkit*, Manchester: Co-operatives UK.
Cornforth, C. and Edwards, C. (1998) *Good Governance: Developing Effective Board-Management Relations in Public and Voluntary Organizations*, London: CIMA Publishing.
Cornforth, C. and Simpson, S. (2002) 'Change and Continuity in the Governance of Non-Profit Organisations in the U.K: The Impact of Organizational Size', *Nonprofit Management and Leadership*, 12, 4, pp. 451–470.
Europe Aid (2009) *Public Sector Reform: An Introduction*, Concept paper 1, Tools and Methods Series, European Commission.

Ham, C. and Hunt, P. (2008) *Membership Governance in NHS Foundation Trusts: A Review for the Department of Health*, London: Department of Health.

Knoke, D. (1990) *Organizing for Collective Action: The Political Economies of Associations*, New York: Aldine de Gruyter.

Kooiman, J. (1999) 'Socio-Political Governance: Overview, Reflections and Design', *Public Management*, 1, 1, pp. 67–92.

Learmount, S. (2002) *Corporate Governance: What Can Be Learned from Japan?*, Oxford: Oxford University Press.

Michels, R. (1949) *Political Parties: A Sociological Study of Oligarchical Tendencies in modern Democracy*, Glencoe, IL: Free Press.

Monks, R. (2005) 'Why is a Corporation Like a Stray Cat? A Conversation with Bob Monks about Responsible Ownership as the Path to Corporate Accountability', *Business Ethics*, Fall, pp. 28–31.

Nyssens, M. (ed.) (2006) *Social Enterprises in Europe: Between Market, Public Policies and Communities*, London: Routledge.

Ostrower, F. and Stone, M. M. (2006) 'Boards of Nonprofit Organizations: Research Trends, Findings and Prospects for Future Research', in W. Powell and R. Steinberg (eds) *The Nonprofit Sector: A Research Handbook* (2nd edition), New Haven, CT: Yale University Press.

Reichart, O., Kane, D., Pratten, B. and Wilding, K. (2008) *The UK Civil Society Almanac 2008*, London: National Council for Voluntary Organizations.

Rhodes, R. (1994) 'The Hollowing of the State', *Political Quarterly*, 65, pp. 138–151.

Rochester, C. (2003) 'The Role of Boards in Small Voluntary Organisations', in C. Cornforth (ed.) *The Governance of Public and Non-profit Organizations: What Do Boards Do?*, London: Routledge.

Sladden, N. (2008) 'Trading Places?' *Caritas*, April.

Social Enterprise Coalition (2007) *Keeping it Legal: A Guide to Legal Forms for Social Enterprises*, London: Social Enterprise Coalition.

Spear, R., Cornforth, C. and Aiken, M. (2007) *For Love and Money: Governance and Social Enterprise*, London: National Council for Voluntary Organisations. (Downloadable from: http://www7.open.ac.uk/oubs/research/project-detail.asp?id=85).

Spear, R., Cornforth, C. and Aiken, M. (2008) *For Love and Money: Governance and Social Enterprise*, London: Governance Hub, National Council for Voluntary Organizations.

Steele, J. and Parston, G. (2003) *Rubber Stamped? The Expectations and Experiences of Appointed Public Service Governors*, London: Office of Public Management.

Tschirhart, M. (2006) 'Nonprofit Membership Associations', in W. Powell and R.Steinberg (eds) *The Nonprofit Sector: A Research Handbook* (2nd edition) New Haven, CT: Yale University Press.

Walsham, M., Dingwall, C. and Hempseed, I. (2007) *Healthy Business: A Guide to Social Enterprise in Health and Social Care*, London: Social Enterprise Coalition.

Wilding, K., Clark, J., Griffith, M., Jochum, V. and Wainwright, S. (2006) *The UK Voluntary Sector Almanac 2006: The State of the Sector*, London: National Council for Voluntary Organizations.

Wood, M. M. (1992) 'Is Governing Board Behaviour Cyclical?', *Nonprofit Management and Leadership*, 3, 2, pp. 139–163.

# PART II

Hybridity in Action

# 5 Volunteers in hybrid organizations: A marginalised majority?

*Angela Ellis Paine, Nick Ockenden and Joanna Stuart*

## Introduction

The involvement of volunteers, both at board and at service level, is one of the defining features of third sector organizations or TSOs (Billis and Harris, 1996; see also Billis, 2003). Indeed, having a human resource structure reliant on volunteers as opposed to paid staff is one of the five key traits identified by David Billis in Chapter 3 as distinguishing associations from bureaucracies.

As other chapters have attested, developments such as the move towards welfare pluralism with the associated increased role for the third sector in public service delivery, increasingly competitive funding regimes and the introduction of performance management have been driving TSOs in the direction of bureaucracy at the expenses of associational features. Volunteering might well be considered one of the associational features to fall victim to these developments. At the very least, the way in which TSOs engage, organize and develop volunteers are likely to have changed as they have responded to the various public policy pressures driving hybridization described in Chapter 2. It is this change in the nature and experience of volunteering, particularly at the service level, which is the focus of this chapter.

Given the centrality of volunteering to the very concept of the 'third sector' and to delivering the 'work' of TSOs, it is somewhat surprising that so little attention has been paid to the implications of these various developments for volunteering (Scott and Russell, 2001; Zimmeck, 2001). While it has been suggested that volunteers are increasingly being replaced by paid staff, and that their roles and terms of engagement are changing (Billis and Harris, 1992), to date there has been relatively little systematic examination of this. There has been limited, if any, research focused explicitly on the changing nature or experience of volunteering within hybrid organizations.

This chapter examines some of the evidence that can help to shed light on these issues. It begins by exploring the growth in the employment of paid staff within TSOs and the implications of this for the role and position of volunteers. It goes on to examine the processes of formalisation within the sector and in particular the transference of workplace management models from the private and public sectors to volunteering within TSOs. It then considers the implications of these developments for the experience of volunteers. The final part of the chapter puts forward an emergent model to suggest that the look and feel of volunteering are somewhat different in organizations according to whether they are classified according to Billis's model (Chapter 3) as associations, shallow or entrenched hybrids.

In exploring these issues this chapter draws on a series of research studies undertaken by the Institute for Volunteering Research over the last few years. In particular, evidence will be drawn from three large-scale national studies of volunteering: *Helping Out*, a survey of 2,700 adults in England (Low et al., 2007); *Management Matters*, a national survey of volunteer management capacity involving 1,248 TSOs (Machin and Ellis Paine, 2008a); and *Reasonable Care?*, a study of risk management amongst 1,124 individuals and 535 organizations (Gaskin, 2005). We will also draw on findings from qualitative case study research into volunteering in community-based organizations (Hutchison and Ockenden, 2008; Ockenden and Hutin, 2008; and other unpublished reports). These studies did not focus specifically on volunteering in hybrids but all provide insights into the nature and experience of volunteering in such contexts.

## Volunteers versus paid staff: The breadth and depth of engagement

The third sector has undergone a period of rapid profession-alisation, with the number of paid staff employed by voluntary organizations increasing considerably over recent years. The UK Labour Force Survey reports that the total number of people employed in the sector increased by 24 per cent between 1997 and 2006, with full-time equivalent staff numbers increasing by 75,000 between 2001 and 2006 (Kane et al., 2009). By 2009, it was estimated that the sector employed 508,000 full-time equivalent paid staff (ibid.). This trend has led some commentators to suggest that paid staff are replacing volunteers in TSOs (see, for example, Elstub, 2006).

Equivalent data is not available for the number of volunteers involved in the sector but evidence suggests that, over roughly the same time period, the number of volunteers active across the country has either stayed static or declined (DCLG, 2008; nfpSynergy, 2008). The Citizenship Survey, for example, reports that while the proportion of people engaging in regular (once a month or more) formal volunteering in groups or organizations rose from 27 per cent in 2001 to 29 per cent in 2005, it had gone back down to 2001 levels by 2007/8 (DCLG, 2008). A majority of these volunteers are active in the third sector, although many are also involved in the public and, indeed, the private sector (Low et al., 2007). One estimate claims that volunteers provide the equivalent of 1.1 million full-time workers to the UK's third sector (Reichardt et al., 2007). This suggests that volunteers continue to represent more than twice the full-time equivalent (FTE) paid workforce (ibid.). At the same time, they are getting involved in a greater number of organizations (Low et al., 2007).

It is hard to get a sense from this national data what this means for individual organizations and the evidence is inconclusive. In one study, a fifth of organizations reported a drop in the number of their volunteers (Gaskin, 2005). Another, which focused on homeless organizations, concluded that the space for volunteering within large 'highly professionalised corporatist' (essentially hybrid) organizations had been eroded, with fewer opportunities for engagement, resulting in an exodus of volunteers (Cloke et al., 2007). The involvement of TSOs in public service delivery has in particular been found to lead to a replacement of volunteers by paid staff (Elstub, 2006), despite government's emphasis on their involvement (see for example, HM Treasury, 2002). Many TSOs have opted to employ paid staff to fulfil their contract obligations rather than involve volunteers to do so.

Other research, however, suggests that it is far from true that volunteers are disappearing from TSOs, even from those that have many of the features associated with 'entrenched hybrids'. Some organizations, including some involved in public service delivery, report involving more volunteers now than ever before. One organization we spoke to reported that as the value of the contracts they delivered had increased three fold since 1997, so too had the number of their volunteers.

Rather than an absolute reduction in the numbers of volunteers in TSOs, the evidence suggests that the change has been relative. While volunteer numbers may in some organizations have increased, the rate of growth of paid staff employed by TSOs has been faster. This seems to be particularly true among hybrid organizations. It is therefore the ratio of staff to volunteers which has shifted within hybrids rather than the extent of volunteer involvement per se (see Geoghegan and Powell, 2006 for similar arguments).

Regardless of the absolute or relative numbers of volunteers involved, however, we need to consider the position and influence of volunteers within organizations. While the involvement of paid staff does not automatically move organizations into hybrid status, the moment at which an organization becomes staff-led as opposed to volunteer-led could arguably be one of the cut-off points. Indeed, Billis argues in Chapter 3 of this volume that taking on paid staff can be seen as a step into hybridity and when those paid staff come to dominate the organization and hierarchical management structures are introduced then entrenchment can be seen to have arrived.

The evidence for the ways in which the role and position of volunteers relative to paid staff may change within hybrid organizations is mixed. Public service delivery and increased competition for funding among TSOs have led to many under-taking an increasing range of functions, which are increasingly delivered by a mix of paid staff and volunteers. In many cases, this has led to a greater breadth of engagement through an increased diversity of roles and opportunities for volunteers, particularly in front line service delivery (Gaskin, 2005; Hutchison and Ockenden, 2008). In some cases, volunteers are being asked to perform work which is 'more complex, more sophisticated and more responsible' as well as more visible (Graff, 2003 in Gaskin, 2005, p. 10), leading to increased workloads and greater demands on volunteers (see for example Gaskin, 2008). These demands have been particularly acute among volunteers in governance positions (see Harris, 2001 for a discussion of the anxieties this may cause, and Wise, 2001; Joseph Rowntree Foundation, 2000; Blacksell and Phillips, 1994 for an account of the debate this is raising about moving to payment of trustees).

In some organizations, however, rather than volunteers being involved across the new roles, a hierarchy is developing in which the more 'risky', 'demanding' or 'intensive' roles have become the realm of paid staff. Geoghegan and Powell (2006), for example, found that volunteers were being asked to perform 'ancillary tasks', leaving 'complex tasks' to paid staff (see also, Gaskin, 2005). At the same time, it would seem that as organizations grow and become more complex, volunteers are less likely to be involved in strategic roles and have less power and influence within organizations (see for example Weeks et al., 1996). Beyond the select group of volunteers in governance positions (and questions have been raised about the actual power that resides with volunteers even at this level), they are often less involved in decision-making processes. They may also be less involved, more broadly, in the internal affairs of organizations. This is in line with other findings about a wider change in accountability within TSOs, upwards and outwards to funders and the like, rather than downwards to members and volunteers (Taylor and Warburton, 2003).

When volunteers do have opportunities to engage at this level, it can be challenging, particularly for long-serving volunteers who have seen the organization change considerably from the one they first got involved in, often leaving many long-standing volunteers feeling isolated and out of touch with the organizations (Leonard et al., 2004; Hutchison and Ockenden, 2008). Based on a study of HIV/AIDS charities, Weeks et al. (1996, p. 114) note that

> Founders and early volunteers often find themselves marginalised and efforts to have volunteer representatives on management committees are sometimes fraught with difficulties as their ambitions for the organisation may differ significantly from those now managing the agency.

In summary, the rapid growth of paid staff within the sector, along with other developments associated with hybridization, has facilitated a greater breadth of involvement for volunteers within many hybrid organizations but, at the same time, it has also led to the substitution or inhibition of deeper forms of engagement. In many hybrid organizations volunteers have been moved out of decision-making and strategic roles into 'less risky' or 'ancillary' front line service delivery roles. Rather than necessarily dominating numerically, paid staff are dominating strategically; they have effectively marginalised the position of volunteers within many hybrid organizations. Volunteers are being positioned as resources to be used rather than as owners, members or even co-producers. It is perhaps the marginalisation of volunteering, rather than the actual scale of involvement of volunteers versus paid staff, which is the critical factor in distinguishing hybrid organizations from their associational origins.

### Formalising volunteer involvement: The growth of modern management

Professionalisation has been accompanied by a shift towards formalisation. Third sector organizations have increasingly adopted the norms and ways of working that are more traditionally associated with their private and public sector counterparts such as a more 'rational' approach to 'business', clearer lines of accountability and authority and a greater emphasis on performance monitoring and management.

For volunteering, this has largely meant the introduction of what are generally considered to be workplace, top-down models of volunteer management (Holmes, 2003). As Zimmeck (2001) argues, 'modern management', with its drive towards standardisation and formalisation, has been imported from private and public sector organizations to replace the more 'home grown', less bureaucratic, approach to volunteer support more typical of associations.

The first (paid) volunteer manager was employed in a hospital in Cambridge in 1963 (Gay, 2000). The third sector was soon to import this model. By 2007, 43 per cent of TSOs reported employing paid staff to manage volunteers (Clark, 2007). A new professional body – the Association of Volunteer Managers – had also been launched with the aim of promoting 'the management of volunteers for the benefit of the public' (www.avm.org.uk). Supporting this new profession, there has been an expansion in the provision of training in volunteer management (see Rochester and Grotz, 2006); the development of National Occupational Standards for the Management of Volunteers (produced by the Voluntary Sector National Training Organization, 2004 and revised by the UK Workforce Hub in 2008); and a burgeoning of volunteer management good practice guidance (see for example, McCurley and Lynch, 1998; Ellis, 2002; Noble et al., 2003; Graff, 2005; Fryer et al., 2007).

A dominant model of volunteer management emerges from across these developments, with a common set of prescribed codes and good practices. These generally include: a volunteer co-ordinator; a written volunteer policy; task descriptions for individual volunteer roles; a recruitment, written application and interview procedure; an induction programme for new volunteers; training; supervision; recognition; and, increasingly, evaluation (see Brudney, 1999, for a summary of these elements and the key texts that have led to their development/promotion, much of which emerges from the US). These principles are codified within the Investing in Volunteers quality standard for volunteer involvement and management, launched in 2004 and awarded since then to more than 200 organizations. In themselves these 'good practice' principles do not necessarily all lead to formalisation or top-down management structures and, indeed, much of the guidance includes cautionary notes about needing to ensure they are applied appropriately, flexibly and informally. Nonetheless, evidence suggests that, in practice, they have contributed to more formal approaches.

A majority of volunteer-involving TSOs report that they have in place these elements of volunteer management (Machin and Ellis Paine, 2008a). In *Management Matters*, three in four organizations, for example, reported having a written policy on volunteer involvement and four in five said they carried out equal opportunities monitoring of their volunteers. They were, however, more common in large organizations (large in terms of income, number of staff and number of volunteers) than smaller ones. Third sector organizations with an income of £1 million or over, for example, were twice as likely as those with a lower income to have written task descriptions and to hold exit interviews. Further analysis shows that among those organizations that had funding for involving volunteers through contracts, they were also more likely to implement these procedures than those who funded volunteer management through other sources or who had no budgets at all for volunteering.

The introduction of this more formalised, workplace-based, model of volunteer management is being driven by a range of external stakeholders, including funders and regulators, and a number of factors, not least ensuring service levels and contract compliance. Hybrid organizations, in particular, are establishing management practices which are more typical of the private and/or public sector organizations that they are trying to win contracts from. More stringent legislation, regulation and risk awareness are driving the move towards formalisation of volunteer management (Gaskin, 2005) and in some organizations, formalisation has also been demanded by the volunteers themselves (Davis Smith, 1998). While these drivers and the resulting move towards formalisation are not exclusive to hybrids, they do seem to be most pronounced within them and the very presence of formal management structures might be considered an indicator of hybridization (Zimmeck, 2001).

Any systematic evaluation of the value and effectiveness of these developments either from the perception of the volunteers or the organizations that employ them is, however, lacking (Hutter, 2005 in Gaskin, 2008). But evidence increasingly suggests that they have impacted on both the position and the experience of volunteers across the third sector. It is to this that we shall now turn.

## The experience of volunteering: Better organized, but too much like paid work

On the surface at least, recent evidence suggests that volunteers are happy with the ways in which their work is organized and supported, and increasingly so. In *Helping Out*, a majority of volunteers were positive about their volunteering experiences. Nine out of ten agreed that they could cope with the things they were asked to do (97 per cent); that their efforts were appreciated (95 per cent); and that they were given the opportunity to take part in activities they liked (91 per cent). Less than one-third (31 per cent) felt that their volunteering could be much better organized (Low et al., 2007). A similar survey conducted in 1997 (Davis Smith, 1998) found that nearly three-quarters (71 per cent) of volunteers had said things could be much better organized, while nearly one-third (30 per cent) could not cope with the things they were asked to do. It would seem that professionalisation and formalisation are contributing to a general improvement in the experience of volunteers (see also Russell and Scott, 1997; Hutchison and Ockenden, 2008).

Despite these positive responses from volunteers and the proliferation of volunteer management practices noted above, however, evidence has consistently revealed an under-resourcing of volunteer involvement. One study reported that 32 per cent of TSOs had no dedicated funding for volunteer support and only 46 per cent resourced it through their core budget (Machin and Ellis Paine, 2008a). The costs of recruiting, training and supporting volunteers are often not fully reflected in contract fees (Scott and Russell, 2001), with contractors consistently underestimating both the potential added value and the cost of involving volunteers (Hutchison and Ockenden, 2008; Neuberger, 2008). Volunteers are often seen as a cost-free resource or even as a way of cutting costs for service delivery and studies consistently suggest that many volunteers are not receiving the support they need or deserve (Gaskin, 2005; Low et al., 2007).

Perhaps more worryingly, overly formal managerial and bureaucratic practices and procedures adopted by organizations can be off-putting and alienating for some volunteers and have impacted negatively on the volunteering experience (Gaskin, 2003; Leonard et al., 2004; Low et al., 2007). Even when they recognise that some regulation and formalisation is necessary, many volunteers do not welcome it (Gaskin, 2003). The *Helping Out* study asked volunteers whether, for example, they felt receiving a role description would be a good thing: two-thirds (65 per cent) of all current volunteers said they felt that it would not and many of them thought that it would make their volunteering too rigid and formal:

> It would be too formal and take the fun out of things because I enjoy the flexibility of volunteering without the restrictions of a written job description. (Machin and Ellis Paine, 2008b, p. 5)

Excessive bureaucratic, formal and inflexible ways of working, too much regulation and 'too much paperwork' are often cited by volunteers as some of the main drawbacks of volunteering. The *Helping Out* study found that nearly one in five volunteers (17 per cent) felt that 'volunteering is becoming too much like paid work', while one in four (27 per cent) felt that there was too much bureaucracy associated with their volunteering. Other research has highlighted similar concerns. One recent unpublished study with a large national (hybrid) TSO, for example, found that more than half of volunteers felt that their volunteering was too bureaucratic:

> As a volunteer group we seem to be threatened with a lot of paperwork/bureaucracy. Most of us have full time office jobs and want to just get out at the weekend and work not spend hours on paperwork.
>
> [I want] to be able to fulfil one of my many ideas for raising funds for our [organization] without being met by a blank wall of bureaucracy and red tape!

For some volunteers, particularly long serving ones, bureau-cracy and more formalised ways of working have been so off-putting that they have left, or at least seriously considered stopping, volunteering. Gaskin (2003; 2005) reports explicit examples of where volunteers have left organizations because they felt their volunteering had become too bureaucratic:

> I was a volunteer at [prison] Visitors' Centre for two and a half years – until it got too bureaucratic. It wasn't what I volunteered for. (Gaskin, 2003, p. 17)

> I was involved with (large national welfare charity) for fifteen years and it gradually become more professional – you had to do this and had to do that...and you think in the end I didn't join it to be like this. (Ibid.)

It is not only the bureaucracy and the paperwork that are off-putting. It is also a more fundamental change in the rela-tionships between volunteers and their organizations. There is a danger that formalisation has meant that 'human process' has lost out to guidelines and standards (Guirguis-Younger et al., 2005). The pressures of contract funding, other demands of professionalisation and the formalisation of volunteer manage-ment have been found to contribute to an erosion of the more social aspects of volunteer support and involvement such as informal get togethers and chats over coffee (Hutchison and Ockenden, 2008). This has implications for the relationships that are formed between staff and volunteers and among vol-unteers themselves. In particular, organizations are reporting divides between 'old' and 'new' volunteers:

> There is a lack of team spirit amongst the volunteers now...We can't get cohesion in the group.

Given that sociability is a key motivator for, and an important impact of, volunteering, such developments have considerable implications. As Gaskin (2005, p. 14) notes, '[the] moti-vation of volunteers is being seriously undermined' by the introduction of work-based management practices.

Overly formal management procedures can also create barri-ers to volunteering for potential new recruits. Indeed, concerns about bureaucracy are more likely to deter people from getting involved in volunteering than to make current volunteers stop. *Helping Out*, for example, reports that nearly half (49 per cent) of those who were not (formal) volunteers but would have liked to start volunteering were put off by too much bureaucracy (Low et al., 2007). In one study, more than one-third of the organizations (36 per cent) said that they now found it more difficult to recruit volunteers (Gaskin, 2005, see also Machin and Ellis Paine, 2008a).

Formalised recruitment and application procedures for volunteers are often perceived to be too formal, lengthy and impersonal (Gaskin, 2003), acting as a barrier to potential volunteers, particularly those from more marginalised groups (see, for example, IVR, 2004). Lengthy application forms, for example, can be intimidating and off-putting to those with literacy or English language issues and those with visual impairments. Equally, the prospect of an interview can be particularly daunting for some socially excluded groups. Formalisation of volunteering, therefore, can lead to the selective recruitment of volunteers (Weeks et al., 1996; Scott and Russell, 2001).

The increasingly stringent training requirements for volunteers can also be off-putting to some potential volunteers (IVR, 2004). Accredited training is on the increase, but while it brings added appeal to volunteering for some – notably young people, it is a deterrent to others – such as older people (Rochester and Grotz, 2006). Some volunteers may get involved, only to drop out half way through what they perceive to be an overly lengthy training programme (IVR, 2004).

Recruitment is increasingly selective not only because the practices and procedures are alienating to particular groups but also because a shift in organizational thinking and ways of working has encouraged the recruitment of volunteers with specific skills and experience which in itself serves to exclude certain groups. In general, this has meant a move away from recognition of the value of experiential learning to a new focus on skills and accredited learning, what Fournier (1999) refers to as 'professional competence' (and see also Bondi, 2004). Russell and Scott (2001) note that this move to skills-based recruitment has led to the development of 'technical' rather than 'social' volunteers. Weeks et al. (1996) found that professionalisation in HIV/AIDS organizations had led to the recruitment of a 'new type of person' not directly affected by HIV or AIDS. This had implications for the 'proximity' of volunteers to the service users. Other evidence suggests that the ability of volunteers to meet the needs of service users and clients has been constrained by increasingly tightly defined role descriptions (Bondi, 2004; Guirguis-Younger et al., 2005).

## An emergent model: Volunteering and degrees of hybridity

So far we have highlighted key developments affecting volunteering across the third sector as a whole, with an underlying proposition that these developments are most pronounced in hybrid organizations. In this section, we attempt to develop this argument further by suggesting that different models of volunteering are emerging within the different kinds of organizations – associations, shallow hybrids and entrenched hybrids – identified in Chapter 3. While we highlight a number of emergent distinguishing factors, we suggest that the most critical of these are the positioning of volunteering within organizations and the associated ethos of volunteering.

It has been argued that pure associations rely solely on volunteers. It is, of course, possible for associations to employ paid staff without being considered hybrids but volunteers clearly remain dominant both in numbers and, most importantly, in decision-making, power and authority. While paid staff may be introduced to perform certain tasks, volunteers are the owners of associations; they are the beginning and the end of the organization. In some cases, there may be no distinction between paid staff and individual volunteers; one individual may occupy both positions, being paid for some of the work they do but not for all of it, depending on the availability of funding. Roles are not clearly defined, or at least they are not defined in terms of tasks, and leaders and followers emerge in an informal and implicit manner. Volunteers identify closely with the organization, and are strongly committed to its aims and values. For leaders, volunteering is likely to go beyond being a spare time activity, to the extent that it is better considered as a vocation or occupation; for them it is part of what Rochester (2006) identifies as the 'serious-leisure paradigm', while for others within associations volunteering can be considered as part of Rochester's (2006) 'civil society paradigm'. To talk of volunteer 'management' is inappropriate, with associations adopting a far more subtle and contingent process of organization and mutual support.

Within shallow hybrids, paid staff begin to take on greater significance and have a more central role in the strategic and operational roles of the organization than in associations. Volunteers are positioned not as owners but as members; they have a role in decision-making and their views are generally taken seriously but they are not the ultimate power holders. Volunteer roles are distinct from paid staff, although there may be some blurring, and their roles are emergent – they develop in response both to organizational need and to the interests of individual volunteers. Volunteers are organized and managed informally, developmentally and inclusively along the lines of Zimmeck's (2001) 'home-grown' model. Indeed, a commitment to inclusivity means that some organizations may invest in their volunteers to an extent that may appear to outweigh the returns in economic terms. Within some shallow hybrids, the general commitment to volunteering reflected in their organizational ethos may lead them to seek to involve their service users as volunteers. Those service users may have additional support needs that require considerable resource input before any immediate or direct benefits can be reaped by the organization. Involving users, however, may directly contribute to the wider 'business' aims of the organization; if an organization exists to improve the lives of disabled people, involving them as volunteers in their organization may help to achieve that end as volunteering is recognised as a route out of social exclusion. Volunteering is then both a means and an end.

Within entrenched hybrids, the balance of power has shifted entirely towards paid staff who occupy roles and positions that are clearly distinct from those of volunteers. While entrenched hybrids may involve vast numbers of volunteers, their involvement is shallow. Volunteers are treated as resources to be deployed by organizations in the delivery of services; they are a means to an end and their strategic role in organizational decision-making is minimal (we are of course, referring here only to volunteers in service roles, not those in trustee positions). Volunteers are recruited to fulfil clearly defined, pre-determined roles. Top-down workplace management practices are applied to paid staff and to volunteers alike, with volunteers subject to standardised, formalised and rigorous selection processes; role descriptions; supervision; and performance management. This is the manifestation of Rochester's (1999; 2006) non-profit or service delivery paradigm of volunteering and of Zimmeck's (2001) 'modern management'. While volunteers in entrenched hybrids welcome the improvement to the ways in which their 'work' is organized, they are less happy about the extent to which it has been formalised with the result that some people have ceased to volunteer and others have chosen not to get involved.

These different models of volunteer engagement are summarised in Table 5.1.

These, however, are ideal types and the model is emergent and tentative. In practice, volunteering is often more complex than is suggested by this, or indeed any, model: its sheer diversity defies categorisation. Within any one organization, volunteering may be positioned, organized and experienced in a number of different ways. Federated organizations or those with a branch network, for example, may demonstrate all three types. Organizations we have studied have exhibited the features of volunteering associated with entrenched hybrids at the head office level, while, at the local level, volunteering has looked and felt much more like the associational model. Even within a much simpler organizational structure, there may be one programme or activity in which volunteers lead, have a strong sense of ownership and autonomy over and a high degree of control of, yet elsewhere and overall across the organization the involvement of volunteers is far more marginal. Examples can be given of many hybrids that have resisted some of these developments; that have kept volunteers at the centre of their organization and have developed more creative and flexible ways of involving and supporting them.

**Table 5.1** Three models of volunteer engagement

| Type of organization | Position of volunteers | Management of volunteers | Engagement of volunteers | Volunteering ethos |
| --- | --- | --- | --- | --- |
| Association | Owners | Implicit – Mutual support | Depth but not always breadth | Volunteering as an end |
| Shallow hybrid | Members | Informal – Home grown and developmental | Breadth and depth | Volunteering as a means and an end |
| Entrenched hybrid | Resources | Formal – Modern, top-down and workplace-based | Breadth but no depth | Volunteering as a means to an end |

Similarly, while many volunteers may be disgruntled by the degree of formalisation within entrenched hybrids, leading to some voting with their feet, others are positively enthusiastic about all aspects of their engagement within hybrids, preferring a shallow form of engagement whereby it is easy for them to dip in and dip out of volunteering. All in all, we end up with a complex mix of multiple and often conflicting dynamics (Wilson, 2001).

## Conclusion

Even acknowledging these complexities, we can conclude that volunteering has come to feel different in hybrid organizations and particularly within entrenched hybrids. While the numbers of volunteers involved may remain high, the further into hybridity an organization slips, the more volunteering feels like an instrument of delivery rather than a force for change. Volunteers are brought in to fulfil specific roles, which are designed to deliver specific services in order to meet a specific need. They are often subject to recruitment and management procedures which feel better suited to paid staff than to volunteers. While the 'organization' of their involvement might on the whole be improving, the quality of their experience does not always match this. Volunteers are increasingly dissatisfied about the bureaucratisation of the activities they feel passionate about as 'their' TSOs have taken on the features of public and private sector organizations. The very nature of volunteering is changing within hybrid organizations, particularly those that deliver so many public services and are so much in government favour. There is a danger that meaningful engagement may only be possible in smaller associational organizations that are 'below the radar', or within those shallow hybrid organizations where volunteering has retained its position as a central part of the organizational ethos. Indeed, it may be the centrality of volunteers to an organization that stops it from slipping any further into hybridity.

We are, however, left with a considerable number of unanswered questions and a challenging research agenda. Further research is needed to test the tentative model we have put forward; to make sense of some of the complexity we have noted; and to understand the dynamics of change. Why is it, for example, that some organizations have resisted the overwhelming drive towards professionalisation and formalisation and have kept the spirit of volunteering alive and central to their organizational ethos, while others have not? Is it all a matter of chance, or is there something more systematic at play? We also need to explore further what makes for 'good' volunteer 'management' in these different organizational contexts. To date, the overwhelming emphasis has been on the implementation of 'modern', top-down management practices but evidence here suggests that these very practices may be serving to weaken volunteering and may be more appropriate in some contexts than others. Too little attention has been given to understanding the need for alternative models of volunteer management and how they can be applied.

## References

Billis, D. (2003) *Sectors, Hybrids, and Public Policy: The Voluntary Sector in Context*, Paper presented at the ARNOVA Annual Conference 2003.

Billis, D. and Harris, M. (1996) *Voluntary Agencies: Challenges of Organisation and Management*, Basingstoke: Macmillan.

Billis, D. and Harris, M. (1992) 'Taking the strain of change: UK local voluntary agencies enter the post-Thatcher period', *Nonprofit and Voluntary Sector Quarterly*, 21(3), pp. 211–225.

Blacksell, S. and Phillips, D. (1994) *Paid to Volunteer – The Extent of Paying Volunteers in the 1990s*, London: Volunteer Centre UK.

Bondi, L. (2004) ' "A double edged sword?" The professionalisation of counselling in the United Kingdom', *Health and Place*, 10, pp. 319–328.

Brudney, J. (1999) 'The effective use of volunteers: Best practices for the public sector', *Law and Contemporary Problems*, 62(4), pp. 219–255.

Clark, J. (2007) *Voluntary Sector Skills Survey 2007: England*, London: The UK Workforce Hub.

Cloke, P., Johnsen, S. and May, J. (2007) 'Ethical citizenship? Volunteers and the ethics of providing services for homeless people', *Geoforum*, 38(6), pp. 1089–1101.

Collin, S. and Nagnoni, T. (2002) 'The governance of voluntary work in the public sector: Institutional differences and invariant trends', *Journal of Management and Governance*, 6(4), pp. 323–341.

Davis Smith, J. (1998) *The 1997 National Survey of Volunteering*, London: Institute for Volunteering Research.

Department for Communities and Local Government (2008) *Citizenship Survey: 2007–08 (April 2007–March 2008)*, London: DCLG.

Ellis, S. (2002) *The Volunteer Recruitment Book*, Philadelphia: Energize Inc.

Elstub, S. (2006) 'Towards an inclusive social policy for the UK: The need for democratic deliberation in voluntary and community associations', *Voluntas*, 17(1), pp. 17–39.

Fryer, A., Jackson, R. and Dyer, F. (2007) *Turn your Organisation into a Volunteer Magnet*, Ontario: Linda Graff and Associates Inc.

Gaskin, K (2003) *A Choice Blend: What Volunteers want from Organisation and Management*, London: Institute for Volunteering Research.

Gaskin, K. (2005) *Getting a Grip: Risk, Risk Management and Volunteering, A Review of the Literature*, London: Institute for Volunteering Research.

Gaskin, K. (2008) *A Winning Team? The Impacts of Volunteers in Sport*, London: Institute for Volunteering Research.

Gay, P. (2000) *Delivering the Goods: A Report of the Work of Volunteer Managers*, London: Institute for Volunteering Research.

Geoghegan, M. and Powell, F. (2006) 'Community development, partnership governance and dilemmas of professionalization: Profiling and assessing the case of Ireland', *British Journal of Social Work*, 36, pp. 845–861.

Graff, L. L. (2003) *Better Safe... Risk Management in Volunteer Programs and Community Service*, Ontario: Linda Graff and Associates.

Graff, L. L. (2005) *Best of All: The Quick Reference Guide to Effective Volunteer Involvement*, Ontario: Linda Graff and Associates Inc.

Guirguis-Younger, M., Kelley, M. and Mckee, M. (2005) 'Professionalization of hospice volunteer practices: What are the implications?' *Palliative and Supportive Care*, 3, pp. 143–144.

Harris, M. (2001) 'Voluntary organisations in a changing policy environment', in M. Harris, M. and Rochester, C. (eds) *Voluntary Organisations and Social Policy in Britain*, Basingstoke: Palgrave.

Holmes, K. (2003) 'Volunteers in the heritage sector: A neglected audience?' *International Journal of Heritage Studies*, 9(4), pp. 341–355.

HM Treasury and Cabinet Office (2007) *The Future Role of the Third Sector in Social and Economic Regeneration: Final Report*, London: HM Treasury.

HM Treasury (2002) *Next Steps on Volunteering and Giving in the UK: A Discussion Document*, London: HM Treasury.

Hutchison, R. and Ockenden, N. (2008) *The Impact of Public Policy on Volunteering in Community-Based Organisations*, London: Institute for Volunteering Research.

Institute for Volunteering Research (IVR) (2004) *Volunteering for All? Exploring the Link between Volunteering and Social Exclusion*, London: Institute for Volunteering Research.

Joseph Rowntree Foundation (2000) *Paying for Good Governance: Is Remuneration for Trustees the Way to Improve Charity Governance?* Report from a Joseph Rowntree Foundation seminar held on 20.06.2000 www.jrf.org.uk/knowledge/responses/docs/good-governance.asp.

Kane, D., Clark, J., Lesniewski, S., Wilton, J., Pratten, B. and Wilding, K. (2009) *The UK Civil Society Almanac 2009*, London: National Council for Voluntary Organisations.

Leonard, R., Onyx, J. and Hayward-Brown, H. (2004) 'Volunteer and coordinator perspectives on managing women volunteers', *Non-profit Management and Leadership*, 15(2), pp. 205–219.

Low, N., Butt, S., Ellis Paine, A. and Davis Smith, J. (2007) *Helping Out: A National Survey of Volunteering and Charitable Giving*, London: Cabinet Office.

McCurley, S. and Lynch, R. (1998) *Essential Volunteer Management*, London: Directory of Social Change.

Machin, J. and Ellis Paine, A. (2008a) *Management Matters: A National Survey of Volunteer Management Capacity*, London: Institute for Volunteering Research.

Machin, J. and Ellis Paine, A. (2008b) *Managing for Success: Volunteers' Views on their Involvement and Support*, London: Institute for Volunteering Research.

Neuberger, J. (2008) *Volunteering in the Public Services: Health and Social Care*, London: Cabinet Office.

NfpSynergy (2008) *Who Volunteers? Volunteering Trends 2007–2007.* Accessed from: http://www.nfpsynergy.net.

Noble, J., Rogers, L. and Fryer, A. (2003) *Volunteer Management: An Essential Guide*, Volunteering SA Inc.

Ockenden, N. and Hutin, M. (2008) *Volunteering to Lead: A Study of Leadership in Small, Volunteer-led Groups*, London: Institute for Volunteering Research.

Reichardt, O., Wilding, K. and Kane, D. (2007) *The UK Voluntary Sector Almanac: The State of the Sector 2007*, London: NCVO.

Rochester, C. (2006) *Making Sense of Volunteering: A Literature Review*, London: The Commission on the Future of Volunteering.

Rochester, C. (1999) 'One size does not fit all: Four models of involving volunteers in small voluntary organisations', *Voluntary Action*, 1(2), pp. 7–20.

Rochester, C. and Grotz, J. (2006) *Volunteers and Training: A Report for the Commission on the Future of Volunteering*, Unpublished report.

Russell, L. and Scott, D. (1997) *Very Active Citizens? The Impact of Contracts on Volunteers*, Manchester: University of Manchester.

Scott, D. and Russell, L. (2001) 'Contracting: The experience of service delivery agencies', Chapter 4, pp. 49–63, in M. Harris and C. Rochester (eds) *Voluntary Organisations and Social Policy in Britain*, Basingstoke: Palgrave.

Taylor, M and Warburton, D. (2003) 'Legitimacy and the role of UK TSOs in the policy process', *Voluntas*, 14(3), pp. 321–338.

UK Workforce Hub (2008) Management of Volunteers: National Occupational Standards, London: UK Workforce Hub.

Voluntary Sector National Training Organisation (2004) *Managing Volunteers: National Occupational Standards*, London: Voluntary Sector National Training Organisation.

Weeks, J., Aggleton, P., McKevitt, C., Parkinson, K. and Taylor-Laybourn, A. (1996) 'Community and contracts: Tensions and dilemmas in the voluntary sector response to HIV and AIDS', *Policy Studies*, 17(2), pp. 107–123.

Wilson, C. (2001) *The Changing Face of Social Service Volunteering: A Literature Review*, Wellington: Ministry of Social Development, New Zealand.

Wise, D. (2001) 'Would the payment of market rates for non executive directors strengthen charity governance?' *International Journal of Nonprofit and Voluntary Sector Marketing*, 6(1), pp. 49–60.

Zimmeck, M. (2001) *The Right Stuff: New Ways of Thinking about Managing Volunteers*, London: Institute for Volunteering Research.

# 6 Faith-based organizations and hybridity: A special case?

## Colin Rochester and Malcolm Torry

### Introduction

In this chapter, we will discuss the ways in which religious and faith-based organizations have experienced the growing pressures towards hybridity during the past decade. We will assess the extent to which they have been influenced by expectations which are specific to them as well as by the general social policy drivers, discussed in Chapter 2, which affect third sector organizations (TSOs) across the board. We will discuss the impact of these pressures on faith-based organizations and consider the extent to which their experience, especially at community level, of resisting or embracing hybridization is different from that of other TSOs. And, finally, we will explore the implications of the distinctive forms that hybridity takes in faith-based organizations for their role in the provision of social welfare.

We need to begin, however, by clarifying our terms and explaining exactly what kinds of organizations the chapter will take as its focus. Even within the boundaries of the broad field of social welfare which have been set for this book, faith-based organizations are a heterogeneous collection. We can offer some examples: the faith communities of a London borough establish a multi-faith workplace chaplaincy in a major new development; a Church of England parish builds a community centre at the back of the church building and the vicar chairs the management committee; members of a church set up an arts trust to organize community drama; and a diocese forms a housing association in order to develop church land for social housing. The two key features these initiatives have in common are (1) a main purpose which is not purely religious and (2) a structural connection to a religious organization.

## Religious organizations

Defining religious organizations in turn is a complex matter (explored more fully in Torry, 2005) but, for the purposes of this chapter, it is sufficient to employ a 'prototype' method of definition (Rosch and Lloyd, 1978; Rosch, 1999) and take the congregation as the prototypical religious organization. A 'congregation' is a group of people gathered for worship and a 'religious organization' can thus be defined as a more or less structured association gathering regularly for worship. This is in line with the definition used by Charlton (2008, p. 267): 'the term will be used to refer to recognized and stable gatherings for religious purposes'. Congregations do, of course, fulfil other functions: 'Congregation members assemble for the primary purpose of worship and religious practice. They collectively practise their faith by caring for those in need and combating social injustices' (Cnaan, 2002, p. 80). In the process they may build social capital in their members and in their communities (Torry, 2005), they may be midwives of voluntary organizations and of voluntary activity (Lukka and Locke, 2000) and they may carry out a significant amount of informal care (Harris, 1998). Their fundamental purpose, however, is worship: an activity always firmly embedded in a particular religious tradition.

This means that religious organizations (Roman Catholic and Anglican parishes, free churches, mosques, gurdwaras, mandirs, temples and Quaker meetings) are also firmly embedded in particular religious traditions and are defined by a particular function. If a church no longer gathers for worship, then it is no longer a church, it is no longer a congregation and it is no longer a religious organization. Because any other function is subsidiary to the religious organization's main purpose and because no other kind of organization has corporate worship as its primary function, religious organizations by their very nature cannot hybridize.

Congregations can be seen as a distinctive form of the archetypal third sector association introduced as part of the conceptual framework developed by David Billis in Chapter 3 of this volume. They have been described as 'special case voluntary associations' (Harris, 1998, p. 186). Much of their organizational behaviour can be explained by key features of the associational form which are markedly different from the practices of the bureaucratic 'world'. In the first place, involvement is 'essentially voluntary' and members will leave if their expectations of material, social or psychological benefits are disappointed. Secondly, their needs and demands are directed to 'expressive social and personal benefits such as friendship, mutual support and exchange of news' (ibid., p. 178) rather than the achievement of instrumental goals. Their leaders have a very limited range of tools for persuading members to follow their suggestions and there is little interest in formal procedures and deadlines.

Unlike other associations, however, members of congregations have little control over their ultimate goals and have to deal with a very special kind of professional staff. Members of congregations can debate and decide comparatively low-level decisions about operational matters but the kind of debate about the organization's overall purposes and long-term aims which are commonplace in other associations simply do not happen: the religious or theological principles underpinning congregations are simply not open to question but accepted as a condition of membership. Religious functionaries like vicars, priests or rabbis do not occupy the same position in the life and work of congregations as lay paid staff. In the first place, they have a special kind of authority which is based on tradition and charisma and is independent of the congregational association. Less profoundly but not insignificantly, in many cases they provide a link across the congregation's boundary into the wider denominational structures of which it is part.

### Faith-based organizations and social welfare

At local level, the contribution of congregations to social welfare is made through three kinds of organizational arrangement – as an integral part of the congregation's work; as a distinct programme or project directly managed by the congregation; or through the establishment of a separately constituted but structurally linked faith-based organization.

In the first instance, members of congregations give and receive care which arises from the informal relationships nurtured within the congregation (Wuthnow, 1990). This kind of 'quiet care' takes the form of 'the less "organized" types of welfare such as mutual aid, social integration and various kinds of informal care' (Harris, 1998, p. 168). Many congregations, for example, provide opportunities for older people to meet on a weekly basis while some of their members will visit those who are ill or unable to leave their houses.

The second kind of organizational arrangement is a little more formal. Typically, some members of the congregation become aware of a social need and take action to meet it. The most common examples of this kind of provision are parents and toddlers groups and activities for young people. While these are undertaken in the name of the congregation and are organized within its governing structure, they have their own governing instruments, however rudimentary; their own personnel; and their own purposes. In our terminology and typology these are 'faith-based organizations' which are 'wholly owned' by the religious organizations within which they have come into being.

The third organizational form involves the establishment of a separate body which has its own constitution and bank account and may be registered as a charity in its own right. These organizations tend to come into being where their activities may be too extensive or their responsibilities too onerous to be comfortably managed by the congregation's governing body (one defining moment is the discovery that the new activities are not covered by the congregation's insurance policy). They may also involve collaboration with other interested parties or significant external funding – or both. Typically, the congregation will be a major stakeholder or 'part owner' of the organization and will nominate some but not all of the members of its governing body. Faith-based organizations of this kind can be seen as a form of the enacted hybrid introduced in Chapter 3 of this volume with its associated complexities of ownership and accountability. The choice of organizational form – which may or may not involve the creation of a separate body – is, of course, essentially an aspect of governance which is discussed more fully in Chapter 4.

While the third kind of arrangement discussed above features a recognisably formally constituted organization, the informal characteristics and reliance on personal interaction of the other forms mean that they may not conform to conventional ideas about organizations: 'organizational theory struggles with these entities because it is not clear that they are "organizations" as understood by contemporary students of nonprofit organization and management' (Cnaan et al., 2008, p. 2). At the informal level, too, it can be difficult to distinguish between religious and welfare functions: the group of older people who meet once a week may pray together as well as benefit from social interaction with their peers. It is, moreover, only in the separately constituted faith-based organization that we would expect to find evidence of even shallow forms of hybridity.

Faith-based organizations do not, of course, operate only at the local or congregational level; they are also established as sub-regional, regional and national bodies. These wider structures can be seen as federations of congregations and as faith-based rather than religious organizations; their key function is not worship but the provision of support and services to the organizations that have that function – the congregations. Faith-based organizations formed and run at the regional or national level to address specific issues have played a major part in the development and implementation of social policy and remain significant players. The churches led the way in the development of the popular educational system in Victorian England – not only providing the school buildings but also training the new elementary school teachers – and have made major contributions to the welfare of children and young people; the provision of housing; and personal social services.

To a great extent the role of these large national and regional bodies in the welfare mix is taken for granted and their religious origins are often forgotten or ignored. In some cases, the process of hybridization has gone so far that their religious roots and values are largely invisible: 'through both commercialization and professionalization, some of these religiously based organizations often end up operating much like their secular counterparts, even if faith ultimately animates the organization's mission' (Frumkin, 2002, p. 15). On the other hand, faith can remain a vital force in some organizations and pose a challenge or barrier to the wholesale adoption of the practices of secular bureaucracies; Jeavons (1994, p. viii) has drawn on his personal experience to highlight the challenge of managing 'in a organizational context in which the affirmation of moral values is as important as the completion of a task' and quoted with approval Hall's observation on an earlier period of philanthropy in the USA that 'Christian charity involves more than the economical provision of services. As, if not more, important was the creation of a community of feeling, a set of human bonds which are in themselves perhaps more valuable than the service' (Hall, 1990, quoted in Jeavons, 1994, p. 69).

While we will return to these kinds of organizations later in the chapter, however, our first concern is faith-based organizations at congregational level. It is the small-scale activity which takes place at local or community level undertaken by people from a wide variety of faiths that is not only the most common manifestation of faith-based voluntary action but also the focus of the current attention of those who shape and implement social policy.

## Social policy and the pressure for greater hybridity

Clearly the impact of the powerful policy streams identified by Margaret Harris in Chapter 2 as the drivers of the third sector as a whole towards greater hybridization has been felt by religious and faith-based organizations and there is no need to rehearse them again here. It is worth noting, however, that some areas of the UK have marked the inclusion of faith-based organizations in the wider sector by changing their terminology to 'voluntary, community and faith sectors' (Jochum et al., 2007).

On the other hand, faith-based organizations are also affected by particular forms of expectation or pressure which are specific to them. A review of public policy documents (Jochum et al., 2007) has identified three reasons why government has been keen to engage with faith communities as a means of delivering public services.

In the first place, they are seen as providing a means of access to and better engagement with black and minority ethnic (BME) communities. Religious and faith-based organizations occupy a central place in the cultural identity of many BME and refugee communities; they provide a key part of their social infrastructure; and their leaders are recognised as important community representatives. This means that they offer a means of engaging with hard to reach groups or, more accurately perhaps, help people to access services which are hard to reach.

Secondly, faith-based organizations have significant human and material resources. The great majority of congregations have the use of some kind of building, many of which – like the almost omnipresent church hall – can be used as community buildings to house a range of activities from playgroups for the under 5s to social clubs for older people. Many of them also benefit from the philanthropic donations of their members: religion is a major factor not only in determining whether someone will give money to good causes and how much he or she is prepared to contribute, but also plays in the selection of which causes to support. But it is the scale and the distribution of their human resources which constitute the most important assets of religious and faith-based organizations. This has three aspects: their members provide a large pool of potential volunteers; those who fill lay leadership roles tend to be remarkably committed, energetic and well-qualified (Harris and Rochester, 2001); and the 'religious functionaries' employed by congregations are found in practically all kinds of communities. In the most disadvantaged communities local clergy may constitute the only examples of local resident professionals.

Thirdly, faith communities are also seen by government as 'repositories and transmitters of social values. These values are seen to be a vital motivation for social action and community involvement... From this perspective, faith is seen as engendering a concern for others and a sense of social responsibility

that can be particularly valuable in disadvantaged neighbourhoods' (Jochum et al., 2007, p. 17). As well as stimulating
action, these values can be seen as shaping the nature of the
response of faith-based organizations to social need. They may
bring a qualitatively different approach to social welfare based
on religious values and commitment to their fellow human
beings rather than the technical expertise of the 'professional'.

## Faith-based organizations and welfare: The evidence

There is no equivalent in the UK literature of Cnaan's (2002)
study of 251 congregations in the US. This found that congregations provided considerable amounts of 'informal care'
but also established 'programs'. The case studies reveal the
programs discussed to be faith-based organizations – that is,
separately constituted organizations, or sometimes organizations within the church's governing structure but having their
own governing instrument, personnel and purpose. The study
also found that involvement in such programmes could renew
congregational life which suggested a more general mutual
reinforcement between the activities of religious organizations
and their faith-based 'programs'. Cnaan and his colleagues
also reported that the content of the programmes was diverse,
although they shared a bias towards social care rather than
social critique. And they also found that the social welfare
activities of congregations benefited the wider community to a
greater extent than their members.

The lack of comparable research findings in the UK has
been noted by the authors of a recent study for the Church
of England (Davis et al., 2008) who felt that they were trying
to develop their analysis of the Church's involvement in social
welfare on the basis of totally inadequate sources of data. That
is not to say that there is no evidence. As part of the government's drive to engage religious and faith-based organization
in the delivery of welfare, there have been, since the turn of the
century, a series of surveys of the scale and scope of the contribution of faith groups to social action. Key findings from some
30 reports of this kind have been collated into a valuable table
by the Church of England (Payne, 2008). The studies vary

not only in terms of the quality of the research on which they are based but also on their geographical scope, size of sample and the questions to which they seek answers. Some of them aim to capture the activities of all faith communities across one of the nine government regions for England, while others are restricted to all or part of a county or a city and may focus on just one denomination. They do not all use quantitative methodology – some focus on the qualitative analysis of case studies but, in any case, differences in methodology mean that the data across surveys are not strictly comparable nor can they be aggregated.

The surveys do, however, provide us with an overview of some salient characteristics of 'faith-based social action' (the term generally used in these studies which we take to be broadly comparable with social welfare as employed in this volume). It is worth noting that response rates were generally high, ranging from 23 per cent to more than 80 per cent and clustering around rather more than 50 per cent. The first key feature is the scale and reach of activity: respondent organizations commonly reported that they were, on average, engaged in two or three social action activities or projects, while in three of the studies the figure varied from 6.5 to 9. Secondly, activities were largely dependent on the work of volunteers; the number of active volunteers per congregation ranged from 12 to 19. Information about the number of paid staff engaged in faith-based social action was harder to come by but a study of London undertaken in 2002 (London Churches Group, 2002) estimated that faith communities were employing 10,000 staff but were involving 45,000 volunteers on some 7,000 social action projects. Thirdly, while the total range of activities was very wide indeed, most congregations focused their activities on two groups – children and older people – while a number also mentioned women and families. References to other groups which included the unemployed, people with disabilities and long-term health conditions, excluded children, refugees and asylum seekers and distressed minorities such as people with alcohol or drug abuse issues were less frequent. Similarly, social, educational and recreational activities were commonplace, while more specific provision such as providing information, advice or counselling, health services and home visiting were reported by minorities among those who responded to the surveys.

As well as providing this very general and schematic overview of congregational activity in the field of social welfare, some of the reports also include case study material or vignettes of projects which can be seen as emergent or actual faith-based organizations. The authors of one of them, moreover, have used their data from a study of the churches in one Anglican diocese to enable them to reflect on the contribution that faith-based organizations can make to social welfare and the limitations of their involvement (Cairns et al., 2007). We are also able to draw on a recent study of organizations providing emergency services for homeless people in England which discusses the role of faith-based organizations in this area of social action (Cloke et al., 2007). Finally, but not necessarily least, we draw on the extensive experience of one of the authors of this chapter (Torry) as an Anglican clergyman working in South East London. These sources inform the next sections of the chapter in which we consider the impact of public policy expectations and the changing organizational environment on faith-based organizations.

## The impact on faith-based organizations at local level

This evidence strongly suggests that local religious and faith-based organizations are making a substantial contribution to social welfare and indicates that this contribution has been growing (although there is no way in which we can quantify that increase). While the investment of congregations in these activities and the development of faith-based organizations as delivery mechanisms have had the effect of supplementing and complementing the public sector provision of welfare, it is important to note that they have been largely driven by the congregations' own agendas.

At the heart of these agendas is a concern for others which goes beyond the boundaries of the congregations' own memberships and which is central to the teaching of all the main faiths. This concern typically finds expression and action is triggered by the discovery of specific kinds of need. A group of parents may identify the need for activities for their own and other children. In more than one example, provision for homeless people has been a response to finding people with nowhere else to go sleeping in the church porch or in the graveyard.

If one of the explanations for social action of the local congregation is the disposition of its members to respond to specific kinds of need that come to their attention, a second is the possession by many religious organizations of physical plant. Congregations are often stewards of buildings which are expensive to maintain and which, in many areas, provide the only premises available for community use. The felt need to make good use of these assets is another important push in the direction of social action and community involvement.

Congregations' own commitment to providing welfare services can be seen as a strong foundation for involving them in an enhanced role in the implementation of public policy. There are, however, some important constraints on their ability to play a larger part and significant difficulties in the way of greater involvement. As we have seen, most of their provision takes the form of small-scale activities run by or heavily dependent on volunteers with limited scope for enlargement and there were comparatively few projects which were mainly staffed by paid workers. While congregations possess governing structures and financial and administrative systems that provide the basic infrastructure for organizing activities and delivering services, they face difficulties in supporting large-scale provision over time.

On one level, this lack of capacity can be characterised as constraints on the time their leaders could devote to management and the limitations of their knowledge and expertise. The ubiquitous problem of finding enough time to devote to the management and administration of welfare activities became more acute with the increasing scale and complexity of some projects. The task became especially onerous when the congregation had secured external funding and employed staff. The requirements for monitoring, evaluation and accountability attached to external funding and the challenge of managing staff not only made heavy demands on people's time but also involved the acquisition of new skills and new kinds of knowledge. A common theme found in the numerous surveys of the contribution of faith-based organizations to social action we briefly reviewed earlier in the chapter is that congregations lack knowledge and expertise of this kind and that this failing needs to be addressed if they are to gain access to funding for welfare provision (see, for example, Smith, 2004; Fentener et al., 2008). This may also explain the fact that the organizational landscape in the UK contains comparatively few examples of the 'faith-based nonprofits' which in the US 'form a significant complement to the informal service activities and social ministries that take place within congregations' (Cadge and Wuthnow, 2006, p. 493).

The failure of congregations to access external – largely governmental – funding and thus to develop hybridized faith-based organizations can, however, be explained not so much by a lack of capacity but by the existence of deep-rooted differences in values. These may be expressed as different behavioural norms and practices: the rules by which external funders and especially statutory agencies expect the organizational game to be played may not be readily compatible with the associational norms of a congregation where leadership is personal and informal, relationships are characterised by mutual trust and roles are shaped by those who occupy them rather than being clearly defined before anyone is recruited to perform their functions.

At a more profound level, moreover, differences about *how* social welfare should be delivered may be based on a different and strongly held view about *why* faith-based groups should be involved at all. Cairns and his colleagues found that those involved in the activities they studied were motivated and guided by theological principles rather than secular ideas about civic responsibility let alone the implementation of public policy:

> The process of providing service and of being an active participant in the local neighbourhood is seen as an end in itself. Concepts such as 'outcomes', 'good practice' and 'public accountability' which drive governmental regulation and monitoring requirements, may sit uncomfortably alongside concepts of divinely ordained injunctions to simply care for neighbours and people in need. (Cairns et al., 2006, p. 427)

An example of the operational expression of this difference can be found in a recent study by Cloke and his colleagues (2007) of the role of volunteers in staffing emergency services for homeless people. They focussed on the roles and motivation of volunteers who were involved in small local agencies which had tended to retain the faith-based characteristics of their origins. Unlike their counterparts in larger agencies in the field which had become secularised and bureaucratic, they were not 'squeezed into corporatist agendas and hierarchies'. The study offers three insights into the distinctive nature of volunteering in faith-based organizations. First, for most of them the disposition to volunteer was rooted in their religious belief. Secondly, people volunteered because they wanted to rather than because of any sense of obligation or civic duty. And, thirdly, they had sought out flexibility; these faith-based organizations offered them the opportunity to express their 'ethical citizenship' without 'the perceived fettering of professionalism, over-training and standardisation in service provision' (Cloke et al., 2007, p. 1093).

## The relationship between religious and faith-based organizations

The definition of 'faith-based organizations' we adopted for this chapter included the criterion that they have a structural relationship with a religious organization and, in this section, we explore the nature of this relationship and raise questions about how – and to what extent – it might impact on the degree to which faith-based organizations may be affected by hybridization. As we have seen, at congregational level, many of the projects or, to use Cnaan's term 'programs', can be seen as 'wholly owned subsidiaries' of the local religious organization, while the ownership of other activities is shared with others. A fairly typical example of the latter set of relationships is a community centre built by the church and managed by a board whose members are made up of equal numbers drawn from the local community; the users of the centre; and the church.

The strength of the ties to the religious organization may change over time either because of a decline in interest on the part of members of the congregation or because of changes in the external environment. One example of this process is provided by the Christ Church Forum which was established by a local church in East Greenwich during the 1980s as a Centre for Integrated Living in which people with and without disabilities could work together in the service of the community. The original parish church building was turned into offices and meeting rooms and a new worship area was built on the end. The vicar was chair of the Forum's management committee (though this was not a requirement of the constitution), several members of the congregation were heavily involved and promotion of religion was one of the Forum's charitable aims. About 10 years ago Christ Church Forum was asked by the local authority to absorb a failing nearby community centre. One of the conditions for the absorption requested by the centre's board and imposed by the borough as a condition for funding for the transition was that the Forum should change its name. The management committee agreed and the organization is now known as the 'Forum@Greenwich'. This has been accompanied by other changes: the vicar is no longer its chair; there are no longer congregational members on the management committee; and religion does not feature amongst the organization's stated objectives.

The history of the Christ Church Forum can be interpreted as an example of the effects of a process of hybridization where the congregation gave up its stake in the organization as the organization tailored its identity to the requirements of the local authority. A similar weakening of the links between congregations and faith-based organizations can be seen in the development of the diocesan social work agency, Wel-Care, which specialises in working with families with children and has a specific expertise in managing contact centres where volunteers supervise contact between parents in cases where unsupervised contact might be problematic. Wel-Care was previously a federation of smaller, borough-based charities each of which was responsible for the provision in each area and controlled by trustees usually drawn from local congregations. It is now a single entity, although it retains a network of local committees to provide a link between the projects and local churches. The change is the result of increasingly close

regulation both of charities and social workers and is the cul-
mination of a more professional approach to the work of
the agency which has also involved increased funding from
local authorities. In contrast to the earlier example, however,
Wel-Care's governance is integrated into the diocesan organizational structure: the trustees are made up of Christians active
in the diocese; the organization still reports to the Diocesan Synod; and, if there is a new director, then she or he is
commissioned by the Bishop.

Our third example from the same part of England highlights the contrasting histories of two housing charities which
have been described as faith-based. The first of these, the Carr-
Gomm Society, was established by its eponymous founder and
a small group of like-minded Christians to provide a small-
scale response to the housing needs of people with mental
health difficulties. The organization grew rapidly in response
to the government's policy of decanting large numbers of
patients from long-stay hospitals into supervised accommoda-
tion provided by TSOs. As it grew, the Carr-Gomm Society
recruited additional staff from other housing associations and
from local authority social services and housing departments.
It came to rely on local authority and NHS funding and
its activities, its systems and its procedures became indistinguishable from those of other organizations in the social
care field. New trustees were recruited for their expertise
rather than for their Christian faith and, in the process,
the organization's connection with its faith roots became
attenuated.

By contrast, the Southwark and London Diocesan Housing Association was set up to enable the two dioceses to
develop social housing on land owned by the church. It is
part of the world of housing associations with funding from
the government's Homes and Communities Agency and paid
staff who are housing professionals but it retains a strong
structural connection with the church (albeit this is with the
dioceses rather than at the local or parish level). The land
on which its houses are built remains under the control of
the dioceses, two archdeacons co-chair the board of directors
and other members of the board are also appointed by the
dioceses.

## Conclusions: Faith-based organizations and hybridity

While the evidence we have presented in this chapter is far from comprehensive, we believe that it is possible to draw from it some tentative conclusions about the distinctive ways in which the pressures for hybridization impact on religious and faith-based organizations and some explanations for this experience.

We began by suggesting that faith-based organizations could be defined as bodies which had a structural connection to a religious organization but whose main purpose was not itself purely religious and that religious organizations were more or less structured associations which gathered regularly for worship. We took local congregations as classic models of religious organizations. In our view, they are examples of the associational archetype of the TSO identified by Billis in Chapter 3 of this volume with some specific characteristics of their own, notably the inability of their members to challenge the overall goals and long-term aims of the organization because they are underpinned by non-negotiable theological principles.

Much of the evidence we reviewed focuses on local forms of social action which are carried out by congregations and the faith-based organizations which are linked to them. We can distinguish between three types of institutional arrangements for these activities. Some of them are undertaken by the congregation as part of their general activities. Others are programmes which, although they are part of the congregation's responsibilities, have their own distinct governing instruments, personnel and purposes. And the third kind of arrangement takes the form of an organization which has an existence outside the congregation and has its own constitutional identity, although it retains strong links with the congregation that established it (such as a board of trustees wholly or partly drawn from members of the religious organization).

The last-named of these variants are clearly, in our terms, faith-based organizations which have dipped their toes in the waters of hybridity and are coming under pressure to move into deeper water. Typically, they are having to manage their relationship with a bureaucratic external funder; fulfil the responsibilities of an employer; and meet a variety of demands from regulatory authorities. These demands seem likely to grow stronger in the wake of the stream of public policy that brings with it a larger and enhanced role for faith-based groups in the delivery of public services. The evidence that we have, however, suggests that the pressure of government expectations and the growing degree of hybridization it might bring are meeting resistance (of a passive kind) from faith-based organizations with strong links to local religious organizations.

Failure to sign up to the new role has been seen by the officers of statutory agencies and researchers alike as the result of a lack of capacity: those leading them lacked the expertise to access external funds and meet the requirements for accountability that come with them. Another possible explanation is the difficulty of scaling-up activities which are generally very small ('parochial' in more ways than one) and dependent to a large extent on the contribution of volunteers.

There is, however, another explanation which we find more convincing. This is that the congregations' commitment to serving their local communities and the government's desire to see them delivering public policy might overlap to some extent but they are not rooted in the same values and operating principles. On one level, we have argued that the rules of the bureaucratic game played by statutory funders are not easily reconciled with the associational norms of the congregation. But the gap between the two approaches is wider than that: the theological imperative of giving service which informs and drives the work of congregations in social action is miles away from the ideas of civic responsibility and public service which underpin public policy and shape the work of those who implement it. In short, we are arguing that the non-negotiable theological principles, on which the specific associational form of the religious organization is based, provide a significant barrier to the hybridization of faith-based organizations at the local level. The example given late in the article of the history of the Christ Church Forum suggests that the door to hybridity is thrown open only when the organization loses or loosens its structural relationship with the religious organization and ownership passes to secular interests.

We stress that these tentative conclusions apply to faith-based organizations working at local or parish level. While we have given scant attention to faith-based organizations which operate at a wider level, we can point to the different circumstances in which they encounter hybridity. We suggest that the diocesan structure of the Anglican Church (and its equivalent, where they exist, in other denominations) might best be seen as a faith-based rather than a religious organization – as a body which supports and provides services to congregations rather than as a group of worshippers. It can be seen itself as a hybrid organization with experience of reconciling its bureaucracy with its congregational roots. Where the diocese has maintained its ownership of hybrid organizations like Southwark Wel-Care and the Southwark and London Diocesan Housing Association, they can be seen as 'attached' faith-based organizations subject to the continuing influence of the Church. Other faith-based organizations which have wandered from their ecclesiastical roots – like Christ Church Forum and the Carr-Gomm Society – are more likely, we suggest, to move into the category of entrenched hybrids in the absence of a countervailing pressure.

We emphasise that these conclusions are tentative. The evidence on which they are based is far from comprehensive and was not collected in order to enable researchers to ask the questions that interested us. Clearly, our ideas need to be tested by further research but we hope they will have part to play not only in shaping the future agenda for research but also in raising doubts about the assumptions made by policy makers about the future role of faith-based organizations as providers of social welfare services. There are important constraints on their enhanced involvement in the government's public service delivery agenda which go beyond the common diagnosis of lack of capacity and have their roots in the distinctive entrenched characteristics of religious organizations.

## References

Cadge, W. and R. Wuthnow (2006) 'Religion in the Nonprofit Sector' in W. Powell and R. Steinberg (eds), *The Nonprofit Sector: A Research Handbook*, Second edition, New Haven: Yale University Press.

Cairns, B., M. Harris and R. Hutchison (2007) 'Sharing God's Love or Meeting Government Goals: Local Churches and Public Policy Implementation', *Policy and Politics*, 35 (3), pp. 413–32.

Charlton, J. (2008) 'Congregations and Communities' in R. Cnaan and C. Milofsky (eds), *Handbook of Community Movements and Local Organizations*, New York: Springer.

Clarke, F. (2004) *Coalfields Regeneration in North East England; the Contribution of Faith Communities*, Durham: North East Churches.

Cloke, P., S. Johnsen and J. May (2007) 'Ethical Citizenship? Volunteers and the Ethics of Providing Services for Homeless People', *Geoforum*, 38 (6), pp. 1089–1101.

Cnaan, R. (2002) *The Invisible Caring Hand: American Congregations and the Provision of Welfare*, New York and London: New York University Press.

Cnaan, R., C. Milo32sky and A. Hunter (2008) 'Introduction: Creating a Frame for Understanding Local Organizations' in R. Cnaan and C. Milofsky (eds), *Handbook of Community Movements and Local Organizations*, New York: Springer.

Davis, F., E. Paulhus and A. Bradstock (2008) *Moral, but No Compass*, Chelmsford: Matthew James Publishing.

Fentener, R., P. Daly, R. Foster and M. James (2008) *Faith Groups and Government: Faith-Based Organisations and Government at Local and Regional Levels*, London: Community Development Foundation.

Frumkin. P. (2002) *On Being Nonprofit: A Conceptual and Policy Primer*, Cambridge MA; Harvard University Press.

Hall, P.D. (1990) 'The History of Religious Philanthropy in America' in R. Wuthnow and V. Hodgkinson (eds), *Faith and Philanthropy in America*, Washington: Independent Sector.

Harris, M. (1998) *Organizing God's Work: Challenges for Churches and Synagogues*, London: Macmillan.

Harris, M. and C. Rochester (2001) *Governance in the Jewish Voluntary Sector*, London: Institute for Jewish Policy Research.

Jeavons, Thomas H. (1994) *When the Bottom Line is Faithfulness*, Bloomington and Indianapolis: Indiana University Press.

Jochum, V., B. Patten and K. Wilding (eds) (2007) *Faith and Voluntary Action: An Overview of Current Evidence and Debates*, London: National Council for Voluntary Organisations.

London Churches Group for Social Action and Greater London Enterprise (2002) *Regenerating London: Faith Communities and*

*Social Action*, London: London Churches Group for Social Action.

Lukka, P. and M. Locke (2000) 'Faith, voluntary action and social policy: A review of research', *Voluntary Action*, 3 (1), pp. 25–42.

Payne, B. (2008) *Recent Surveys/Mapping Exercises Undertaken Across the English Regions, Scotland and Wales to Measure the Contribution of Faith Groups to Social Action and Culture* accessed 10 March 2009 at www.cofe.anglican.org/about/builtheritage/ buildingfaith/regionalreportstable.pdf.

Rochester, C., T. Bissett and H. Singh (2007) 'Faith-Based Organisations As Service-Providers' in V. Jochum, B. Patten and K. Wilding (eds) (2007) *Faith and Voluntary Action: An Overview of Current Evidence and Debates*, London: National Council for Voluntary Organisations.

Rosch, E. (1999) 'Reclaiming Concepts' in W. Freeman and R. Núñez (eds), *Reclaiming Cognition, Journal of Consciousness Studies*, 6 (11–12), pp. 61–77.

Rosch, E. and B. Lloyd (1978) *Cognition and Categorization*, New Jersey: Lawrence Erlbaum.

Smith, K. (2004) *Faith in the North East: Social Action by Faith Communities in the Region*, Newcastle upon Tyne: Voluntary Organisations Network North East.

Torry, M. (2005) *Managing God's Business: Religious and Faith-based Organizations and their Management*, Aldershot: Ashgate.

Wuthnow, R. (1990) 'Religion and the Voluntary Spirit in the United States; Mapping the Terrain' in R. Wuthnow, V. Hodgkinson and associates (eds), *Faith and Philanthropy in America*, San Francisco: Jossey-Bass.

# 7 Community anchor organizations: Sustainability and independence

## Romayne Hutchison and Ben Cairns

### Introduction

This chapter will focus on 'multi-purpose' community-based organizations, otherwise known as 'community anchor organizations' (Home Office, 2004; HM Treasury, 2007). As well as being important in terms of their increasing role in the delivery of public services, they also offer an especially interesting example of the effects of hybridization. With their roots in the associational world, but with the addition of a strong service-providing role, they straddle the worlds of association and bureaucracy that are described in Chapter 3 of this volume; they could thus be described as shallow hybrids. Drawing on our own recent research, the chapter will discuss some of the ways in which community anchor organizations are becoming more hybrid in nature before considering some of the strategies which these organizations might employ to meet the challenges of hybridity.

### Community anchor organizations

The enhanced role played by the third sector in public services delivery since the election of the New Labour government in 1997 is discussed elsewhere in this volume. More specifically, recent government policy documents have stressed the role of community anchor organizations in both public services delivery and the building of strong communities (DCLG, 2007,

2008; HM Treasury, 2007). These organizations have been described as 'strong, sustainable community-based organizations [that] can provide a crucial focus for community development and change in their neighbourhood and community' (Home Office, 2004, p. 19).

They range from relatively small community centres, village and church halls to large settlements, social action centres and development trusts that run a number of activities and often act as hosts to other organizations and projects (Thake, 2006). Many have a long tradition of community development work with local people in an attempt to improve their lives and to try to tackle the causes and effects of poverty and disadvantage. They are often involved in the provision of informal services and the organization of activities with and for local communities as well as running more formal services funded under contracts or service level agreements with local authorities (IVAR, 2006). Their role in providing advocacy or 'voice' for local people has also assumed greater prominence in recent years (Home Office, 2004). Some larger community anchor organizations may describe themselves as 'social enterprises' (Spear et al., 2007; and see Chapter 8 of this volume). Those that incorporate a strong service-providing element employ paid staff, sometimes in considerable numbers, while their involvement of volunteers tends to be focused on governance and on the organization and running of particular events rather than direct service provision (Thake, 2006). While some have developed into extremely large undertakings, most can still be considered as falling into one of National Council for Voluntary Organisation's (NCVO's) categorisations of third sector organizations (TSOs) as small or medium (Kane et al., 2009).

## Pressures on third sector organizations

There is little published research focused specifically on these multi-purpose organizations, and none that concentrates on the effects of hybridization. However, research on the wider third sector discusses various relevant factors that may lead TSOs to become increasingly formalised, less independent and more hybrid in nature. These include co-option by the state of TSOs as vehicles for public service delivery and public policy implementation (Smith and Lipsky, 1993; Salamon, 1995, 2002); greater regulation by contracting bodies and increased pressure to be accountable (Rochester, 2001; Cairns et al., 2005); requirements to restructure and change their management (Wallis and Dollery, 2005) or adopt terms and conditions of service delivery that are not in line with their organizational values or systems (Lewis, 2005); and the challenge of working across organizational or sectoral boundaries to provide services in collaboration with other – public, private and third sector – agencies (Sullivan and Skelcher, 2003; Harris et al., 2004).

These pressures may in turn lead to the incorporation of TSOs as an arm of the state (Etherington, 2004; Charity Commission, 2007; Commission for the Compact, 2008) or to isomorphism, taking on the characteristics of the government agencies with which they work (Harris, 2001; Kelly, 2007). A closer relationship to government might also undermine the distinguishing features of the third sector: 'voluntary governing bodies, advocacy, volunteering – which constitute the "authentic core" or "soul" of the sector' (Harris and Billis, 1996, p. 244). In such cases, organizations may be prone to mission dilution or mission drift (Weisbrod, 2004; Jones, 2007) and of becoming more hybrid in nature with little planning or foresight.

For community anchor organizations, the pressures towards hybridity are particularly acute. Whilst many have their roots in the associational world of groups that come together to address social problems, some have begun to exhibit the features of more than one sector – either the public or the private sector, or both – and therefore can be considered as shallow hybrids. They may straddle the boundaries of the third sector and the private sector through, for example, their development of enterprise activities such as community cafés or bars, or renting out of office space. Others may have ventured so far into the provision of public services that they have become virtually indistinguishable from statutory providers; in such cases, they could be considered to be entrenched hybrids.

In the light of these trends and the heightened policy interest in both their service delivery function and their role in providing voice for local communities (HM Treasury, 2007), the ways in which community anchor organizations negotiate and manage the challenges of hybridity deserve more attention.

## The evidence

Our discussion is informed by the findings from two separate studies of community anchor organizations carried out by the Institute for Voluntary Action Research (IVAR) in 2006 and 2007. All the quotations which appear in this chapter are from participants in those two studies. One study explored the contribution of community anchor organizations to public services delivery and civil renewal, while the other looked at the ways in which these organizations performed an advocacy role with and on behalf of individuals and groupings of local people. Both studies focused on organizations which provided services and activities for a broad range of people: these included educational classes, childcare, lunch clubs and other activities for older people, legal and other advice services, groups for drug users, various services for young people and so on. A total of 30 organizations, based in a variety of mainly urban locations around England, were studied. All employed paid staff, with numbers of (part or full-time) employees ranging from 1 to 120. Their funding levels were between a few thousand and over 2 million pounds. The larger organizations often derived their income from several sources that might include different statutory sector contracts, grants, charitable trust funding, fees for services provided and individual donations.

We highlight the ways in which these organizations are becoming more hybrid in nature first through considering the pressures on them to move away from their original mission and purpose; we then describe some of the factors influencing their decisions about prioritisation of services and in particular the challenges to their performance of an advocacy function. We move on to discuss their organizational responses to the pressures of public service provision and greater alignment with statutory bodies. As Chapter 3 suggests, some of them may at this stage in their organizational life be considered shallow hybrids; for others, the changes are such that they might more appropriately be described as entrenched hybrids.

## Shifts in organizational mission and purpose

Many community anchor managers and leaders have experienced difficulty in recent years in maintaining an independent strategic vision and community focus and in holding on to key aspects of their mission in an environment which stressed a substantial public service delivery role for TSOs, including community anchors. They felt that this environment had been created by central government: some referred explicitly to central government's desire to see TSOs take on an enhanced role in the provision of public services, while others were less direct in their references, but nevertheless indicated an awareness that changes at the local level, such as a move from grants to service level agreements or contracts, emanated from central government.

While some organizations felt that they were *not* public service providers – 'we are not a substitute arm of local or central government' – others acknowledged that this was their status because they delivered services funded by means of a contract with the local authority. Some viewed their organizations as being explicitly about the provision of public services: 'the concept of being a public services provider very much fits'. Others saw their mission as having slipped by default into public service provision: 'it's almost as though we're a community association distracted by public services'. Anxiety about the possible erosion of the sector's distinctive features was summed up thus: 'the more you move towards commissioning/contracting, the more difficult it is for the sector to add value and contribute its own "something"'.

The mission and purpose of community anchor organizations was widely perceived by their leaders as being about meeting the needs of individuals through the provision of services: 'our mission and purpose is to provide services for the local residents through the different work streams we have' rather than in terms of facilitating individuals' engagement in communal activities or performing a community development role, which many of them had done in the past. Although the word 'empowerment' was often used when talking about their work with individuals, this was generally in relation to helping people improve their quality of life through the acquisition of opportunities, skills or resources rather than enhancing their ability to be involved in political or community development processes. While services and activities were usually developed in response to perceived local need, the idea of being community-led did not feature strongly and this provides evidence of their drift away from their associational roots and their provision of a voice role for local communities.

For many community anchor organizations, this gradual move away from their associational roots and accountability to local communities has been further exacerbated by the substantial increase in the accountability and monitoring requirements placed on them by statutory agencies, both funders and other regulatory bodies. In some instances, this was the result of increasing demands from existing funders for more detailed information, while elsewhere it followed the acquisition of one or more new sources of funding. Those who run community anchor organizations do not object to monitoring and regulation in themselves, but they are concerned that these activities take up ever-increasing amounts of their time: 'too many people want a piece of you and you have to spin too many plates'. They consider themselves to be accountable to a diverse group of external stakeholders and regulatory bodies as well as to their own governing body, the local community and their users.

## Changes to organizations' prioritisation of services and activities

The availability of funding for some, but not other, areas of their work led community anchors to focus on particular aspects of their organizational mission rather than others, and to prioritise services for which funding was available. These were not necessarily the services most wanted, or needed, by local people. Organizations might concentrate on running vocational training courses rather than recreational courses, and discontinuing organizing social events for local people, because of funding constraints: 'services have to be viable; we can't do them just because local people want them'. This frequently meant that the aspects of their work that could be considered as contributing to community cohesion were in decline: 'there's a danger that we might end up just providing services that we can afford to run. So we might lose our social agenda which is to look after those most in need. There's a danger that accountants might start to run the organization in the same way as they run a business'.

The services and activities which they provided were those in line with government priorities and local (statutory) funding criteria: 'there is no statutory money for innovative or development work any more or work that doesn't help the council achieve their floor targets; there are some things you just cannot get funding for, e.g. advocacy, legal advice, general support'. In some instances, services which were considered important had been cut because funding was not available: these included 'legal representation, help with accessing housing and support services for people with mental health difficulties. We've had to turn away a number of people with mental health concerns and alcohol issues'.

Those involved with community anchor organizations are also aware that the ways in which they delivered services, as well as the services themselves, have been affected by government policy relating to specific client groups. This was particularly true of organizations working with children and young people, which needed to work in line with the Every Child Matters agenda and several different pieces of legislation. While the increased array of government initiatives in relation to the welfare of children and young people were welcome, they had some unintended consequences such as a reduction in parental involvement as a result of the need to have more paid staff. In such situations, it could be argued that some of the distinctive, more informal, aspects of voluntary childcare provision are being eroded, making it little different from services and activities offered by childcare providers in the public or private sectors.

Community anchor organizations' ability to act as community development agencies – which, as we noted earlier, is for many an important part of their history and mission – has been weakened because of the difficulty in securing funding for this area of work. Some had previously benefited from the availability of funding streams such as the Neighbourhood Renewal

Fund and used it to resource their community development work: 'it enabled us to get back to the traditional community development work we did back in the 60s, which had reduced'. When this relatively flexible form of funding was no longer available, their ability to undertake community development work was much reduced.

There is only limited funding for community anchors to use at their own discretion to provide services and activities which local people want or need. There are numerous examples of the adverse effect on the ability of organizations to set their own goals and the adoption of public sector characteristics. In endeavouring to counter this by developing a more entrepreneurial approach to income generation, some organizations appear also to be taking on attributes of the private sector. They are thus simultaneously being pulled in two different directions but in both instances away from their traditional roots in the associational world. It seems increasingly likely that those that did manage to survive in the current climate would do so at the cost of their distinctive features. Some organizations were described as slipping into a 'market model – the model used by private industry'. Here, community anchor organizations can be seen moving towards a more entrenched model of hybridity.

## Challenges to the performance of community anchors' advocacy function

Advocacy on behalf of individuals and communities can, as we noted earlier, be considered one of the distinctive features of TSOs; indeed the provision of advocacy for local communities has been described by policy makers as a key priority for community anchor organizations (HM Treasury, 2007). They, along with TSOs in many fields of activity, have been active in attempting to influence policy makers to adopt policies favourable to their client group and they also often seek to enhance citizen involvement in influencing decisions (Schmid et al., 2008).

There are, however, a number of barriers to their ability to act as advocates on behalf of local people. These include the availability (or non-availability) of funding to support anchor organizations' advocacy work; their own organizational capacity; and their relationships with the local authorities which were often the focus of their advocacy work. These challenges threaten to squeeze the advocacy function out of the heart of their operations and break community anchors' link to the associational world.

Funding mechanisms generally do not recognise the advocacy function. Although advocacy is an integral part of many organizations' work, it is often invisible to funders, and even at times to the organizations themselves. Advocacy work is usually subsumed within the chief executive's time or in particular project workers' roles alongside other activities or dispersed across many staff members' and volunteers' roles: 'We don't get any funding...it's seen as part and parcel of [the CEO] job to make sure it happens. Others described how the funding was squeezed from other resources: 'It's more a case of being funded to do something else but the commitment of staff is to look wider than the issues you are dealing with, so you do it.' The work is usually an add-on to other work that did receive funding or is 'funded from underspend on other budgets.'

The availability of funding is part of a broader problem of lack of organizational capacity to perform an advocacy function. Advocacy was described as an increasingly resource-intensive and complex activity which needed considerable investment of specific expertise and time. It was suggested that organizations could undertake more advocacy work if the role was formalised more strategically in the organization: 'it's done because we do it, or rather we've decided to do it'. However, retaining those skilled staff who were able to undertake high quality work was difficult when funding was insecure; this threatened both service delivery and advocacy work: 'working in the sector is not secure, so when you get people who are really sharp they tend to get drawn out of the sector.' In some organizations, staff and trustees were preoccupied with organizational survival, and felt that they needed to concentrate some of their resources on advocating for their own organizational existence.

Uncertainties on the part of local authorities and other funders over the respective roles of community anchors and statutory organizations have created further barriers in some localities. The staff of community anchors might be reluctant to act in any way that appeared critical of the local authority while they were, at the same time, applying for commissioned work. In some areas: 'the local authority does not want to hear local people ... we don't have a good relationship with officers' or 'voluntary organizations think the local authorities don't understand what they are doing'.

As their advocacy function becomes increasingly squeezed through lack of funding and organizational capacity and is at times misunderstood by local authorities who prefer to see them concentrate on a service-providing role, community anchors risk losing one of the features which distinguishes them from statutory service providers.

## Organizational responses to the pressures of public service provision

The opportunity to act as public service providers has been welcomed by a small number of organizations. Most, however, have been reluctant to embrace public services provision wholeheartedly, and tried to find ways to retain their roots in the associational world: 'you can respond to the changes that are happening, but keep your ethos, which is what we are doing. There is no question of changing what we are doing; instead we consider how to respond to changes around us. Most statutory agencies accept that the Centre is an independent body'.

Strategies to manage the service delivery agenda included the adoption of new strategic plans against which organizations could assess whether funding opportunities and possible new work matched their mission and strategy. Some organizations had changed their management structure in order to help them to be more aware of the policy environment or to develop more of an external focus, spending more time on marketing and developing links with other local organizations.

The development of an independent funding base can be seen as another means of maintaining mission and developing strategy: 'we have a funding base in our own trust fund.

This makes us behave slightly differently to other organizations that worry about where the next penny is coming from. We consider – do we want to be part of this? Is there another way of doing this?' However, the route to an independent funding base more often came through enterprise activity and the world of income generation, even if it was not necessarily in line with their ethos: 'we've become more enterprising; we have been pushed in that way a little bit but it's been a benefit'. For such organizations, their funding mix now included a substantial amount of money generated not only from more traditional activities such as room hire and renting out of office space, but also from nursery and other childcare fees, running a café, a bar, doing catering for other organizations and, in some instances, charging individual service users: 'the star of social enterprise has risen'; 'a big change has been the increase in self-generated income, which we believe is the future'.

There are a variety of views among community anchor managers about entrepreneurial approaches; some organizations consider it to be a positive development but others believe that it potentially risked distorting their mission by moving their focus away from meeting community need – the very reason for which many of them had been established: 'I can't bear the idea of being forced to sell shoes to fund a legal advice service'. The difficulties of trying to meet need and at the same time make a profit were an ongoing struggle: 'everything is about the good of the community, but we have to make a profit'. Organizations that had started charging community groups for the hire of premises found that those that could not afford the cost had simply gone elsewhere. Asking users for payment had a similar outcome: 'we're dealing with people who are on a very small income. Some people just can't afford to pay the extra, or to pay anything at all. We have to be aware that charging prevents some people from coming. This means they never get out at all and become totally isolated and cut off from the community'.

In some situations, these income-generating activities can be viewed as an alternative means of fulfilling the ultimate organizational goal of meeting the needs of local communities and individuals. Elsewhere, however, income generation has become a goal in its own right and has taken the organizations in new directions, away from their original mission and purpose, making them, at least superficially, little different from commercial service providers.

For some community anchors, then, their attempts to maintain their original mission and purpose, and not to become too closely aligned with the public sector, have taken them away from the associational world in which many of them had their origins and towards a form of hybridity in which they acquired some of the features of the private sector. For organizations which might already be considered as shallow hybrids, this process of adopting the characteristics of other sectors could result in a more entrenched form of hybridity.

## Discussion

In this chapter, we have drawn on our recent research on community anchor organizations in the third sector to consider the issue of hybridity in relation to organizational challenges which they experience around their mission and purpose; goal-setting; and advocacy work. Taken together, these research findings confirm that there are numerous factors which are contributing to a process of creeping and deepening hybridization, whereby organizations are coming adrift from their moorings without adequate preparation or deliberation. In the final part of this chapter, we briefly discuss particular aspects of this process which can be seen to be problematic. We conclude with some tentative observations about strategies which community anchor organizations might employ to meet the challenges of hybridity.

Our research has confirmed that funding is increasingly more readily available for those activities which adhere to governmental priorities; constitute delivery of services; meet individual rather than community needs; and/or are subject to strict accountability and monitoring requirements. Within this emerging funding framework, the potential of community anchor organizations to act as agents of community change, or as advocates for their local community, seems to be restricted by their adoption of a service-providing role and by a lack of availability of funding for community development activities.

Whilst the governmental rhetoric is of 'community cohesion', the effect of current funding regimes seems closer to 'community fragmentation' as organizations are compelled to ignore some local groups in need at the expense of others for whom funding may be available (Cantle, 2001). In having to prioritise statutory requirements over community responsiveness, the primary locus of community organizations' accountability can be seen to shift away from their core constituency – local people and the communities in which they live – towards statutory and regulatory bodies of various kinds. This effectively expands the group of 'principal owners' and risks diffusing the responsibility for the organization's strategy and sustainability.

There is also evidence to suggest that advocacy work (which traditionally has acted as a bridge between citizens and the state and can be regarded as a core function of community anchor organizations) is being squeezed out. Many organizations remain keen to hold on to their mission of providing choices and opportunities to help local people improve their quality of life by carrying out their advocacy function alongside the provision of publicly funded services; they may be understood as shallow hybrids. Other organizations, however, are finding it increasingly difficult to resist pressures to be deflected away from their primary focus and have become public services providers at the expense of their voice role; such organizations can be described as entrenched hybrids. This move between different types of hybridity generally occurs without planning or preparation.

In response to these pressures, community anchor organizations are attempting to seek independent funding and self-generated income through entrepreneurial activities in order to continue providing activities which are part of their mission and valued by their local communities. Whilst this strategy might yield short-term benefits – for example, the continuation of services otherwise threatened with closure – the world of enterprise has its own set of rules and expectations which may, over time, require organizations to take on some of the characteristics of private sector organizations. As with the effects of shifting governmental funding priorities, this may also trigger a process of unplanned hybridization.

How then might we explain the reasons for this creeping hybridization? Concerned by the prescriptive nature of funding, the risks of entrepreneurialism and the decline of advocacy, few of the organizations we studied were able to see how they might achieve greater control over an environment that appears increasingly hostile to their multi-purpose nature. They were also unable to envisage how they might deal with the multiple accountability demands of the public services delivery agenda at the same time as enabling their organizations to retain their autonomy and their ability to make appropriate strategic choices. It would seem therefore that many organizations are being driven towards considerable, yet unplanned, organizational change. This 'emergent' change seemed to be an underlying force, shaping organizational policies and procedures (Hasenfeld, 1992). Community anchor organizations risk drifting away from their founding mission and losing the multi-purpose, community-focused approach which enables them to make their distinctive contribution to their local communities. Here, then, a creeping process of hybridization can be seen as a direct threat to the distinctive contribution of community anchor organizations to community fabric, precisely because it privileges the demands of public agencies over the needs of local communities.

The set of management skills required in this operating environment is far removed from the characteristics of organizations with their roots in the associational world. Although some of the organizations we studied had grown significantly in size, many 'have become what they are without ever quite thinking about the questions of what they are and what they want to become' (Milofsky, 2007). Whilst chief executives were often knowledgeable about wider national and local policy affecting the third sector, some senior staff and trustees remained unclear about key themes such as 'public services delivery' and unaware of their organizations' roots in community action. Furthermore, some trustees had little knowledge of, or interest in, structure and management strategies – in keeping with earlier findings about community-based associations (Smith, 1997a; 1997b). One consequence of this mismatch – between the *internal* interests and skill-sets of organizations and the *external* demands of an increasingly complex policy environment – is that community anchor organizations lack the necessary resources within their governance arrangements to retain independent control of their goal-setting, and to avoid excessive co-option by policy and funding requirements.

## Concluding remarks

In conclusion, we can identify a chronic tension within community anchor organizations. On the one hand, there continues to be serious commitment to the potential for community development to 'create the pre-condition for positive social change – through new ideas and understandings; through new confidence and personal esteem; through new desires and new moods, through a new political will; and through new forms of participation in social life' (Flecknoe and McLlelan, 2004, p. 7). On the other hand, it can be argued that this community development approach and the traditional role of community anchor organizations are in danger of being lost in the organizational change forced on them by the pressures of the current policy and funding environment.

The cumulative effect of these pressures is already evident in the way in which organizations are being pulled away from their associational roots, and in particular from approaches and activities which foster local social interaction. Increasingly, they do not display characteristics traditionally associated with these kinds of organizations – for example, collectivist and egalitarian styles of governance, and a commitment to ideology taking precedence over managerial technique (Milofsky, 2007). In these circumstances – of strategic vulnerability and strategic inertia – there is a real risk that community-based organizations may, by default, slip into a model of entrenched hybridity by becoming full-scale public services providers or social enterprises, without having any prior positive intention to become so.

Hybridity itself is not necessarily to be avoided. Our research does, however, highlight the need for community anchor organizations to be aware of its implications. For if these organizations – which have deep roots and occupy trusted boundary-spanning places in local communities – lose their community accountability or wither by neglect, it may be expensive and time consuming to recreate these characteristics at a later date.

Those organizations which are able to exercise choice and direction over the change process are characterised by having taken strategic steps to preserve their autonomy over mission, goals and activities. In such cases, organizations have been able to survey the environment for opportunities and threats and devise proactive strategic responses, modifying structure and adapting practice as appropriate (Pietrobugo and Wernet, 2004; Strichman et al., 2008). Elsewhere, we have seen third sector infrastructure bodies take decisive steps to increase the levels of policy awareness within their membership and to encourage local organizations to develop more of a policy-shaping role (Harris et al., 2004; bassac, 2007).

Our research also suggests a need for community anchor organizations to develop a more articulated understanding of their function and accountability – in relation to public and private agencies as well as to wider civil society – in order to manage their hybrid status. Such an understanding might include the following: an awareness and appreciation of their history and roots (Billis, 1991); the difficulty of managing accountability to multiple and sometimes divergent stakeholders; and the concept of 'sector blurring' and its implications and possible consequences for organizations as they move into different organizational worlds (Billis, 1993; Taylor, 2002). To support the building of this organizational and environmental consciousness, further consideration will need to be given to the organizational strategies which community anchor organizations might employ and how, in particular, they reconcile ideology with strategy, community needs with policy priorities and founding values with management processes (Milofsky, 2006).

## References

bassac (2007) *Calling for Change: The Evidence for Supporting Community Voices to Speak Out*, London: bassac.

Billis, D. (1991) 'The roots of voluntary agencies: A question of choice', *Nonprofit and Voluntary Sector Quarterly*, vol. 20, no.1, pp. 57–70.

Billis, D. (1993) *Sliding into Change: The Future of the Voluntary Sector*, CVO Working Paper 14, Centre for Voluntary Organisation, London: London School of Economics.

Cairns, B., Harris, M., Hutchison, R. and Tricker, M. (2005) 'Improving performance? The adoption and implementation of quality systems in UK nonprofits', *Nonprofit Management and Leadership*, vol. 16, no. 2, pp. 135–151.

Cantle, T. (2001) *Community Cohesion: A Report of the Independent Review Team*, London: Home Office.

Charity Commission (2007) *Stand and Deliver: The Future for Charities Providing Public Services*, Liverpool: Charity Commission.

Commission for the Compact (2008) *The State of Independence: A Research Study into Independence and the Compact*, Birmingham: Commission for the Compact.

Department for Communities and Local Government (2008) *Communities in Control: Real People, Real Power*, The Empowerment White Paper, London: DCLG.

Department for Communities and Local Government (2007) *Third Sector Strategy for Communities and Local Government*, Discussion Paper, London: DCLG.

Etherington, S. (2004) 'Public services and the future of the UK voluntary sector', *International Journal of Nonprofit and Voluntary Sector Marketing*, vol. 9, no. 2, pp. 105–109.

Flecknoe, C. and McLlelan, N. (2004) *The What, Why and How of Neighbourhood Community Development*, London: Community Matters.

Harris, M. (2001) 'Voluntary Organisations in a Changing Social Policy Environment', in M. Harris and C. Rochester (eds), *Voluntary Organisations and Social Policy in Britain*, Basingstoke: Palgrave.

Harris, M. and Billis, D. (1996) 'Conclusion: Emerging Challenges for Research and Practice', in D. Billis and M. Harris (eds), *Voluntary Agencies: Challenges of Organisation and Management*, Basingstoke: Macmillan.

Harris, M., Cairns, B. and Hutchison, R. (2004) ' "So many tiers, so many agendas, so many pots of money": The challenge of English regionalization for voluntary and community organizations', *Social Policy and Administration*, vol. 38, no. 5, pp. 525–540.

Hasenfeld, Y. (1992) *Human Services as Complex Organizations*, Newbury Park, CA: Sage.

HM Treasury (2007) *The Future Role of the Third Sector in Social and Economic Regeneration*, London: HM Treasury.

Home Office (2004) *Firm Foundations: The Government's Framework for Community Capacity Building*, London: Civil Renewal Unit, Home Office.

Institute for Voluntary Action Research (2006) *Servants of the Community or Agents of Government? The Role of Community-Based Organisations and Their Contribution to Public Services Delivery and Civil Renewal*, London: IVAR.

Jones M.B. (2007) 'The multiple sources of mission drift', *Nonprofit and Voluntary Sector Quarterly*, vol. 32, no. 2, pp. 299–308.

Kane, D., Clark, J., Wilton, J., Lesniewski, S., Pratten, B. and Wilding, K. (2009) *The UK Civil Society Almanac*, London: NCVO.

Kelly, J. (2007) 'Reforming public services in the UK: Bringing in the third sector', *Public Administration*, vol. 85, no. 4, pp. 1033–1022.

Lewis, J. (2005) 'New labour's approach to the voluntary sector: Independence and the meaning of partnership', *Social Policy and Society*, vol. 4, no. 2, pp. 121–131.

Milofsky, C. (2006) 'Small Towns and Mass Society', in R. Cnaan and C. Milofsky (eds), *Handbook on Community Movements and Local Organizations*, New York: Springer.

Milofsky, C. (2007) Address to the *Philanthropy Forum: How Nonprofit Organizations Create Community Program*, Washington DC, June.

Pietrobugo, J. and Wernet, S.P. (2004) 'Joining forces, fortunes, and futures: Restructuring and adaptation in nonprofit hospice organizations', *Nonprofit Management and Leadership*, vol. 15, no. 1, pp. 117–137.

Rochester, C. (2001) 'Regulation: The Impact on Local Voluntary Action', in M. Harris and C. Rochester (eds), *Voluntary Organisations and Social Policy in Britain*, Basingstoke: Palgrave.

Salamon, L. (1995) *Partners in Public Service: Government-Nonprofit Relations in the Modern Welfare State*, Baltimore, MD: Johns Hopkins University Press.

Salamon, L.M. (2002) *The Tools of Government: A Guide to the New Governance*, New York: Oxford University Press.

Schmid, H., Bar, M. and Nirel, R. (2008) 'Advocacy activities in nonprofit human services organizations implications for policy', *Nonprofit and Voluntary Sector Quarterly*, vol. 37, no. 4, pp. 581–602.

Smith, D.H. (1997a) 'The rest of the nonprofit sector: Grassroots associations as the dark matter ignored in the prevailing "flat earth" maps of the sector', *Nonprofit and Voluntary Sector Quarterly*, vol. 26, no. 2, pp. 114–131.

Smith, D.H. (1997b) 'Grassroots associations are important: Some theory and a review of the impact literature', *Nonprofit and Voluntary Sector Quarterly*, vol. 26, no. 3, pp. 269–306.

Smith, S.R. and Lipsky, M. (1993) *Nonprofits for Hire: The Welfare State in the Age of Contracting*, Cambridge, MA: Harvard University Press.

Spear, R., Cornforth, C. and Aiken, M. (2007) *For Love and Money: Governance and Social Enterprise*, London: Governance Hub, NCVO.

Strichman, N., Bickel, W.W. and Marshood, F. (2008) 'Adaptive capacity in Israeli social change nonprofits', *Nonprofit and Voluntary Sector Quarterly*, vol. 37, no. 2, pp. 224–248.

Sullivan, H. and Skelcher, C. (2003) *Working Across Boundaries: Collaboration in Public Services*, London: Palgrave.

Taylor, M. (2002) 'Government, the Third Sector and the Contract Culture: The UK experience so far', in U. Ascoli and C. Ranci (eds), *Dilemmas of the Welfare Mix: The New Structure of Welfare in an Era of Privatization*, New York: Plenum Press.

Thake, S. (2006) *Community Assets: The Benefits and Costs of Community Management and Ownership*, London: DCLG.

Wallis, J. and Dollery, B. (2005) 'The impact of alternative styles of policy leadership on the direction of local government reform', *International Journal of Social Economics*, vol. 32, no. 4, pp. 291–306.

Weisbrod, B.A. (2004) 'The pitfalls of profits', *Stamford Social Innovation Review*, vol. 2, no. 3, pp. 40–47.

# 8 Social enterprises: Challenges from the field

*Mike Aiken*

## Introduction

This chapter examines some of the challenges facing social enterprises and considers these in the light of some of the theory of hybridity presented in Chapter 3 of this volume. Social enterprises provide useful material for this discussion as even the terminology is highly suggestive of mixed approaches. Some accounts have typified them as exemplars of a hybrid form which intertwine within one organization the 'different components and rationales' of state, market and civil society (Evers, 2004, p. 8). An examination of social enterprises – considering both the dynamics of their operating environment and the internal organizational tensions they face – could be illuminated by a consideration of some theoretical ideas about hybridity. The policy and funding environment has encouraged the development of social enterprises and has seen them as convenient entrepreneurial vehicles for delivering welfare services formerly managed by the public sector. Meanwhile, practitioners within social enterprises have pointed to the internal organizational challenges of a 'conflict in culture between "care" and "business"' within their governance and operations (Social Firms, 2009). This chapter considers to what extent such tensions can be understood by considering them as hybrids which draw on operating principles from different sectors.

The remainder of this introduction offers a brief overview of the rise to prominence of social enterprises and discusses some of the ways they have been conceptualised. The second section examines the operation of social enterprises in a particular policy field and presents three organizational case studies. The third section provides an analysis of the different challenges these organizations face using the idea of hybridity. The conclusion considers ways in which these theoretical ideas can be utilised by practitioners, policy makers and researchers.

There have been significant changes in the policy environment. Until recently explicit recognition and support for the social enterprise model was rare. Less than 15 years ago, Thake could write of the role of social enterprises in the urban field that 'what is surprising, perhaps, is that so many organizations have survived or emerged when the policy frameworks have not been supportive' (Thake, 1995, p. 66). Government policy can be characterised as having moved from benign neglect in the early 1980s to active engagement from the late 1990s onwards. This has not been merely as a result of a change in the governing party in 1997: the previous Conservative administration was, for example, undertaking case studies of Development Trusts (DoE, 1987) well before the advent of New Labour.

The New Labour administration, which took office in 1997, explicitly promoted social enterprises. It established a government Social Enterprise Unit in 2001 which, in May 2006, became part of the Office for the Third Sector within the Cabinet Office. A rapid flow of policy statements began with the Social Enterprise Plan (DTI, 2002). The then Prime Minister, Tony Blair, neatly balanced business and social purpose when he spoke of the role of social enterprise organizations as

> ...combining strong public service ethos with business acumen...we can open up the possibility of entrepreneurial organizations – highly responsive to customers and with the freedom of the private sector – but which are driven by a commitment to public benefit rather than purely maximising profits for shareholders (DTI, 2002, p. 5).

A few years later, the bundling together of organizations from different sectors was put in stronger terms when the Prime Minister described the role of TSO's as sitting alongside business and public sector entities. He envisaged them making 'greater strides to social justice, working more easily with conventional businesses and the public sector' (OTS, 2006a, p. 13). There has been a rapid succession of policy, guidance and funding documents encouraging social enterprises. These have included the following: the Community Interest Company legal form established in 2004; adjustments to public procurement policies (HMT, 2006a; OTS, 2006b); initiatives to transfer public sector assets to third sector organizations (Quirk, 2007); the work of the Commission on Unclaimed Assets (2007); various capacity building initiatives such as Hubs (later National Support Services); and pilot projects, such as the Adventure Capital Fund, promoting investment and growth (Thake, 2005). Meanwhile, the Conservative Party in opposition suggested that social enterprises were 'putting the power of business growth behind the objective of social change' (Conservative Party, 2008, p. 44). The Social Enterprise Coalition, an umbrella organization established in 2002, responded to nearly 30 government policy initiatives that same year. In short, social enterprises appeared to offer policy makers both enterprise and social credentials – a union of ideas which, in earlier epochs, would have appeared to belong to distinctive professional and sectoral realms. So far there seems little evidence that the collapse of financial institutions in 2008 will mark a change in this overall approach.

The term 'social enterprise' is not uncontested. The broad notion of organizations 'having a social purpose' which aim to achieve this in part by 'engaging in trade in the marketplace' (Pearce, 2003, p. 30) is still a helpful orientating statement, although the nature of what constitutes the market remains under-explained. In such accounts, social enterprises are described as being one 'wedge' within the 'third system' because they have a different mode of production and values to the 'first' (private profit) and 'second' (public service) systems (Pearce, 2003, p. 24), but they are also close to business organizations because they trade in markets. The government's definition suggests they are 'a business with primarily social objectives whose surpluses are principally reinvested for that purpose in the business or in the community' (OTS, 2006a, p. 13). Meanwhile the Social Enterprise Coalition summarised them as 'businesses set up to tackle a social and/or environmental need' with any profits reinvested (SEC, 2009). In contrast to these approaches, social enterprise can be understood as a way of working – an orientation rather than an organization – which may be embedded within one part of an agency or even operate in the spaces between organizations such as in networks.

The general approach taken in this chapter is to use an analytic framework proposed by Borzaga and Defourney (2001, pp. 17–18) as a guide. These authors suggested a set of nine criteria which would help to identify social enterprises. The aim was to encompass aspects which were both economic/entrepreneurial (taking economic risks; a continuous production of goods or services; having a high degree of autonomy; and some paid workers) and social in nature (explicit community benefit; launched by citizens; decision-making not based on capital ownership, some degree of participatory decision-making for users; and limited profit distribution). Social enterprises can thus be understood as organizations which seek to mix the often distinct third sector traditions of philanthropy and mutualism (Aiken, 2007).

## Social enterprises in the work integration field

In order to examine some of the challenges facing social enterprises, and to see how these can be explained using some of the ideas about hybridity discussed in this volume, we will focus on the policy field of work and training for disadvantaged people, sometimes termed 'work integration'. There has been a long history of third sector activity in this arena (Aiken, 2007). Community Programmes, sponsored from the late 1970s by government agencies, enabled TSO's to recruit staff on short-term contracts in community projects (Addy and Scott, 1987) involving over 20,000 places at one stage (Spear, 2001, p. 244). As contracting processes intensified from the late 1990s, larger national charities with social enterprise or trading wings began to bid for contracts alongside private organizations (such as Reed) and long-established quasi-public sector organizations (such as Remploy). Increasingly regional and national social enterprises, and quasi-public organizations, have been competing with national or international commercial organizations – at times with obscure ownership – in a multi-million training and work industry (Davies, 2006; Aiken, 2006b).

Social enterprises in the work integration field have sought to combine the logics of welfare for disadvantaged groups as part of their values and mission (by providing a supportive environment, training and employment) with an economic enterprise (by undertaking productive work which could yield an income to the organization). Many initiatives from the era of 'benign neglect' were small scale and local and sought to combine local social inclusion with work, volunteering or training (Aiken and Bode, 2009). Examples of social enterprises undertaking this work have included worker co-operatives, social firms, intermediate labour market organizations, community-based enterprises, semi-independent units embedded within community centres or national charitable organizations (Spear and Aiken, 2003; Aiken, 2006c). Economic activity has occurred in niche markets (e.g. recycling or food co-operatives), labour intensive areas (e.g. childcare, landscape gardening, retail and catering) which, with supervision, provided entry-level work.

Alongside the New Deal, introduced in 1998, social enterprises have taken advantage of and moulded a series of policies and programmes including initiatives focused on as follows: disabled people (DWP, 2002), claimants on incapacity benefit (DWP, 2002); and skill improvement (HMT, 2006b). The influential Freud Report (2007) has argued for further welfare-to-work reform. Amidst the 2008 financial crisis, its author – banker-turned-welfare reformer, David Freud – was arguing that TSO's could help the long-term unemployed back into work because 'the people who have the main expertise with the very hardest to help are the 3rd sector ... but because they don't issue shares they lack capital, you have to find hybrid ways of doing that to allow them to grow ...' (Freud, 2009).

Similar work integration activities have taken place around the world. There were over 3,600 Community Development Corporations engaged in job creation and regeneration work in the US in 1998 (Price, 2008). Local development and social economy WISE were active in Ireland (O'Shaunhessy,

2006); legal frameworks encouraged the growth of social co-ops in Italy (Borzaga and Loss, 2006, p. 75); and the legal form of the *enterprise d'insertion* or EI acted in a similar way in Belgium (Nyssens and Platteau, 2006). In Germany, organizations active in this field included entities which are municipally owned or sponsored by welfare associations as well as co-operatives, social firms and others (Bode et al., 2006). In Latin America, government funding to support third sector employment initiatives for indigenous groups provides further evidence of an international trend (CDI, 2007).

## Three work integration cases

The cases which follow have been selected from more extensive investigations undertaken over the previous 8 years including joint research with colleagues from other European countries (Spear and Aiken, 2003; Spear and Aiken, 2006; Aiken, 2006a; 2006b; 2007). The aim is to understand some of the challenges facing social enterprises in this field and this selection seeks to be illuminative and analytic. Three social enterprises are chosen to illustrate different characteristics and the contrasting challenges they face. Hence, for each case, a concise profile is offered which considers in turn basic details about their origin, legal status, income, staff and volunteers; the activities undertaken in the work integration field; sources of income; and governance arrangements. This is followed by a discussion of the challenges and tensions these organizations face in achieving their missions.

---

### Daily Bread: Profile

**Basic details**: Daily Bread is a worker's co-operative in Northampton which was established by its members more than 25 years ago. It is registered as an Industrial and Provident Society and has 20 staff, a few volunteers and a turnover of more than £1 m.

**Activities**: The co-operative operates a shop selling whole-foods to the general public. It specifically employs a quota of people with mental illness as part of its ethical values and aims to engage them as fully as possible in the democratic working of the co-operative. The activity with the disadvantaged workers is small in terms of number – less than 20 per cent of the workforce – and there is no inclination to scale up. However, these are not temporary placements – paid and permanent work is offered – although a few have, at times, elected to undertake voluntary work.

**Income sources**: Daily Bread's financial resources come from the sale of goods to the public. There are no public sector contracts or grants.

**Governance arrangements**: As with other worker co-operatives, the members are simultaneously owners, managers and staff of the enterprise. The general meetings, to which members come, constitute the main formal decision-making forum.

## Daily Bread: Tensions and challenges

Daily Bread does not use grants or contracts from the public sector hence the work integration activity is funded, in business terms, from profits.[1] With their own income from customers, Daily Bread operates with greater freedom in terms of choosing which disadvantaged staff they wish to appoint. They are little affected by the designated target groups, specified outcomes and strict time limits associated with managerialist-inclined public sector programmes. They have also been resistant to offering more full-time posts as these would be at the expense of part-time posts which offer better opportunities for disadvantaged people seeking employment.

Despite the work integration activity and their other social commitments, they cannot afford to undermine business imperatives. They need to strike a balance with the proportion of disadvantaged people in their workforce if they are to maintain a successful business. They recognise that they are supported by an increasing public awareness – a social movement even – around food and heath issues. Nevertheless, the most crucial factor in their financial survival is the customers purchasing items in the shop. For this reason, they emphasise their business credentials: 'People who come to see what Daily Bread does . . . think Daily Bread are sandal wearing hippies but not a real business!'

An expansion of the business could present a threat to the character and practices of a small organization such as Daily Bread. It has deliberately not sought a high growth strategy as this is not seen as a central aim. Where it has initiated growth, this has been through nurturing a semi-independent sister organization in a neighbouring town based on similar values. Daily Bread is clearly an unusual, although not unique, organization but the selection and integration of new people into the principles of the co-operative remain an important challenge. Values play an important role and these can be seen as an organizational resource which steers action:

> . . . values . . . around food, Christian values, co-operative princi-ples, the importance of wholefoods, treating people fairly and of equal worth . . . it is also about fairness in pricing . . . if some-thing has gone down in price we should put the price down rather than see what price the market can stand.

In summary, Daily Bread is a small and successful worker co-operative, originating from local people. It operates in the private sector retail field, undertaking work integration as part of its ethical commitments. Permanent jobs are offered and it sits largely outside of the extensive policy frameworks in the field. Members of the co-operative need to combine the roles of member, staff, manager and owner – which can take considerable skill and application.

---

### Bolton WISE: Profile

**Basic details**: Bolton WISE was initiated in 1997 with a strong impetus from a local authority which initially seconded senior staff. It is now a company limited by guarantee with charita-ble status. In 2008, it had an income of nearly £1.7 m, and employed 52 core staff and involved 5 volunteers.

**Activities**: The organization can be understood as offering short-term transitional work and training while undertaking productive work using an Intermediate Labour Market (ILM) model. Work integration is undertaken through a sub-division, Wise-Works, which offers services to clients on contract such as maintenance of grounds, gardening, small building works and erecting fencing. In 2008, it could claim 60 per cent of those leaving the ILM project had gained employment and 32 per cent had gained qualifications in excess of contractual requirements.

**Income sources**: Financial resources come mainly from contracts with public sector agencies such as Job Centre Plus, Learning and Skills Council, Sure Start and an arms-length public sector housing company.

**Governance**: The board encompasses representatives from all three sectors but leans more to the public sector. It includes two councillors but also a senior figure from the local voluntary sector.

## Bolton WISE: Tensions and challenges

Maintaining good relations with the public sector, in particular key departments in the local authority, has been an important strategy.[2] This has been especially true because recent public policy has tended to emphasise moving unemployed people directly into employment, rather than through an intermediate labour market. Such relations have also been crucial as the majority of their resource streams originated from public sector bodies.

There have been tensions concerning the conditions attached to resources for social objectives. Targets for the number of trainees that were required to achieve certain qualifications, and time limits determining when they needed to be found permanent jobs, had placed pressures on the organization. The workfare regime meant that some trainees had not joined the programme through choice and arrived poorly motivated. High professional standards amongst the management and staff needed to be in place for inspiring trainees:

> ...they have been mandatorily sent here – our first job is to change their perspective on life and work – it's a tall order...So we need to challenge them – to have the confidence to want to chose something. 'Inspirational' means a wide range of opportunities to capture their imagination...

Finding ways to combine business and social objectives was vital. While work integration was rated as a primary aim, providing products and services for clients to a high standard was clearly of importance, hence the need to integrate these different imperatives. They were frank in acknowledging that they had to balance goals between a variety of stakeholders including funders. They needed to provide projects that met the needs of trainees but also to undertake work relevant for the local economy.

> The other factor which determines the project is [to] secure funding to do work that is of social benefit...so it is not all based on the needs of our primary customers – it is also based on the needs of our funders and the wider community out there and the services they need.

In summary, Bolton WISE is a specialist organization providing short-term work and training for disadvantaged people who undertake productive work in their locality. It originated from the public sector, with which it maintains close relations, and is highly dependent on such programmes for resources to fund the training element of work integration activities. The needs of funders and local community need to be carefully balanced.

---

**Tomorrow's People Trust Limited: Profile**

**Basic details**: Tomorrow's People Trust Limited, based in Hastings, was founded in 1984 by a private sector company, Grand Met (Diageo), and later registered as a charity in 2004. It had an income in 2008 of £7.2 m, employed around 170 core staff, with no volunteers involved apart from board members.

**Activities**: It is a specialist organization providing advice, training and placements for disadvantaged people and operates across the UK. It does not provide work directly but acts as a broker to enable disadvantaged people to gain employment. This is undertaken through a wide number of projects delivered by local staff (well regarded by evaluations) via public sector contracts for employment-related schemes. It claims to have helped over 400,000 people across the UK (nearly 13,000 in 2008). The organization also takes part in advocacy activities and works with other large providers to lobby for improvements in contracting processes.

**Income sources**: Its income has come from public sector programmes (including DWP, and Government Office for London). In addition, there have been donations from Diageo, Laidlaw Foundation, PricewaterhouseCoopers, Esmee Fairbairn, Rank Foundation and others.

**Governance arrangements**: It retains close connections to the private sector and the 10 person board is drawn mainly from this sphere such as Diageo, Lloyds of London, CBI, BT, a law firm, a consultancy organization, as well as the Cricket Board, Parole Board and Business in the Community (TP, 2009). It is a highly engaged board with many of the London members actively participating in the work.

## Tomorrow's People: Tensions and challenges

Tomorrow's People has identified one of the major risks it faces as the need to have sufficient reserves in the event that it is unable to win public sector contracts or is subject to abrupt changes in policy. In addition, if a financial downturn persists, there could be challenges arising from the significant investment it receives from the private sector. Tomorrow's People, which only became legally independent from Diageo in 2004, has been shaped and supported by its private sector 'parent.' Diageo described the support it had offered as including the 'transfer of business and other relevant skills, including those of senior management, as well as providing funding' (TP, 2004, p. 1). It had also continued to play

a critical role in the continued operations and development of Tomorrow's People, investing £25 million in today's
prices...without the initial ideas and this ongoing support
Tomorrow's People is unlikely to exist in its current form (TP,
2004, p. 5).

The chief executive of Tomorrow's People also praised Diageo for helping her 'to understand how they operate at the
highest level...you could say that it is our corporate guru'
(O'Hara, 2005) and she emphasised that an important factor in their recent success was the way they had 'applied the
business principles we learnt' (New Start, 2009).

The range of clients helped and their depth of disadvantage
has been questioned at times with suggestions of 'creaming'
clients (PCS, 2006). It has, however, been a charity award
winner, praised by Gordon Brown, and gained favourable evaluations for the care it takes with job seekers (RAND, 2006).
At the same time, the 'robust corporate support and dynamic
leadership from Tomorrow's People' on their programmes has
been cited favourably in evaluations (TP, 2006).

In summary, Tomorrow's People is a national charity which
is a specialist in placing people into jobs at considerable scale. It
is heavily involved in contracting for public sector programmes.
The organization maintains strong relations with the private
sector, from which it originated, and continues to gains funds
and expertise from that source.

## Discussion

To what extent can such tensions and challenges presented
from these three contrasting cases be understood by considering the notion of hybrids? First, we will consider where
we locate the three organizations in terms of sectors. It is
worth reminding ourselves that these organizations can all
be counted, formally, as TSO's: two are registered charities
and one is an industrial and provident society. None of them
have private shareholders or distribute profits. In addition,
they all, more or less, fit within Borzaga and Defourney's
(2001) framework, although Tomorrow's People and Bolton

WISE would have difficulties fitting the criteria of being established by citizens. Figure 3.1, in Chapter 3 of this volume, provides a more detailed guide by mapping the three sectors and their hybrid zones. Daily Bread exhibits hybrid properties of the third and private sector (combining social and business purposes) while originating from local citizens – hence could be located in zone 6 of the figure – a third/private sector hybrid. Bolton WISE displays characteristics of the third and public sector (undertaking charitable activities for disadvantaged people with close ties and funding from the public sector contracting). It also undertakes productive work in the local community which suggests it has an element of private sector engagement. Its origins from the public sector suggest it be placed in zone 1 of the figure – a public/third sector hybrid. Tomorrow's People might be seen, at first sight, as displaying third and public sector hybridity as it undertakes work legally deemed charitable and has close ties to the public sector via funding as well as advocating on programme issues. Nevertheless, it has a close dependence on the private sector for management expertise, board members, funding as well as for inspiration. Hence, it could be placed in the central area of the diagram as a private/public/third hybrid originating from the private sector (zone 8).

This underlines that functional definitions such as 'legal identity' and 'formal governance arrangements', while of great importance, cannot on their own locate an organization in a given single sector. Research is needed to uncover issues such as the resource mix in and the informal power influences on an organization. This leads us to ask if we can gauge, in practice, if organizations exhibiting hybrid characteristics have a primary allegiance to one particular sector and thus exhibit a corresponding set of overarching principles. The five core elements proposed in Chapter 3 of this volume (namely, ownership; governance; operational priorities; human resources; and other distinctive resources) could help to distinguish a primary orientation for each organization.

For reasons of brevity, we concentrate on one aspect: ownership. Who are the 'principal owners' in these three cases – for example, who *really* has the power to close or radically shape them? In Daily Bread this would, formally and actively, be the members of the co-operative – who collectively own the business – enacted through the general meeting. To illustrate the complexity of the situation, however, let us conduct a brief thought experiment. The co-operative members would be expected to be most active as their livelihoods are at stake but it would be unsurprising if some members were not more influential than others. The organization remains young enough to still have contact with founders and they might exert informal authority from a distance in crucial discussions. We could also look beyond the organizational boundary to consider how some major ideological decisions might attract attention from outsiders such as shoppers, wholefood suppliers, social movement activists or Christian groups. Such actions might strongly – even decisively – influence decisions at a key general meeting. This illustrates that even with a small worker co-operative, where ownership is clearly defined compared to charities, the nature of 'principal owners' – while probably identical to 'formal' and 'active' owners – might need to be examined. It also suggests that principal owners may not always be fixed: shifting power balances and mobilisation may reveal new alliances.

In the case of Bolton WISE, while the board of trustees constitute the 'formal' owners, 'principal owners' might be found amongst key people in the local authority who, by withholding support at a crucial point in contracting arrangements, might seriously undermine the organization. Indeed, rapidly changing policy priorities in the work integration field combined with a high dependence on public sector contracting appear to have presented some social enterprises in the field (such as Necta, Sheffield ReBuild, Enprove) with little alternative but to close or merge. Similarly, for work integration social enterprises trading mainly in goods, a rapid market change (for example, a collapsing price differential between new and recycled items) occurring alongside other challenges may prove fatal (Recycle IT). This can occur regardless of the role of any key individual. At Bolton WISE, nevertheless, there was evidence that senior staff played critical roles in shaping the organization, particularly in relation to managing the multiple accountabilities towards public sector funders, trainees and community. Staff may be considered to form part of the 'active' owners. Considering the principal owners of Tomorrow's People presents some intriguing questions. While 'formal' owners could be the trustees, experienced senior staff may be the 'active owners' who would play a significant steering role in a calamity and even steer the organization in a new direction. Nevertheless, the shadow of the private sector originator might be revealed as the decisive 'primary owner' in a crisis.

There are two important issues to raise before proceeding. In relation to identifying principal owners in the case of Tomorrow's People and Bolton WISE, regulation also plays a role. A charity can be considered to be a public benefit organization held in trust by law, for a disadvantaged group, via a board of trustees. In a terminal crisis the regulator may intervene to modify or close the organization, distributing the assets appropriately. In the light of this discussion, principal owners may need to be understood more broadly to encompass, in a given situation, entities ranging from regulatory bodies through to social movements. In relation to one of the other elements in the five part formulation, namely, the 'other distinctive resources,' Daily Bread, for example, cites the importance of organizational values. In order to maintain their orientation, these are likely to be a resource they utilise and, by implication, they would need to find ways of reproduce both their membership (Stryjan, 1989) and their organizational values (Aiken, 2002).

No decisive view will be presented here on who the principal owners may be in these three organizations – this would need further empirical research – although a range of possibilities have been discussed. The aim has been to illustrate how this idea can be utilised and expanded in real settings. The theory, as outlined in Chapter 3, suggests that a better understanding of this aspect, along with an analysis of the other four elements, would bring us closer to clarifying to which sector they owed primary allegiance and thus which operating logic or 'rules of the game' were operating. A codicil must be added here concerning sector principles in relation to co-operatives. Daily Bread operates from a mutual tradition, while the other two organizations are formally aligned to a philanthropic or charitable tradition. While the term 'third sector' encompasses both – especially since the inception of the UK's Office of the Third Sector's – these do have certain distinctive differences particularly in relation to governance.

We can now consider the degree of hybridity organizations may exhibit compared to a Weberian ideal type non-hybrid. If we accept that a great many organizations beyond a very small scale will be hybrids, as understood in this book, *to some degree*, we can proceed to discuss their depth of hybridity. Factors such as the extent of the professionalised staff team, paucity of volunteers, board membership from different sectors and degree of public sector contracting suggest that Tomorrow's People exhibits signs of entrenched hybridity as does Bolton WISE, albeit to a much lesser degree. Both organizations can be described as enacted – from the private and public sector, respectively. A further observation should be made here. Tomorrow's People, a nationally constituted organization, has many locally recruited workers but it is not clear if they play a significant role in national strategy. Bolton WISE displays strong roots in, and awareness of, the locality – both community and public sector institutions – and this may be an additional aspect in considering the degree of entrenchment. Daily Bread, perhaps appropriately in terms of its product lines, could be seen as an organic hybrid that has grown slowly to a 'shallow' degree. This can be argued from the nature of its democratic structures in which owners, managers and staff are united; relatively small team of workers with little formal hierarchy; and the absence of public sector contracting. One final point should be made on the presence or absence of volunteers which may be seen as of high importance in an ideal model of a voluntary association but is not present in Borzaga and Defourney's conceptualisation of a social enterprise.

## Conclusion

The examination of social enterprises in the work integration field was undertaken against the background of two trends: the promotion of this model and the externalisation of public services in a reconfigured welfare state. Both of these developments have tended to encourage hybrid forms. Three case studies were selected to consider how far a theory of hybridity could assist in understanding the tensions they were facing. By considering the diagram of three overlapping circles to represent sectors and their hybrid zones and analysing some data about the organizations, it was possible to illustrate three distinctive hybridization tendencies. Daily Bread was proposed as a third/private, Bolton WISE as a public/third and Tomorrow's People as private/public/third sector hybrid. These present not just descriptive labels but offer clues as to their organizational origin and possible trajectory. The notion of principal owners enabled us to consider influences beyond the formal owners and look at the role of various actors in addition to the official boards. In addition, the idea that in any hybrid a dominating operating logic from one sector may apply was used to consider, in a preliminary way, the primary affiliation of these organizations. The distinction between entrenched and shallow and enacted and organic provided a vocabulary which enabled us to consider, respectively, the depth of hybridity and the process of hybridization.

If hybridity is to become increasingly common, it will be important for policy makers and practitioners to understand how social enterprises manage the tensions between competing principles. First, it will be important to analyse the depth of hybridity in social enterprises building on the factors suggested in the theory outlined in Chapter 3. Second, it will be of value to understand how fixed the nature of the hybridity is within given social enterprises by exploring settings where the logic shifts from one sector to another. For example, we could consider a public/third sector work integration hybrid (which emerged from, and was principally managed by, public sector principles) which transformed over time into a third/public sector organized (principally managed by third sector principles). Third, it will be important to understand if the imperatives and operating logics from different sectors are impossible to reconcile in one agency. In work integration social enterprises, this has sometimes been attempted by separating imperatives from private and third sectors in different professional jobs, departments or board members (Spear and Aiken, 2003; Cornforth et al., 2008). The theory discussed in this volume implies that principles or 'rules of the game' from one sector are likely to dominate sooner or later. Hence, both the extent and ways in which social enterprises seek to manage different sectoral principles – and the degree to which these are sustainable in critical moments – offer an opportunity to explore a theoretical question in an empirical setting. This can also begin to illuminate the question of whether hybrid organizations are, in practice, able to develop management approaches which combine distinctive features from all three sectors.

One effect of the enshrinement of the term 'third sector' in public policy has been a danger of reification and the assumption that common characteristics can be found amongst all the entities now captured inside a concept which may be 'chaotic' (Sayer, 2000). There is a particular problem here with (sensibly) sheltering the philanthropic and mutualist traditions under one umbrella if the result is to (confusingly) conflate their distinctive governance patterns and objectives. The co-operative form (ICA, 2009) may provide the ideal type in the mutualist tradition as an analogue to the role played by the association in the philanthropic tradition. The members of the co-operative, as 'protagonists in their own destiny' (Whyte and Whyte, 1991), are activists in, and beneficiaries of, their organization. One way to view social enterprises is that they seek to combine mutual and philanthropic traditions which could present examples of 'entrenched hybrids...established from within the [third] sector' (Billis, this volume, p. 61).

## Notes

1. Some portions of this profile draw on Spear and Aiken, 2003.
2. Some portions of this profile draw on Spear and Aiken, 2003.

## References

Addy, T. and D. Scott (1987) *Fatal Impacts: The MSC and Voluntary Action*, Manchester: William Temple Foundation.

Aiken, M. (2002) Managing values: The reproduction of organisational values in social economy organisations, PhD thesis, Open University, Milton Keynes.

Aiken, M. (2006a) *Labour Market Policy and Decentralisation: Structural and Developmental Tendencies Emerging from the Emdela Research: The UK Country Report* http://technology.open.ac.uk/cru/publicatold.htm

Aiken, M. (2006b) 'Contracting with the private sector for services: New challenges for the third sector?' Voluntary Sector Studies Group (VSSN) Day Conference Wed 16th May 2006, at South Bank University, London, http://technology.open.ac.uk/cru/publicatold.htm

Aiken, M. (2006c) 'Towards market or state?', in Nyssens, M. (ed.), *Social Enterprises. Between Markets, Public Policies and Community*, London: Routledge.

Aiken, M. (2007) 'Think Piece on the role of social enterprise in creating and maintaining employment for disadvantaged groups', Commissioned by Department of Communities and Local Government, November 2007.

Aiken, M. and I. Bode (2009) 'Killing the golden goose? Third sector organisations and back-to-work programmes in Germany and the UK', *Social Policy and Administration*, vol. 43, 3, pp. 209–225.

Billis, D. (1989) *A Theory of the Voluntary Sector: Implications for Theory and Practice. Working paper No 5*, London: LSE.

Billis, D. (1993) *Organising Public and Voluntary Agencies*, London: Routledge.

Bode, I., A. Evers and A. Schultz (2006) 'Where do we go from here? The unfinished story of WISE in Germany', in Nyssens, M. (2006) *Social Enterprise*, London: Routledge.

Borzaga, C. and J. Defourney (2001) *The Emergence of Social Enterprise*, London: Routledge.

Borzaga, C. and M. Loss (2006) 'Multiple goals and multi-stakeholder management in Italian social enterprises', in Nyssens, M. (ed.), *Social Enterprise*, London: Routledge.

CDI (2007) *Acciones de Gobierno para Desarrollo Integral de los Pueblos Indígenas, Informe 2007*, Mexico: Comision Nacional para el Desarrollo de los Pueblos Indígenas, Estados Unidos Mexicanos.

Commission on Unclaimed Assets (2007) *The Social Investment Bank: Its Organisation and Role in Driving Development of the Third Sector*, London: Commission on Unclaimed Assets.

Conservative Party (2008) *A Stronger Society: Voluntary Action in the 21st Century, Responsibility Agenda*, Policy Green Paper No. 5, p. 30 Millbank, London SW1P 4 DP.

Cornforth, C., R. Spear and M. Aiken (2007) *For Love and Money: Governance and Social Enterprise*, London: The Governance Hub and Social Enterprise Coalition, published by NCVO.

Davies, S. (2006) *Third Sector Provision of Employment-Related Services: A Report for the Public and Commercial Services Union (PCS)*, June, Cardiff School of Social Sciences, Cardiff University.

DoE (1987) *Creating Developing Trusts*, London: HMSO, Department of the Environment.

DTI (2002) *Social Enterprise: A Strategy for Success*, London: Department of Trade and Industry DTI URN 02/1054.

DWP (2002) *Pathways to Work: Helping People into Employment*, CM 5690, London: Department for Work and Pensions.

Evers, A. (2004) 'Mixed Welfare Systems and Hybrid Organisations – Changes in the Governance and Provision of Social Services' Sixth International Conference of the International Society for Third Sector Research, 11–14 July, Ryerson University and York University, Toronto, Canada.

Freud, D. (2009) 'David Freud interviewed on the Today Programme' BBC Radio 4, 8.35 a.m. 4/2/2009.

Freud, D. (2007) *Reducing Dependency, Increasing Opportunity: Options for the Future of Welfare to Work*, London: DWP.

HMT (2006a) *Improving Financial Relationships with the Third Sector: Guidance to Funders and Purchasers*, London: HM Treasury.

HMT (2006b) *The Leitch Report: Prosperity for all in the Global Economy – World Class Skills*, London: HM Treasury.

ICA (2009) 'Statement on the Co-operative Identity' International Co-operative Alliance, http://www.ica.coop/coop/principles. html Last searched 9/3/2009.

New Start (2009) 'Cash boost will help Tomorrow's People expand' Posted on Thursday, 26/2/2009 Source: www.newstartmag.co. uk/blog/article/cash-boost-will-help-tomorrows-people-expand/ Last searched 6/4/09.

Nyssens, M. and A. Platteu (2006) 'Profiles of Workers in Belgium WISE', in Nyssens, M. (ed.) *Social Enterprise*, London: Routledge.

O'Hara, M. (2005) 'Leading questions: Debbie Scott, Tomorrow's People chief executive and deputy chair of the Tories' Social Justice Commission, The Guardian, Wednesday 21/12/2005 www.guardian.co.uk/society/2005/dec/21/guardiansocietysupplement4 Last searched: 6/4/2009.

O'Shaughnessy, M. (2006) 'Irish social enterprises: Challenges in mobilising resources to meet multiple goals', in Nyssens, M. (ed.), *Social Enterprise*, London: Routledge.

OTS (2006a) *Social Enterprise Action Plan: Scaling New Heights*, London: Cabinet Office: Office of the Third Sector.

OTS (2006b) *Partnership in Public Services: An Action Plan for Third Sector Involvement*, London: Cabinet Office: Office of the Third Sector.

PCS (2006) *Third Sector Provision of Employment Related Services*, prepared by Steve Davies for the Public and Commercial Services Union, PCS 160 Falcon Rd., London.

Pearce, J. (2003) *Social Enterprise in Anytown*, London: Calouste Gulbenkian Foundation.

Price, R. (2008) 'Evidence Review of USA Community ownership or assets', unpublished paper by Ruth Price, NY.

Quirk, B. (2007) *Making Assets Work: The Quirk Review of Community Management and Ownership of Public Assets*, London: Department for Communities and Local Government.

RAND (2006) *Benchmarking of the Use of Personal Advisors in Job Centre Plus*, A report prepared by Stolk, C., Rubin, J. and Grant, J. for the Audit Office.

Sayer, A. (2000) *Realism and Social Science*, London: Sage.

SEC (2009) 'Voice 09' Social enterprise Coalition Conference, www.socialenterprise.org.uk/pages/events.html Last searched 6/2/2009.

Social Firms (2009) 'What are the Main Issues Facing Social Firms?' www.socialfirms.co.uk/index.php/Section99/page46.html Last searched 5/2/2009.

Spear, R. (2001) 'United Kingdom: Labour market integration and employment creation', in Spear, R., Defourney, J., Favreau, L. and Laville, J-L. (eds), *Tackling Social Exclusion in Europe*, Aldershot: Ashgate.

Spear, R. and M. Aiken (2003) *Country Report on the Perse Project*, www.emes.net Last searched 20 November 2008.

Spear, R. and Aiken, M. (2006) 'Factors influencing the development of social enterprises: Five cases' 3rd Annual UK Social Enterprise Research Conference, London: London South Bank University, 22–23 June 2006.

Stryjan, Y. (1989) *Impossible Organizations: Self Management and Organizational Reproduction*, Connecticut: Greenwood Press.

Thake, S. (1995) *Staying the Course*, York: Joseph Rowntree Foundation.

Thake, S. (2005) *Adventure Capital Fund Round 2: Baseline Report Defining the Market*, London: London Metropolitan University.

TP (2004) *Twenty-Year Evaluation of Tomorrow's People Trust Limited*, Executive Summary, September 2004, Oxford: Oxford Economic Forecasting.

TP (2006) 'Getting London Working, Delivering Jobs and Opportunities to London's Unemployed', end of programme evaluation by TANK Consulting, London EC1R 3BW June 2006. www.tankconsulting.com Last searched 31/3/2009.

TP (2009) 'Tomorrow's People Board' www.tomorrows-people.org.uk/our_board.htm Last searched 28/2/2008.

Whyte, W. F. and K. K. Whyte (1991) *Making Mondragon: The Growth and Dynamics of the Worker Co-operative Complex*, New York: Ithaca.

# 9 Hybridity in partnership working: Managing tensions and opportunities

*Joanna Howard and*
*Marilyn Taylor*

## Introduction

Recent years have seen a move from 'government to governance' which has involved new actors alongside the state in governing. The significance of this change has been flagged up in the introduction to this book and in Chapter 4. Many commentators have been critical of these new arrangements, suggesting that third sector organizations (TSOs) can easily become co-opted onto state agendas through the demands on their time and resources and through 'rules of the game' that are dictated by the state.

Our own research[1] suggests that there may be a more complex story to be told. In it we set out to explore the experience of non-governmental actors in what we called 'new governance spaces', the new partnerships and other forums into which TSOs have been invited to participate over recent years. We wanted to identify the tensions and opportunities in these 'spaces' and explore how non-governmental actors addressed them, focusing particularly on the extent to which TSOs were able to maintain an independent and distinctive voice in such settings. But what seemed a fairly straightforward exercise became much more complicated when we realised that some of the non-governmental organizations we had chosen to study could equally well be defined as a governance space themselves. Rather than regarding these as rather difficult-to-code aberrations, we decided that we should examine them in more detail, partly because, as far as we were aware, this form of hybridity had not been widely studied and partly because it was in these organizations that the tensions of partnership working might be most strongly manifested.

Drawing on this research, this chapter begins by introducing two examples of these partnership hybrids: a regeneration partnership and a healthy living centre. We then discuss both the opportunities and challenges that result from this hybridity. We end by returning to some of the issues raised in the introduction to this book and exploring the wider implications of this form of hybrid for welfare and governance.

## The case studies

In studying citizen participation, Cornwall (2004) has distinguished between 'invited' spaces – state sponsored top-down decision-making fora into which non-state actors have been invited – and 'claimed' or 'popular' spaces – bottom-up fora which TSOs set up for themselves. Our study suggests, however, that there are a growing number of spaces that, though initiated by or in response to state initiatives, cannot be seen simply as a state-sponsored 'invited space' because they also operate as a TSO in their own right. Some are set up independently from the start, but cannot be regarded as totally independent because they are set up in response to a state policy initiative that will only fund a partnership between the public, third and private sector. They are thus heavily dependent on state funding and legitimation. Others begin life as a state-sponsored partnership – an 'invited space' set up by the local authority to carry out a particular programme, such as Sure Start, the New Deal for Communities or a Neighbourhood Management Pathfinder. They have, however, reconstituted themselves as non-statutory entities in order to establish their independence; to access new funds; and/or simply to keep themselves going beyond an initial state-sponsored period. Both types of partnership are likely to have a mix of publicly appointed and non-governmental trustees and a mix of staff managed by the state, by the organization itself and sometimes by other actors. Sometimes the local authority remains the accountable body, responsible for the administration of the funds. They thus operate at the 'interstices of power' between state and civil society (Gaventa, 2004).

There were two organizations in our research that fitted this pattern. The first was a regeneration partnership in Wales, which was set up by the local state in response to a Welsh Assembly initiative but which reconstituted itself as an independent development trust. Its executive director was, however, still employed by the local authority, which also continued to act as the accountable body for the trust's government funding. The second was a Healthy Living Centre (HLC) in England, set up by non-state actors in response to a central government initiative. Both had both state and non-state actors as staff and trustees. The trust is still state-funded (with some additional self-generated funds), while the centre was initially funded by the National Lottery and closed when this funding finished.

## The trust

The area in which the trust now operates was selected in 1998 as a pilot area for a Welsh Assembly regeneration initiative called 'People in Communities'. The initial impetus came from a housing association which was looking for a joint approach to dealing with high levels of antisocial behaviour and void properties in the neighbourhood. The local authority's director of housing took up the initiative and applied for People in Communities funding. A year later, the local authority employed a coordinator to set up a local partnership. This individual came from the Welsh Cooperative Centre with extensive experience in both business and community development. He worked with local agencies, groups and individuals to create a loose partnership. After 2 years of working in this way, the partnership chose to constitute itself more formally. At this stage, it became the trust – a limited company with charitable status, with a board consisting of nominated representatives from the public sector (local authority, health and police), TSOs and local residents and councillors. It also regularly convened a broader forum to report on its work to the wider community. After 3 years, the People in Communities funding finished and a new Welsh Assembly initiative called 'Communities First' was introduced. The local authority applied for Communities First status for the area and the trust was invited to continue as the host organization since it was the existing regeneration partnership in the area, and already fulfilled the Welsh Assembly's 'three thirds' criteria for Communities First partnership boards (the requirement to have equal representation of residents, TSOs and the state). The coordinator (now known as the 'Executive Director of the Trust') continued in post, still employed by the local authority but accountable in principle to the trust.

The trust's work focuses on community development and supporting and developing local community organizations as well as facilitating the regeneration partnership. It is a membership organization with around 150 members living or working in the area who may attend bi-monthly open meetings and the annual general meeting (AGM). Community representatives are elected to the board by the AGM. While attendance by public sector members of the board has been sporadic (except for the police and local authority housing), there is a good attendance from public sector services (primary care trust [PCT], police, youth services and housing) at the bi-monthly public forums that the trust facilitates. Representatives are appointed to the board by third sector partner organizations which include two long-standing organizations working with families and children, a church and a community dance organization. The trust also runs a training and activity centre which offers courses such as computer skills. It employs 11 staff, including a full-time manager for the centre and a community development worker (while the coordinator continues to be employed by the local authority) and involves a number of volunteers in its work.

### The centre

The English Healthy Living Centre Programme was funded by central government through the New Opportunities Fund (NOF). This was set up as part of the National Lottery to 'distribute grants for projects related to health, education and the environment as determined by the government' (National Lottery Act, 1998). Applicants for funding had to demonstrate that their centre would be 'supported by a broadly based partnership which includes statutory, voluntary, community and private sectors' (NOF, 1998, p. 112). The initiative to set up a centre in our case study area came from experienced local community activists responding to perceived local health needs and inequalities. In 2001, they invited local and city-wide TSOs together with public bodies including the city council and the primary care trust to join them in the necessary partnership. The centre was established as an independent legal entity early in 2003 with representatives from the public and third sectors and an operational agreement with the Department of Health. A large local TSO which had been involved in the bid process was chosen to be the accountable body for the contract and took on the management and administration of the contract including the line management of the centre director.

The centre's core team comprised eight staff, most of whom were employed by the various partner organizations which each delivered their own project (for example, Sure Start delivered the healthy eating component of the work). The centre's work in addressing health inequalities was wide-ranging and covered diet, exercise, community safety and even employment and training. Partner organizations were highly disparate, with officers from the city council and the chief executive of a large and well-funded TSO sitting alongside fellow board members representing tiny community organizations on a governing body with a TSO majority. In 2007, when the funding ran out, the centre closed.

Table 9.1 summarises the key features of the two organizations:

**Table 9.1** The two case studies

|  | The trust | The centre |
|---|---|---|
| The 'trigger' | State initiative | State initiative |
| Initiated by: | The state | Local community sector professionals |

**Table 9.1** (Continued)

|  | The trust | The centre |
|---|---|---|
| Governance | Stakeholders from public, third sector and local residents | Stakeholders from public and third sector. TSO acts as accountable body |
|  | Local authority acts as accountable body | Widespread uncertainty about exact constitutional nature |
| Membership | Wider community either as paid-up or symbolic members | No wider membership |
| Accountability | Director accountable both via the local authority to the Welsh Assembly government and to the Trust Board. Felt accountability to the community | Not formally constituted. Manager accountable to the grant recipient TSO. Unclear horizontal accountabilities |
| Distinctive human resources | Mixed paid staff: local authority and Trust. Executive Director employed by the local authority. Volunteers | Mixed: seconded from TSOs and the National Health Service and direct appointments |
| Distinctive other resources | Welsh Assembly Government plus sundry other smaller income streams | Government via the National Lottery |
| Closure | Still going | End of Lottery funding |

In terms of the framework set out in Chapter 3, both organizations could be described as enacted hybrids, set up to serve a particular government purpose by TSOs in the case of the centre and by the local authority in the case of the trust. Despite their dependence on government funding, both had consciously set themselves up at arms-length from the state and clearly adopted a third sector identity as opposed to that of a state-sponsored partnership. On the other hand, both were also acting as a 'governance space' into which other TSOs – alongside public sector bodies – were invited. Both also participated in other partnership forums and governance spaces in their locality. This hybridity posed a number of interlinked challenges – in relation to management, identity, accountability and control.

## The challenges of hybridity

### Management and authority

Hybridity can offer space for innovation, flexibility and risk taking, but the two case studies suggest that this is likely to depend on commitment from all sides to a clear vision for the organization and a clear overall structure. Without this, different interpretations and understandings can create tensions and even lead to collapse. Both the trust and the centre were partnerships that were striving to develop and sustain an identity as a single autonomous organization. In both organizations, however, there was evidence that, instead of combining different logics in new and productive ways, key players continued to operate according to the rules and operating cultures of the organization they originally came from. Thus in our first case study partnership the decision to constitute as a trust followed a long period of debate, involving all partners. As a Welsh Assembly sponsored partnership, it had adhered to the three thirds principle. But as the trust became more independent, the local authority found it more difficult to cooperate with it. This was partly because of the trust's wish to take over Grant Recipient Body status from the local authority and thus receive funding directly from the Welsh Assembly and partly because the local authority's legal department was uncomfortable with councillors' liabilities as board members of a limited company. More generally, there was a feeling that the local authority, despite holding onto its Grant Recipient body status, was only partially committed to membership of the Trust:

> ... from the beginning, I saw that the council should be a member of this partnership. And that it should be an equal member. Yes, it is also the grant recipient body. It funds staff. But it's got to wear two hats. An equal partner around the table, and then a local authority externally, if you like. It hasn't quite worked that way.

There are a number of possible causes for the ambivalence of those involved in the organizations. In the case of the centre, it might have been because partner organizations were hedging their bets in case the new hybrid was not sustainable – seconded staff may have expected in any case to revert to their originating organizations at some point. Alternatively, in both examples, it may be because professional partners found it difficult to handle the uncertainty of these new organizational forms and were more at ease falling back on familiar ways of operating.

While relations with the council have been strained at times, the trust has remained internally coherent with – as our interviews identify – clear agreement over the aims and objectives of the organization and effective procedures in place for staff and partners to work together. Once the partnership became a development trust, the partners signed up to the constitutional agreement and board members became directors of the company limited by guarantee.

This was not the case with the centre where, although relationships worked well at the individual project and the day-to-day level, the overall partnership arrangements became increasingly difficult to manage:

> The team is spread out between organizations ... as opposed to being HLC ... centrally ... which is where some of the lines of management and so forth has gotten very complicated (Centre director)

There was a strong feeling that the centre, while set up with good intentions, lacked the structures, procedures and contracts that were needed to underpin a free standing partnership and help it to manage times of conflict:

> Now this was a group of organizations put together and we assumed we'd all get on and we'd all act reasonably and fairly.

Prior to becoming the centre, respondents felt that relations between local organizations had been good and there had been an agreed vision. However, once funding was secured, the vision of this new partnership organization was not revisited, nor were the internal relationships between the centre director and the various partners clarified. At the time of interview, some respondents were very unclear about the status of the organization and its board, particularly in relation to the TSO that was acting as accountable body. Individual accountabilities were also unclear: some staff were seconded and some were directly appointed while some groups preferred to remain autonomous while others were happy to be managed through the centre. Some of the organizations that had been involved in writing the original partnership proposal left, while others changed the individual delegated to sit on the partnership; this meant that a clearer contract and terms of engagement were required to replace the personal commitment of the original members. However, this clarification did not happen and the lack of established agreement about management lines left the director unable to act when problems arose:

> A good partnership relies on good infrastructure and unfortunately you can't put it into place after the event. Nobody's going to turn round and say, 'Oh yes, let's commit ourselves to something when we don't have to'. And the fundamental issue within the centre was that there was no partnership agreement. Not a proper one and when people turned round and said, 'Well I don't want to do that'. How do you force them to? (Centre director)

This meant that neither the trustees nor the directly appointed staff could enforce decisions, leading to organizational paralysis. In addition, a grievance between one particular individual and the board stretched the informal organizational understandings and initial goodwill almost to breaking point.

The centre director was unable to intervene as the centre did not directly employ any of the relevant parties and so no grievance procedures were in place. A centre board member reflected that this could only have been overcome by setting up legally binding procedures. Initial goodwill was not enough for the long haul:

> It's taught me that goodwill needs to be underpinned by legality. It's taught me that there are people in the world who assume power to themselves when they have none and I have been absolutely amazed at how that has happened. Because, in actual fact, there was a period when the powerful organizations sitting round the table were absolutely powerless and where there was a spirit of intimidation in the board and it didn't come from the powerful partners.

The situation was aggravated by the fact that both the line manager at the accountable body and also the chair of the centre's board changed several times. Eventually, in an attempt to reduce the conflict on the board, the managing director of the accountable body TSO took over the chair. However, his concern – in response to the criticisms by one member – not to allow his own organization to dominate the partnership meant that, although he was able to act to contain the conflict, he was unable to resolve it.

These internal conflicts and confusions contributed to the failure of the centre to survive beyond the end of its dedicated state funding. The increasing problems and tensions generated by the hybrid nature of the organization meant that there was little enthusiasm amongst partners to find any other way of keeping it going – or, in the terminology of Chapter 3, there were no principal owners willing to 'stand up and be counted'. Nobody cared enough whether the organization lived or died and it was the ghosts at the table – in this case the funders – who controlled its destiny.

### Identity and accountability

All this created problems with identity and accountability. While the parent organizations of the seconded staff found it useful symbolically to be associated with the centre, when there were difficulties those staff could choose to revert to their 'real' identity – and the associated lines of accountability – with their parent organization, effectively abandoning the centre as an organization. While there was an assumption of shared values – as we saw in the previous section – they were not strong enough to bind people into a sense of identity with the centre once problems emerged.

Similarly, the centre director felt that she had to be accountable to the TSO that held and managed the centre's grant even though her accountability was formally to the board. A manager at the TSO felt that there was also a tension between his organization and the local authority:

> the local authority in this instance believe they were better placed to provide the services and administer the programme itself and I think we've got . . . we've had our own issues in terms of personalities from our side and there was a genuine clash.

Conflicting accountabilities and identity were also an issue for the trust but here they were focused in the role of the director: the accountability of the staff was much clearer. The chair described the tension that their executive director's double role (as executive director of the trust and coordinator of the Communities First Partnership) brought with it: 'that is where there is the tension for X's post in that he's employed by the council but he's here to carry out the decisions of the trust'. He went on to describe their strategy to deal with this:

> Well, it will be a dual approach sometimes . . . He has the face-to-face contact or the regular contact with them [government]. But [the vice-chair] and myself will attend the meetings if there's anything serious they need to discuss . . . So that the Welsh Assembly are aware of that sort of difference, and also the local authority . . . If X is being asked to do something, or if X is doing something, it's because the trust has asked him to do so.

This seems much more straightforward than the situation at the centre, and no more than any TSO might do to guarantee the accountability of the board and to protect its workers. However, while it might have been clear to the chair and board of the trust where accountability lay, it was not always so clear to the local authority, who saw the executive director primarily as the coordinator of their regeneration initiative:

> He [the director] got into some serious trouble and problems with the council who were his employers, or who are his employers and who line manage him. Obviously he's in a difficult position because he's supposed to represent the trust's views to the council and yet he's answerable to the council. (Board member, third sector)

A respondent suggested that there were conflicting visions about the ownership and purpose of many Communities First partnerships: people in the local authority believed the partnerships should be accountable to them as funders, while frontline workers believed the accountability should primarily be to the wider local community as part of the objective of transferring power and ownership to its members. In helping the partnership to develop as a limited company and to become independent from the local authority, the director of the trust strongly believed that he was facilitating a transfer of ownership:

> We had a loose partnership and after many months of discussion, and a few visits to other communities and advice from various sources . . . we adopted the company limited by guarantee structure. We tailored our aims to suit what we were doing. We felt that as a movement we would be growing stronger in this community and we would employ people.

Certainly, he no longer saw it as a government initiative:

> So I think it is a good independent movement that understands the need to stay close to the local authority and those with the greatest resources. But they won't be bullied and they won't be told what to do by the local authority and I think that is a strength that they have always had. They always saw themselves as an independent movement. It may be the cause of some misunderstandings and antipathy with the local authority.

In this sense, hybridity may be a temporary or transitional phenomenon – part of a progression from an identity as a state-sponsored partnership to one as an autonomous movement. But in the interim, the executive director and other Communities First workers saw themselves as working 'in and against the state' (LEWRG, 1980), a position which would always create tensions for accountability and identity.

However, the problem doesn't end here, for while the director perceives himself as representing the community, there are some community members who see him as an agent of the state:

> He doesn't live on the estate either. 'He's an outsider', that's what they say to me; 'he's another outsider'.

## Autonomy and control

Control over its own resources might be seen as the *sine qua non* of an autonomous agency. But in the case of the trust, attempts to take control of its funding were rejected by the local authority:

> We made moves to become our own Grant Recipient Body and we met with some reluctance from the council, because they thought that they could keep control of us as long as they had control of the money. (Board member, community)

In the city council's view, the trust was not professional enough to take responsibility for its own funding. When the trust applied more pressure, feeling that this lack of confidence was not justified, an overt power struggle ensued and a senior officer threatened to remove local authority-funded staff from the trust.

We have already described these partnership hybrids as occupying the 'interstices of power' (Gaventa, 2004). They are linked into governmental power structures and as such they inevitably challenge the way government works. Where a local authority is able to cede some control, it will be better able to play a constructive part in community partnerships. But this means discarding top-down cultures of working:

> I think the bottom line of this...is how the council actually sees itself. I know it has a legal requirement...to support

community regeneration. But it's how the council interprets that. Whether it interprets this as being the lead partner or whether it sees itself as being a partner. For many, many years it saw itself as being the lead partner. Now it's beginning to appreciate that it can't be...that it doesn't have the capacity to be the lead partner in every partnership. (Trust board member)

If a local authority is not sufficiently flexible to accommodate this changed role, it may simply withdraw its support, as we saw earlier. Or it may, as the accountable body, appeal to the need to comply with the rules and regulations of the more distant funder – the 'ghost at the table' – thus making the organization more 'governable' (Carmel and Harlock, 2008) and entrenching it firmly within the operational culture of the public sector.

This kind of hybridity does raise unanswered questions about democratic accountability, transparency and exclusion. Was it reasonable of the trust to expect its councillors to accept the same conditions and constraints as other board members? Is it naïve to expect councillors to set aside their role and enter the board as individuals, not as elected members of the city council? In partnerships, the role of the local authority as a democratically elected mediator of different local interests is clear, but once its representatives become trustees alongside others of a separately constituted organization, their role and democratic responsibility become blurred.

### The opportunities that hybridity offers

*Links into government*

Both organizations felt that the presence of state actors inside the organization offered privileged opportunities for influence. Respondents from the trust argued that their proximity to government could give them power to influence the way people within government think and to use the blurring of boundaries to challenge oppositional attitudes on both sides:

> I'd like to think that the likes of [the trust] and . . . other partnerships like it, do break down that 'us and them' that has existed with councils for donkey's years.

The centre also benefited from the presence of public sector partners from the local authority and primary care trust on its board. These linkages were seen by TSO board members to offer opportunities to influence public services at the planning stage:

> We also have had some board members who are strategically quite important. So we had a guy from the primary care trust who was on our board; we had the guy from the city council on our board. So by being part of the board, we could influence them as well in terms of the direction of their organizations when they went back.

In the case of the trust, the fact that its director was technically still an employee of the local authority gave him – and the trust itself – privileged access:

> So yes there's still that link. I mean we have got a direct link and we've been around for, well as a structured organization I think we've been around for six years now, five years, as a registered company. So the council can't refuse to deal with us point blank.

### The best of both worlds

Working as a limited company as well as a partnership also has considerable advantages. It has allowed the trust to have the best of both worlds, to protect its staff, to apply for a wider range of funding and to maintain the special linkages with the local authority provided by its partnership status:

> If we are going to take on staff, then the individuals in the unincorporated association that was the People in Communities partnership needed protection. So limited liability gives them that. Other benefits as well, for example, the trust now

can contract with people, because it is a legal entity, whereas the association was not.

It also offers flexibility to public sector partners, if they are willing to make this leap. However, as we have seen, local authority partners – particularly local councillors – often feel uncomfortable with these hybrid organizations rather than welcoming them as an opportunity to try out new ways of working.

## Broader implications

There has been considerable debate in the third sector literature about the encroachment of public and private sector principles and cultures into the third sector and the dangers that this may be eroding its distinctive characteristics. Much of this has focused on partnerships which are led by the public sector. In this chapter, we have been looking at what happens with partnerships which, though state-initiated, are either consciously located within the third sector from the outset or migrate there as a result of the need to sustain activities beyond the life of a state initiative. Our research suggests that some of these spaces, although triggered or initiated by the state, manifest at least some of the characteristics of independent TSOs. It also suggests that hybridity is not always a question of TSOs being sucked into a state agenda, but that sometimes the impetus and influence can be in the opposite direction. Thus, actors in the trust have embarked on a process of turning what was a (temporary) state-sponsored forum into a sustainable TSO while retaining the multi-actor involvement of the governance space.

As partnerships develop across a range of policy fields and as the state continues to outsource its functions, this is likely to become an increasingly familiar phenomenon. We are interested in the challenges this poses. Our research suggests that such organizations will need to address three main issues which, while not confined to these particular hybrids, are highlighted by their experience: the role and skills of leaders; the ability of the state to manage multiple roles and accountabilities; and the need to remain focused on a joint mission.

## The role of key individuals

The role of individuals who cross or span boundaries and their impact on hybrid organizations are discussed at more length in Chapter 11 of this book. Here we focus on the part played by key individuals in the formation and the operation of the two partnerships.

Managing and resolving conflict between different interests is an essential skill for those in key positions in hybrids of this kind. In the trust, the skills and vision of the director and chair and the relationship between them, together with the continued service of the director – from the earliest days of forming the loose partnership and throughout the process – have been critical for working through both the inevitable 'storming' stage and clashes between personalities and positions:

> I think he's been an extremely good co-ordinator. And we're very fortunate at the moment in our chair as well. And I do think they're both very calm individuals...their public face is calm. And I think they have done an incredible job in bringing, initially, the organizations together, so that internecine strife is gone. And then gradually, I think, the community is becoming less combative, really. Because this community was very, very divided eight or nine years ago.

In the centre, we were told that the role of the chair was vital in containing the conflicts that emerged as a result of the grievance and ensuring that the much looser partnership here could continue to operate.

Operating in this ambiguous and hybrid space requires people who can hold the tensions and perform difficult balancing acts. Their role as boundary spanners is critical to the success of the organization. This role requires a particular resilience both in dealing with competing demands, but also – as we saw in the case of the trust – in accepting that they will often be perceived by both sides as 'not one of us'.

## Learning to manage multiple roles and accountabilities

To a degree, councillors are also experiencing the tensions discussed above and have the potential to share the difficult leadership roles involved. As we have seen, however, this is often not the case:

> I got the feeling that they [local councillors] felt that [the trust] was in competition with them, or was trying to undermine them...they weren't happy about some of the members, the board members of the trust who they saw as rabble rousers and local stroppy people, community activists.

Thus, despite the powerful rhetoric calling for civil renewal and engaged civil society from European, UK central and Welsh national governments, those who are trying to put this into practice on the ground via hybrids such as the trust often encounter resistance to working in these new ways:

> We're trying to create a new democracy where a local community has a stronger voice, and can sit around the table as an equal partnership...Well, some councillors don't quite like that, or haven't got used to that, even after seven years.

Faced with the weight of legal and financial requirements as well as the monitoring demands of many central government programmes, local authorities tend to be cautious and even defensive rather than exploratory. These hybrid forms can, we have suggested, offer more flexibility but only if these defensive cultures change. Otherwise it is likely that they too will become enmeshed within regulatory regimes that stifle innovation. On the other hand, the involvement of councillors does raise issues of legitimacy and accountability which are not easy to resolve and we will return to this in our conclusions.

Nor were problems of commitment confined to public sector players. The TSOs too can be reluctant partners, wanting to maintain their own autonomy, especially in a competitive environment where their funding and member support depend on their maintaining their individual brand.

### Staying focused on mission

The third – related – issue is the need to ensure that the complexities of hybridity do not consume all the organization's energies and divert it from its mission. The centre illustrates how ambiguity of organizational form and purpose can bring about tensions that undermine the purpose and legitimacy of a community partnership:

> But... you're not to forget who you're providing the service to. We became a mini-organization in our own right. With management, directors, members of staff and all the tensions that comes with it. That's not what a board's supposed to be about. A board's supposed to be energetic, lively, full of ideas, a bit of risk taking and an enjoyable place to be. Something you genuinely do for good reasons in your own time.

The trust meanwhile fears that, despite the efforts to innovate and to get the best of both worlds, it ends up doing the same as ever, perhaps because power inequalities between people and role confusions have not really been addressed:

> I feel that we're just playing old games over and over again. There needs to be something radical and a new approach and people have dismissed this as some new-aged model rubbish, but I really do believe that we're missing a trick when we play these old structures over and over again. What's important is human interaction, individual interaction and I think if we... if we look at that, rather than this idea of partnership, which... partnership has a kind of an obligatory role and a contractual nature to it and I think you're already in a bad game if you're doing that. (Chair of the trust)

## Conclusions

While hybridity is a tendency that appears to be on the increase, it is too early to say whether these particular new hybrid forms are a success story and whether they have the potential for radically new approaches to welfare provision and governance. Our research did not allow us to evaluate their effectiveness on the ground, which must be the ultimate test of any organizational form. In any case, it suggests that we need to take a long-term view of their potential. Whereas the centre has collapsed under the weight of conflicting expectations and commitments, the trust is clearly an organization in transition. The skills that are needed of key personnel are evolving and are still not fully recognised. And as the trust illustrates, some stakeholders – particularly from the public sector – still feel more comfortable working inside their own sector, and are uncomfortable and ill-equipped to deal with hybridity. All ambiguity of organizational form and identity inevitably creates tensions. What is interesting is that some of these tensions turn into conflict and others into opportunities. Our research suggests that it is the skills and experience of particular individuals which make some organizations better equipped to navigate these tensions and to take advantage of their strategic position at the interface with governmental power.

It may be that the kind of hybrid we have been studying is a transitional phenomenon and thus, while they will always exist and have to grapple with these tensions and challenges, this will not have a wider significance. However, Leach and Scoones, in their analysis of citizenship and social movements (2007, p. 15), argue the opposite that 'in a world increasingly influenced by the dispersing and fragmented effects of globalisation, there is a need to go beyond state-centred or even pluralist accounts of citizenship' which suggests that their experience is highly significant. They cite Ellison (1997) to argue that the multiplication of identities, affiliations and forms of solidarity in their world vision requires the dissolving of more conventional boundaries between the public and private, the political and the social, arguing for a more integrative vision of 'practised engagement through emergent social solidarities'. This might be seen to hold out the promise of new forms of hybrid TSOs which can meld together some of the best aspects from several sectors whilst diminishing some of the well-known drawbacks of each form of sector organization. But if this is to be the future – and especially in the transition between the world in which we currently operate and this new phenomenon – then the tensions we have described around management and authority, identity and control are likely to become commonplace.

At one level, there are implications about effectiveness and sustainability. For, while there is a potential for social solidarities to emerge in these community partnerships, there is also a danger that the tensions generated by hybridity will overwhelm the organization altogether. But Leech and Scoones' vision raises broader questions about democratic accountability – and particularly the ambiguous position of local authority councillors – which have been a constant problem for the trust in particular. From one perspective, boundary crossing organizations like the trust offer important opportunities to build community power at the interface with government – opportunities which are in tension with the state's tendency to control. But from another, they challenge conventional and fundamental notions of democratic accountability through the electoral process, which will need to be addressed as they become more commonplace.

## Note

1. This study was funded by the Economic and Social Research Council as part of its Non-Governmental Public Action Programme (its reference number is RES-155–0058 and more information can be found on the ESRC's web site: www.esrcsociety today.ac.uk).

## References

Carmel, E. and Harlock, J. (2008) 'Instituting the 'third sector' as a governable terrain: partnership, procurement and performance in the UK', *Policy and Politics*, 36.2, pp. 155–71.

Cornwall, A. (2004) 'Spaces for transformation? Reflections on issues of power and difference in participation in development', in S. Hickey and G. Mohan (eds) *Participation: From Tyranny to Transformation*, London: Zed Books.

Ellison, N. (1997) 'Towards a new social politics: Citizenship and reflexivity in late modernity', *Sociology*, 31.4, pp. 697–717.

Gaventa, J. (2004) 'Towards participatory governance: assessing the transformative possibilities', in S. Hickey and G. Mohan (eds) *Participation: From Tyranny to Transformation*, London: Zed Books.

Ingamells, A. (2007) 'Community development and community renewal: tracing the workings of power', *Community Development Journal*, 42.2, pp. 237–250.

Leach, M. and Scoones, I. (2007) *Mobilising Citizens: Social Movements and the Politics of Knowledge*, Brighton: Institute for Development Studies.

London Edinburgh Weekend Return Group (LEWRG) (1980) *In and Against the State*, London: Pluto Press.

New Opportunities Fund (1998) Guidance for Applicants to the Healthy Living Centre Programme.

# 10 Housing associations: Agents of policy or profits in disguise?

## David Mullins and Hal Pawson

## Introduction

Social housing is a field in which the third sector role has been transformed beyond recognition over the past quarter century. This can be depicted as a process of shifting governance. Assets and strategic policy levers have been progressively stripped away from local government, with responsibility for both delivery and management of social housing increasingly vested with the boards of independent organizations (Mullins, 2006a). This progression has had two main components. First, since the mid-1980s, virtually all new publicly funded social housing has been constructed by housing associations rather than local authorities – around half a million new homes have been built in this way since 1980. Second, since 1988, over 150 local authorities have transferred their entire housing portfolio to housing associations (Pawson, 2006).

This chapter examines the rise of housing associations over the past 25 years, analyses their changing position on the public–private spectrum and discusses the extent to which it remains accurate to portray associations as part of the voluntary sector. It discusses changing forms of hybridity in relation to finance, governance, structure and activities. The chapter then explores the shifting public/private boundary, growing pains associated with the emergence of a hybrid sector of very large organizations and the impact of the post-2007 economic downturn on the hybrid model. In conclusion, we consider the relevance of the two faces of hybridity: 'for-profits in disguise' and 'agents of policy' in understanding English and Dutch housing associations.

## Housing associations: Their origins, constitutions and accountabilities

### Origins

The social origins of housing associations have been widely studied and, following Salamon and Anheier (1998), have been related to shifting welfare regimes (Mullins, 2000a). Some associations trace their genealogy back to medieval almshouses. Less contentiously, the roots of some of today's associations can be traced back to the liberal welfare regime of the late nineteenth and early twentieth century including the philanthropic housing companies of the Victorian era and the new generation of public utility societies established in the 1920s (Garside, 2000).

Post-World War II, in line with the social democratic character of the emerging welfare state, the major responsibility for social housing being was taken by local authorities with housing associations adopting a more shadowy role (Mullins, 2000a). However, the 1960s and 70s saw the 'rediscovery of poverty' and campaigns to reform the welfare state to meet the needs of excluded groups such as homeless people and new migrants. This agitation spawned a new generation of associations associated with Shelter and the Churches. The origins of Scotland's community-based housing associations are similar in some respects (Clapham and Kintrea, 2000).

As Kendall (2003) has observed, the early 1970s saw a 'fortuitous coincidence' for housing associations in which disillusion with council housing and with markets converged with increasing interest in the potential of Third Sector Organizations (TSOs). In this climate successful lobbying for core funding under the Housing Act 1974 led to the establishment in the later 1970s of a cohort of associations to undertake inner city regeneration. They found themselves in what was effectively a risk-free environment, with 100 per cent publicly funded approved capital spending. This enabled associations to accumulate assets which supported later expansion through private borrowing. From 1988 onwards, local authorities responded to anti-municipalist policies by forming new local stock transfer housing associations (Mullins et al., 1995). The modern housing association sector has thus originated from a number of distinct historical roots. Throughout its history, however, the sector has seen considerable organizational fluidity, with existing associations being absorbed – sometimes taken over – by others (Mullins, 2000a; Pawson and Sosenko, 2008). Thanks to the ongoing impacts of this sector restructuring some contemporary associations have origins in two or more of the eras cited above.

By 2006, housing associations had expanded to own 2.2 million homes – a fourfold increase on the early 1980s, and representing more than 8 per cent of the national total. This expansion has brought England into line with other European countries where social housing is delivered primarily or exclusively by TSOs (Kleinman, 1993). In the main, the rise of housing associations since the late 1980s has been directly at the expense of council housing, through the transfer of the ownership of council-constructed homes. Mainly motivated by financial considerations, the 20 years to 2008 saw some 1.3 million tenanted properties being passed from local authority into housing association ownership across Britain. Consequently, by 2008, barely half of England's 354 local authorities retained a landlord role.

### Constitutional forms and accountability

Historically, housing associations have been constituted as Industrial and Provident Societies with shareholder memberships who have purchased non-tradable shares priced at a token £1. Committee members are formally accountable to this membership but, in practice, it is widely acknowledged that such accountability lacks substance. Committee elections are typically staged so that positions are uncontested, with the shareholder membership endorsing candidates solicited by senior staff and/or existing committee members. Associations are frequently criticised as 'self-perpetuating oligarchies'.

Since the mid-1990s, most newly created stock transfer housing associations have been set up as companies limited by guarantee (CLG) under a local housing company (LHC) format. In CLGs the association's members are limited to the members of the board itself – usually (at least initially) designated in equal numbers from three constituencies, tenants, council nominees and 'independents'. The influx of bodies constituted as CLGs cuts across the notion advanced in Chapter 3 that the membership association is a core feature of TSOs.

The LHC model addressed criticisms that stock transfers from local authorities were eroding democratic accountability (Davies and Spencer, 1995, Skelcher, 1998). Because tenants are usually guaranteed a third of board places, it is argued that they have a greater say than in most local authority landlords and that greater legitimacy results. However, critics (such as McKee and Cooper, 2008) point to regulatory guidance stressing that board members (whether tenants or local authority nominees) must prioritise the interests of the organization rather than acting as representatives of their constituency (Housing Corporation, 1998). Thus tenant (and councillor) board members become 'representatives without the means to represent' (Clapham and Kintrea, 2000, p. 547). In the case of stock transfers, Ginsberg contends that: 'Whether tenants exert any more collective influence than they did within local electoral politics is highly debatable' (Ginsberg, 2005, p. 124).

Tenant governorship has also been a feature of the community-based housing association model promulgated in Scotland and in the small sub-sector of housing co-operatives throughout Britain. In the majority of traditional associations, however, tenants have generally played little direct role in governance. In 2003, while tenants accounted for 18 per cent of all board members, the vast majority of these (88 per cent) were from stock transfer associations (Cairncross and Pearl, 2003). Implicitly, tenants accounted for under 5 per cent of board members in 'traditional' associations. This follows from the 'top-down philanthropy' ethic underlying many longer-established associations (Malpass, 2000).

The co-operative sector provides an alternative mutual governance model for housing (Birchall, 1992; Rowlands, 2009).

Rowlands identifies three main eras of co-operative housing: co-partnership in the early twentieth century; co-ownership from the 1960s; and common ownership in the last 30 years. Recently, this had included the exploration of new governance models for tenant-controlled stock transfers in Wales and England (Confederation of Co-operative Housing, 2003; Bromily et al., 2004). The Housing Corporation itself was initially set up to promote co-ownership models (Murie, 2008). Nevertheless, these models enjoyed only limited adoption, and by 2008, Rowlands (ibid.) estimated that 243 part ownership co-operatives owned less than 1 per cent of housing association stock.

## Hybrid characteristics of housing associations

### Finance

Perhaps the most significant determinant of hybridity has been the resource dependence of housing associations on public funding and private finance secured on commercial terms. Among the pioneers of the mixed economy of welfare, housing associations claim to be the most successful exponents of public–private partnerships. The Housing Act 1988 dramatically altered the way associations were funded. Since 1974, they had been essentially publicly financed bodies insulated from commercial risk. Subsequently, private borrowing became the dominant source of income for the acquisition and development of new and existing homes, with £50 billion of loan facilities being secured and £38 billion drawn down (Social Housing, March 2008) alongside £30 billion in public subsidy.

Until the credit crunch, the system had developed such that just 30–40 per cent of the cost of new social housing (in England) was funded from public subsidy, while the remainder was met from reserves, new borrowing and cross-subsidy from sales and other commercial activities. In this respect, the English social housing sector had moved towards the hybrid model that underpins Dutch social housing (Ouwehand and van Daalen, 2002).

Although much of the Dutch housing association stock, which comprises a third of all housing in the Netherlands, was historically financed partly by government loans, these loans were written off in 1995 in return for an ending of such subsidy for the future. Dutch housing associations therefore operate as revolving funds in which inherited assets are exploited to maintain social housing. This has led Dutch associations to focus on asset and portfolio management and to develop commercial activities to cross-subsidise social housing in a Robin Hood style of hybridity (Gruis, 2008). Rising property values over the decade from 1995 enabled Dutch associations to develop a strong housing market foothold, largely independent of government. However, the limited ability of government to steer decision-making in these independent hybrids was becoming a problem by the time of the national election in 2007 and the Government imposed taxes on associations' social as well as commercial activities. The consequences of financial hybridity in the Netherlands were mixed, creating a gap between associations and government which associations tried to manage by constructing a 'social entrepreneurial' identity.

In England, much has been written about the impact of private funding on the character and ethos of housing associations. It has been argued that it has led to a shift in focus from people to property and tougher tenancy management and that transfers to associations represents privatisation (Walker, 2000; Ginsberg, 2005). While large private loans have influenced business plans, financial management and organizational culture, there is little evidence that organizational indebtedness has led to harder nosed management. Indeed, Pawson (2004) found that transfer associations (the most heavily indebted sub-group) recorded eviction rates well below those of local authorities and traditional associations.

Private finance has facilitated a degree of independence from government by reducing resource dependency on public funds. Appreciation in the capital value of stock subsidised through historic public subsidy had, until 2007/08, provided housing associations with assets that could be harnessed for independent purposes. In practice, however, government was keen to see such equity recycled to underpin investment in new housing and reduce new public subsidy. A key contrast to the Dutch position described above has been the greater leverage available to government through continued public funding and intensive regulation and inspection.

## Governance – Housing associations as 'voluntary housing'

Historically, housing associations were often differentiated from council provision by the term 'voluntary housing'. Kendall and Knapp saw housing associations as 'characterised by a meaningful degree of voluntarism in terms of money or time through philanthropy or voluntary citizen involvement' (Kendall and Knapp, 1996, p. 18). The main voluntary input to housing associations has however come from board members. Voluntary governance has itself been contested for some time, reflecting the wider debates about governance models discussed by Cornforth and Spear in Chapter 4 of this volume. An inquiry established by the National Federation of Housing Associations in 1994 noted 'strongly held but opposing views' on the subject (Ashby, 1997, p. 72). Some respondents from voluntary sector backgrounds favoured a clear distinction between voluntary board members and paid staff. Others with industrial experience 'took unitary boards for granted', feeling that executive and non-executive members should sit alongside one another on equal terms (ibid., p. 74). A few years later, Malpass argued that 'Management committees were, and to a large extent still are, rather strange hybrid bodies, reflecting the position of housing associations between the public and private sectors, deeply rooted in the historical traditions of voluntary housing, and arguably ill-suited to the challenges of the present period' (Malpass, 2000, p. 256).

Following the logic of the advocates for change, in 2003, the Housing Corporation allowed English associations to pay board members (Ayton, 2006). In Scotland, by contrast, the (then) regulator, Communities Scotland, rejected calls for a similar change in 2005, citing evidence that the balance of opinion was strongly opposed (Communities Scotland, 2005; Pawson et al., 2005). By 2006, almost a quarter of English associations (excluding those owning fewer than 1,000 dwellings) had adopted board member payment, with a small further increase by 2008 (Pawson et al., 2009).

Board member payment could be seen as part of more professionalised governance. Cairncross and Pearl (2003), for example, identified a rising proportion of university-educated board members. There has also been an increasing emphasis on business management and professional skills as the criteria for board member recruitment and the increased use of appraisals to reinforce expectations of paid non-executive directors.

One of the main growth pains experienced by associations has been in the perceived roles of non-executive directors and their executive peers as the size of organizations has increased and style of organizational management has changed. In terms of the theories presented in Chapter 3, it would appear that large associations have moved away from the membership association model, and that this represents a transition in the principal ownership of associations from non-executive to executive directors; albeit within an external context in which principal ownership is, as we argue in our concluding section, further contested between state and market institutions.

## Structures

Quite apart from stock transfers, the housing association sector has been substantially restructured over the past 25 years. In the period 1974–2000, there was a continuous flow of transfers of engagements (that is, mergers) averaging about 1 per cent of the sector each year (Mullins, 2000a). Two peaks in activity reflected adjustments to legislative and funding changes – namely, the introduction of public funding post 1974–76 and the inauguration of the mixed finance regime post-1988. In the later 1990s, there was a shift in the form of restructuring with the emergence of group structures of associations and other charitable and non-charitable subsidiaries controlled by parent bodies. Initially stimulated by corporation tax changes, the establishment of group structures was subsequently also motivated by other considerations including ring-fencing risky of specialist activities and accommodating local stock transfer subsidiaries (Audit Commission and Housing Corporation, 2001). In England, a further and more intense process of sector restructuring was triggered by 2004 reforms which concentrated development funding on the 70 or so 'best developing associations' under the Housing Corporation's Investment Partnering procurement initiative (Mullins 2006b, p. 9).

From a governance perspective, an important result of sector restructuring has been the gradual unravelling of the initially close geographical fit between post-stock transfer local authorities and their successor landlords. Ultimate control over a body of tenancies may move from a locally-specific organization to a larger and geographically remote body. Critical here is the relatively fluid nature of the housing association sector and the scope for organizations to regroup.

Although new associations have continued to be established to facilitate local authority stock transfers, there has been a reduction in number of associations and an increase in their size. In the 6 years to 2007, for example, stockholdings of the typical English housing association grew by 50 per cent (from 800 to 1,200 dwellings), while the proportion of national housing association stock in the ownership of the 20 largest providers grew from 26 to 29 per cent (Pawson and Sosenko, 2008).

There have also been changes to the internal structure of large housing association groups, reducing the number of separate legal entities to simplify internal governance (fewer boards to service) and reduce regulatory burden (fewer regulatory returns and annual accounts). Indeed the growing pains associated with moving to unprecedented levels of organizational scale may, we believe, be at the heart of the hybridity debate.

## Activities

A slightly different trend has involved the creation of special purpose subsidiaries to manage new, and potentially risky, activities. Commercial subsidiaries have been established by many charitable associations to take on non-charitable activities such as the construction of housing for sale. In keeping with a scenario discussed in Chapter 3, such moves could be seen as a form of increased hybridity brought about by growth via diversification. Initially, such diversification was viewed quite cautiously by the Housing Corporation as sector regulator in England. To restrict perceived risks, a limit (initially 5 per cent of turnover) was imposed on the proportion of activity beyond core social housing functions (Housing Corporation, 2000). However, over the next few years, the policy climate shifted to encourage diversification, particularly into regeneration which became an expected element of stock transfer business plans, and the definition of 'core activities' broadened accordingly (Pawson et al., 2009).

The sector trade body, the National Housing Federation (NHF) actively promoted associations' contribution to community well-being as part of its rebranding as 'In Business for Neighbourhoods' (National Housing Federation, 2003). It undertook an audit of members (National Housing Federation, 2008b) to estimate the scale and scope of activities such as employment and enterprise, well-being, poverty and social exclusion, community safety and cohesion, environment and neighbourhood services. The revenue costs of these neighbourhood services totalled £435 million, of which £272 million came from associations' own resources. Nearly 7,000 services, employing 4,500 staff, benefited the equivalent of 5.5 million people across England.

The promotion and quantification of these activities by NHF can be seen as part of the construction of a hybrid identity for the sector based on social investment performance. There are similarities with attempts to promote a social entrepreneurial identity by Dutch housing associations and with diversification by housing associations across Europe in the face of retreating welfare states (Brandsen et al., 2006). The relationship with government was an underlying issue prompting the NHF audit at a time when increasing regulation of community and neighbourhood activities was being proposed in draft legislation. By demonstrating the existing volume of activity, the survey made the case against regulating these 'discretionary' services. This leads us back to one of the main tensions associated with hybridity – the relationship with governments.

## Emerging tensions and responses to hybridity

### Tensions around the public/private divide

Through its powers as regulator and (partial) funder of housing associations, government has powerfully influenced change in the sector and the roles of its constituent organizations. Thus, while housing associations have always occupied a space somewhere between the private and public sectors, their exact position has shifted over time to reflect changing ministerial priorities. The Housing Act 1974 marked the start of a period when associations could be characterised as quasi-public bodies. Not only were they obliged to submit to state regulation of rents, but also were largely state funded and their role during this period was as 'instruments of housing policy' (Malpass, 2000, p. 155).

With the passage of the Housing Act 1988, however, associations were subject to 're-privatisation' (Randolph, 1993). This introduced a new funding regime which treated associations as non-public bodies with significant commercial freedoms including the ability to leverage private funds against the asset value of their existing stockholdings without affecting public borrowing. Hand in hand with greater autonomy, the new regime exposed associations to financial risks from which they had previously been insulated. For example, cost over-runs in the course of development had to be absorbed by associations themselves. This was seen as incentivizing efficiency (Randolph, 1993).

Campaigners against stock transfer contend that the switch from council landlordism to housing association ownership amounts to 'privatisation' (Mullins and Pawson, 2009). Paradoxically, others have seen housing associations' independence threatened by state control. Even in 2000, it could be contended that 'at the end of the (20th) century (housing associations) are little more than agents of the state ...' (Malpass, 2000, p. 259). In part, this argument is directly connected with the role of (some) housing associations as stock transfer vehicles, as the transfer process has become increasingly tightly controlled and orchestrated from the centre (Malpass and Mullins, 2002; Mullins and Pawson, 2009).

Subsequently, housing associations have been edged towards re-incorporation within the public sector as a result of a series of legal rulings and case law. The 2004 ruling that associations are public bodies for the purposes of EU procurement rules followed from associations' heavily regulated status rather than the extent of public funding underpinning their development programmes (Wilcox, 2004). Concerns were expressed that this might lead to the re-classification of housing associations as public bodies for the purposes of the UK national accounts and that 'this would challenge not only the financial rationale for stock transfers, but also the financial rationale for housing associations to be the predominant vehicle for the delivery of new affordable housing' (Wilcox, 2004, p. 60).

Cowan and McDermont (2006) illustrated the role of the Inland Revenue, the courts and the charity commissioners in the 1970s in specifying the legitimate sphere of activity for housing associations. More recent court pronouncements have further limited genuine independence from the state. The 2002 *Poplar HARCA v Donohue* case found that functions performed by associations assisting local authorities to discharge statutory duties towards homeless persons were public in nature (Bryant, 2008). The 2008 case of *Weaver v London and Quadrant Housing Trust* (Queen's Bench Division, 2008) found that in relation to 'the management and allocation of housing stock' the association was performing 'functions of a public nature' within the meaning of the Human Rights Act and were therefore subject to challenge under the Act and might also be contested via Judicial Review. The Judge's view in this case was that housing activity is 'not simply subject to detailed regulation, but is permeated by state control' (para. 55).

Partly stimulated by these developments, fierce debate accompanied parts of the 2008 Housing and Regeneration Bill which strengthened regulation and political control over housing associations. The NHF criticised proposed regulatory reforms as vesting too much power in ministerial hands. Echoing Wilcox's concerns above, the moves were seen as compounding the risk of associations crossing the threshold into the public sector, and thereby threatening associations' ability to lever in private finance (National Housing Federation, 2008a).

## Growing pains: Large housing associations and hybridity

Notwithstanding the diversity of the housing association sector discussed earlier, much of the sector's activity is now accounted for by a new breed of super organizations. New organizational archetypes are evolving to manage the premier league of associations with 20–50,000 homes in management following growth through merger and group structure. In England, the top 20 associations now control almost 30 per cent of total stock and the process of agglomeration is continuing, albeit gradually. These larger associations appear to mark the emergence of hybrid organizations as a sector in their own right for which new forms of organization and governance are deemed to be required. For example, a commission set up by one of the largest English housing associations aimed to address the problem of 'nineteenth century constitutions (that) are no longer adequate to govern twenty-first century organizations' (London and Quadrant Group, 2005). This Commission on the Future Shape of the Sector argued that 'there is a real difference between managing an organization of 30,000 . . . one of 50,000 homes' and that new 'structures, methods, technology and mindsets' are required for such organizations to operate effectively (ibid., p. 5).

Moreover, recent years have seen substantial consolidation and streamlining of existing housing association groups. As well as cutting the numbers of regulated entities (see above), such changes have reduced the numbers of non-executives, brought payment of non-executives and involved the appointment of more executive directors to boards. All of this is transforming the governance of these organizations in the interests of government-defined notions of efficiency and enhanced flexibility to do commercial deals.

Increasingly, therefore, it is possible to argue that larger housing providers are a distinct sector with different organizational logics to the remainder of the sector. Indeed, critiques of the market dominance and procurement efficiencies of this sub-sector contrast the Tescopoly (Simms, 2006) approach to growth and market and supply chain dominance with the 'community anchorage' (Wadhams, 2006) logic of local partnerships favoured by smaller, more locally based and networked TSOs.

We can sketch the archetypal large hybrid association in relation to the following dimensions:

- *Systems-based approaches*: replace traditional relationship-based approaches to operate on a larger scale in less place-specific ways;
- *Engagement with regulation*: an emphasis on ability to manage regulatory burden through scale and to meet regulator expectations through standardisation and consistency;
- *Procurement*: buying big to secure economies, even if this leads to fewer choices for residents and less potential for local economy multiplier effects from housing association spending; and
- *Customer relationships*: emphasis on a menu of consumerist measures rather than collective engagement of consumers in governance.

Political disenchantment with the large-scale archetype surfaced in parliamentary debates on the Housing and Regeneration Bill. Parallels can be drawn with the political criticism facing the Dutch hybrid sector depicted by one chief executive as a crisis of steering: 'it's not that we are doing a bad job but that they can't control us' (interview, July 2007). In England, signals to support neighbourhood community engagement and 'place shaping' compete with those to enhance efficiency and procurement costs (buying big) by increasing scale.

Concepts of accountability are also being challenged as these organizations move towards consumerist rather than representational models of accountability to tenants and reduce the role of local structures such as subsidiary boards and local authority nominees in strategic decision-making. The challenge is to link the undoubted organizational capacity of these large organizations to tackle entrenched urban regeneration challenges with the local anchorage required to meet community expectations, in short to become 'close neighbours, not distant friends' (van Bortel et al., 2008). There appears to be a strong commitment amongst these organizations to prove right Bubb's (2007) claim that large organizations can remain closely in touch with clients and communities. New ways in which this is being attempted include the development of private sector style corporate social responsibility strategies; the recycling of efficiency savings into community investment projects; the measurement of social performance; and the formation of partnerships with social enterprise and third sector agencies (for example, to generate employment opportunities).

## Hybridity in an economic downturn

As Chapter 3 notes, times of crisis can often clarify sector identities and principal owners. It is important to recognise the importance of the wider economy for the housing hybrid model. The post-2007 credit crunch and economic downturn is posing significant tests for housing associations, alongside other TSOs, and arguably some of these challenges touch on core elements of hybridity.

A key challenge has been the availability and terms on which non-state finance is available. For charities in general, the downturn has impacted on philanthropic giving and hit investment income, both as a result of exposure to bank collapses (for example, the Icelandic institutions) and rapidly falling interest rates. Given their dependence on borrowing from banks and building societies, the main impact for housing associations has been funders' post-2007 reluctance to extend or amend loan agreements without substantial increases in interest rate margins. In proceeding with existing plans to issue bonds, some very large associations have reduced their dependence on bank lenders, thereby sidestepping these problems. Indeed, between July and November 2008 – at the very peak of the credit crunch – associations raised over £1 billion from bond issues (Peter Marsh quoted in Inside Housing, 28 November 2008, p. 25).

However, even the largest associations have been hit by lenders' changed approach to existing loans as banks have attempted to offset risk exposure. Ability to manage assets is affected by resource dependence on private loans, the terms of which deteriorate if any adjustments are made to existing arrangements. The slump in the value of land and unsold housing for sale and shared ownership must be reflected in annual accounts under rules on impairment. Published accounts, in turn, affect the financial ratios and covenants that have been previously agreed with lenders, potentially triggering the need to amend loan agreements. Not surprisingly, lenders have been keen to exploit opportunities to set new terms for the entire package of lending affected and thereby stabilise their own business. This has highlighted the degree of external control of housing association business plans, casting in sharp relief a critical – and previously largely ignored – vulnerability of hybrid finance arrangements.

More fundamentally, the Robin Hood strategy is clearly undermined if commercial activities become unprofitable. In the context of the post-2007 housing market downturn, it has been widely argued that the model of cross-subsidy of new social rented homes from outright sales and shared ownership is broken, or at least inoperable, during a period in which people are unable or unwilling to purchase such properties from associations (either failing to secure mortgage finance or unwillingness to risk a loss in a declining market).

Finally, the economic downturn affects relationships between the hybrid sector and government. The disappearance of the ability of associations to cross-subsidise rented homes from sales income has required the rethinking of ambitious build targets agreed only a year earlier. Associations argued that, as part of its social investment response to the downturn, ministers should bring forward future spending on housing to enable construction to proceed in the short term at higher rates of subsidy. Government has been mindful of the overhang of unsold privately constructed homes and has encouraged associations to purchase these properties, repeating the housing market package used to similar effect in the earlier 1992–93 downturn. Having learned from this earlier experience, however, associations have been reluctant to take on properties seen as too small or poorly constructed to withstand the higher wear and tear of social tenancies compared with home ownership.

As in the private sector, the ultimate impact of the sustained downturn for hybrids is the need to shed staff or risk bankruptcy. Reports of association staff layoffs, particularly in development departments, have become commonplace during the downturn. The sector tradition of larger associations stepping in to rescue failing associations to avoid placing tenants at risk of losing their homes has continued. However, it is reported that the impairment impact of taking on failing businesses is now dissuading larger associations from engaging in this activity, notwithstanding their general financial strength to do so (Inside Housing, December 12th 2008). One reported solution was for financially robust associations to substitute for the banks, encouraged by the regulator to provide soft loans for ailing peers (Inside Housing, January 16th 2009).

## Conclusions

In both England and the Netherlands, housing associations are nowadays generally large, bureaucratised organizations, with paid staff becoming the principal owners of strategy as well as operations. In this sense, the sector is characterised by entrenched hybridity as defined in Chapter 3. This scenario is furthest developed in the super-league of very large associations that has seen the biggest transition from its associational model origins. As organizations have grown, there has been a constant search for new models of organizational structure constitutional arrangements; governance; and management and a conscious construction of new sector and organizational identities. This process of transition has not been without pain, and tensions have arisen in relation to governance and the differing assumptions held by non-executives and executive directors, perhaps over principal ownership matters.

More generally, we can see the two national case studies discussed in this chapter as falling in rather different zones in Figure 3.1 on page 57.

As the Dutch sector has become a private/third sector hybrid, it has been increasingly concerned to protect itself from the 'for profits in disguise' critique by cultivating a social entrepreneurial identity and developing explicit societal benefits (Gruis, 2008). The language of hybridity is now commonplace and there has been an active construction of a values-based social entrepreneurial sector identity. Nevertheless, it has seen its tax advantages and competitive advantage with the private sector eroded by European competition directive challenges and by tax interventions by the Dutch government to treat even the social activities of associations as if they were profit-making.

In England, hybridity is also evident in relation to resource dependencies and funding arrangements; in sector and organizational structures; and in the diverse range of activities undertaken and emphasised in sector identities. However, the English sector seems closest to the public/private/third zone nowadays and this explains the robust defence against the dangers of simply becoming agents of public policy and generally positive presentation (at least before the credit crunch) of its leverage of private funds and know-how. While subject to an increasingly similar financial model to the Dutch, the mission of domestic housing associations appears to be challenged more by government steering than by marketisation. Early drafts of the 2008 Housing and Regeneration Bill were described as 'the greatest ever threat to the independence of housing associations' and arguments for a level playing field with the private sector were made in the opposite direction to the Dutch with a claim for more even-handed regulation of shared ownership activities (National Housing Federation, 2008a).

Further research might develop the questions of types of hybridity, notions of principal ownership and transition processes stimulated by this volume. The impact of external crises such as economic recession in redefining principal ownership will require more considered research as the process unfolds. However, it seems that in England the value added by the housing association (HA) hybrid model has been severely challenged because cross-subsidy models no longer work, exposure to private borrowing now has less favourable impacts and principal external ownership by government has become more apparent. In the Netherlands, by contrast, it seems that the private/third sector identity had become sufficiently entrenched to provide a greater resilience to recession (greater asset cushion, less financial gearing and less government leverage).

## References

Ashby, J. (1997) 'The inquiry into housing association governance', in P. Malpass (ed.), *Ownership, Control and Accountability: The New Governance of Housing*, Coventry: Chartered Institute of Housing.

Audit Commission and Housing Corporation (2001) *Group Dynamics. Group Structures and Registered Social Landlords*, London: Audit Commission.

Ayton, A. (2006) *Board Payment: The First Year*, Housing Corporation Sector Study 36, http://www.housingcorp.gov.uk/server/show/conWebDoc.3442 (accessed 10 April 2009).

Birchall, J. (1992) *Housing Co-operatives in Britain*. Department of Government Working Papers No. 21, London: Brunel University.

van Bortel, G., V. Gruis, D. Mullins and N. Nieboer (2008) *Close Neighbours, not Distant Friends. Neighbourhood Focused Housing Associations in England and the Netherlands*. http://www.curs.bham.ac.uk / research_consultancy / communitiesx / close_neighbours.shtml (accessed 15 March 2009).

Brandsen T., R. Farnell and T. Cardoso Ribero (2006) *Housing Association Diversification in Europe – Profiles, Portfolios and Strategies*, Coventry: Rex Group.

Bromily, R., D. Adamson and S. Connolly (2004) *Housing, Mutuality and Community Renewal: A Review of the Evidence and its Relevance to Stock Transfer in Wales* Cardiff: Welsh Assembly Government. http://new.wales.gov.uk/dsjlg/research/0404/reporte.pdf?lang=en.

Bryant, J. (2008) *The Weaver Case: The 'Public Functions' of Housing Associations*, National Housing Federation Briefing Note, August 2008. http://www.housing.org.uk/Uploads/File/Policy%20briefings/nslg2008br11.pdf

Cairncross, L., C. Morrell, J. Darke and S. Brownhill (2002) *Tenants Managing: An Evaluation of Tenant Management Organisations in England*, London: ODPM.

Cairncross, L. and M. Pearl (2003) *Taking the Lead: Report on a Survey of Housing Association Board Members*, London: Housing Corporation. http://www.housingcorp.gov.uk/CFG/upload/pdf/4103aatakingthelead.pdf (accessed 10 April 2009).

Clapham, D. and K. Kintrea (2000) 'Community-based housing organisations and the local governance debate', *Housing Studies*, 15(4), pp. 533–559.

Confederation of Co-operative Housing (2003) *Empowering Communities*, Coventry: CIH.

Communities Scotland (2005) *Research on Governance Within Registered Social Landlords: A Response from Communities Scotland*, Edinburgh: Communities Scotland.

Cowan, D. and M. McDermont (2006) *Regulating Social Housing: Governing Decline*, Abingdon: Routledge-Cavendish.

Davies, H. and K. Spencer (1995) *Housing Associations and the Governance Debate*, Birmingham: University of Birmingham.

Garside P.L. (2000) *The Conduct of Philanthropy: The William Sutton Trust 1900–2000*, London: Athlone Press.

Ginsberg, N. (2005) 'The privatisation of council housing', *Critical Social Policy*, 25(1), pp. 115–135.

Gruis, V. (2008) *Organisational Archetypes for Dutch Housing Associations*, Environment and Planning Government and Policy (26), pp. 1077–1092.

Housing Corporation (1998) *Guidance for Applicants Seeking to Become Registered Social Landlords – Stock Transfer Applicants*, London: Housing Corporation.

Housing Corporation (2000) *Regulating a Diverse Sector. The Housing Corporation's Policy*, London: Housing Corporation.

Kendall, J. (2003) *The Voluntary Sector*, London: Routledge.

Kendall, J. and M. Knapp (1996) *The Voluntary Sector in the UK*, Manchester: Manchester University Press.

Kleinman, M. (1993) 'Large scale transfers of council housing to new landlords: Is British social housing becoming more European?', *Housing Studies*, 8, pp. 163–178.

London and Quadrant Group (2005) *Future Shape of the Sector Commission*, London: L & Q Group.

Malpass, P. (2000) *Housing Associations and Housing Policy*, Basingstoke: MacMillan.

Malpass, P. and D. Mullins (2002) 'Local authority stock transfer in the UK: From local initiative to national policy', *Housing Studies*, 17(4), pp. 673–686.

McKee, K. and V. Cooper (2008) 'The paradox of tenant empowerment: Regulatory and liberatory possibilities', *Housing, Theory and Society*, 25(2), pp. 132–146.

Mullins, D. (2000a) 'Social origins and transformations: The changing role of English housing associations', *Voluntas*, 11(3), pp. 255–276.

Mullins, D. (2000b) *Constitutional and Structural Partnerships: Who Benefits?* Housing research at CURS No. 8, Birmingham: University of Birmingham.

Mullins, D. (2006a) 'Exploring change in the housing association sector in England using the Delphi method', *Housing Studies*, 21(2), pp. 227–251.

Mullins, D. (2006b) 'Competing institutional logics? Local accountability and scale and efficiency in an expanding non-profit housing sector', *Public Policy and Administration*, 21(3), pp. 6–21.

Mullins, D. and H. Pawson (2009) 'The evolution of stock transfer: Privatisation or towards re-nationalisation?', Chapter 5 in P. Malpass and R. Rowlands (eds), *Housing, Markets and Policy*, London: Routledge.

Mullins, D. and H. Pawson (2010) *After Council Housing: Britain's New Social Landlords*, Basingstoke: Palgrave.

Mullins, D. and M. Riseborough (2000) 'Non-profit housing agencies: Reading and shaping the policy agenda', in M. Harris and C. Rochester (eds), *Voluntary Organisations and Social Policy*, Basingstoke: Palgrave.

Mullins D., P. Niner and M. Riseborough (1995) *Evaluating Large Scale Voluntary Transfers of Local Authority Housing*, London: HMSO.

Murie, A. (2008) *Moving Homes: The Housing Corporation 1964–2008*, London: Politico's.

National Housing Federation (2003) *In Business for Neighbourhoods*, London: National Housing Federation.

National Housing Federation (2008a) *Housing Bill Puts Half a Million New Affordable Homes at Risk*, National Housing Federation press release, 14 January/2008. http://www.housing.org.uk/default.aspx?tabid=232&mid=1150&ctl=Details&Article ID=841

National Housing Federation (2008b) *The Scale and Scope of Housing Association Activity Beyond Housing*, London: National Housing Federation.

Ouwehand, A. and G. van Daalen (2002) *Dutch Housing Associations: A Model for Social Housing?* Delft: DUP Satellite.

Pawson, H. (2004) 'Reviewing stock transfer', in Wilcox, S. (ed.), *Housing Finance Review 2004/5*. Coventry and London: Chartered Institute of Housing and Council of Mortgage Lenders.

Pawson, H. (2006) 'Restructuring England's social housing sector since 1989: Undermining or underpinning the fundamentals of public housing?', *Housing Studies*, 21(5), pp. 767–783.

Pawson, H. and C. Fancy (2003) *Maturing Assets – The Evolution of Stock Transfer Housing Associations*, Bristol: Policy Press.

Pawson, H. and F. Sosenko (2008) *Sector Restructuring*, Housing Corporation Sector Study 61. http://www.housingcorp.gov.uk/server/show/ConWebDoc.14472 (accessed 10 April 2009).

Pawson, H., E. Davidson, J. Morgan, R. Smith and R. Edwards (2009) *Second Generation: The Impacts of Stock Transfers in Urban Britain*, Coventry: Joseph Rowntree Foundation.

Pawson, H., M. Satsangi, M. Munro, L. Cairncross, F. Warren and D. Lomax (2005) *Reviewing Housing Association Governance*, Edinburgh: Communities Scotland.

Queen's Bench Division (2008) Weaver v London and Quadrant Housing Trust. http://www.bailii.org/ew/cases/EWHC/Admin/2008/1377.html (accessed 10 April 2009).

Randolph, B. (1993) 'The re-privatisation of housing associations', in P. Malpass and R. Means (eds), *Implementing Housing Policy*, Buckingham: Open University Press.

Rowlands, R. (2009) *Forging Mutual Futures – Co-operative, Mutual and Community Based Housing in Practice*, Birmingham: University of Birmingham. http://www.curs.bham.ac.uk/publications/downloads.shtml (accessed March 15 2009).

Salamon, L. and H. Anheier (1998) Social origins of civil society. Explaining the non-profit sector cross-nationally, *Voluntas*, 9(3), pp. 213–248.

Skelcher, C. (1998) *The Appointed State: Quasi-governmental Organizations and Democracy*, Basingstoke: Macmillan.

Simms, A. (2006) *Tescopoly: How One Shop Came Out Top and Why it Matters*, London: Constable & Robinson Ltd.

Wadhams, C. (2006) *An Opportunity Waiting to Happen. Housing Associations and Community Anchors*, London: Housing Associations Charitable Trust.

Walker, R.M. (2000) 'The changing management of social housing: The impact of externalisation and managerialisation', *Housing Studies*, 15, pp. 281–299.

Wilcox, S. (ed.) (2004) *UK Housing Review 2004/05*, Coventry and London: Chartered Institute of Housing and Council of Mortgage Lenders.

# 11

# Encountering hybridity: Lessons from individual experiences

*David Lewis*

## Introduction

In the past 20 years, the concept of the 'three sectors' in which the landscape of institutional life is divided into the public, private and 'third' sectors has become well established. From the UK Home Office to the World Bank in Washington DC, forms of this model have guided policy makers in the ways they have tried to develop and implement their ideas in both industrialised and developing country contexts. A belief in the third sector's special capacity to deliver certain types of social services, or to foster community-level participation, has been central to mainstream policy thinking across many national and international contexts. The model offers us a useful analytical framework but, as most people involved on the ground will also know from their experience, the everyday realities of life within third sector organizations are complex and messy, and, as many of the chapters in this volume suggest, may be becoming more so. Furthermore, as Billis (Chapter 1, this volume) argues, the structures and identities of organisations within the third sector have become extremely complex during the past decade, leaving the coherence of the very idea of 'sector' ever more open to question.

The contributors to this volume have mostly provided structural analyses of increasing organizational hybridity and sector blurring. This chapter approaches these issues somewhat differently. It explores mainly internal organizational aspects of sector blurring, analysed at the level of the perceptions and experiences of individuals, drawing on research on the phenomenon of 'sector boundary crossing', in which individuals from either the third sector or the public sector make short-term or long-term transitions over to the 'other' sector during their professional careers. Anecdotal data suggests that, in the past decade or so, there has been an intensification of cross-sector movements of this kind both in the UK and elsewhere.

There has so far been very little specific research on the sector boundary crossing issue in the UK context. One exception is Little and Rochester's (2003) useful study of six individuals brought into government in order to help inform its policy towards the third sector, which found evidence that these people could ameliorate but not influence or shape government policy. Another is Leat's (1995) formative research on the organizational implications of the movement of private sector managers from the for-profit sector to the third sector. Leat concluded that sector difference at the level of organization and management issues was not clear-cut, and that there was considerable diversity within the two sectors that she studied, as well as important differences between them. However, this work focused on a different area of the sector boundary to that covered within the present chapter.

The chapter aims to address two main issues in relation to the broader themes of this book. The first is to explore further the ideas set out in Chapter 3 of this book that tensions may exist between the 'ideal model' of the sector and the every-day realities of particular organizations. The data demonstrates ways that these tensions are played out within the lives of those individuals who move from one sector setting to another, generating processes that often contribute to the shaping of hybrid organizations. The second issue is the more macro-level observation that despite, or perhaps because of, this hybridization process, the sector concept and in particular the idea that a boundary exists between sectors, continues to play an important role in the ways individuals confront and manage different sector realities.

The data presented in this chapter is drawn from a recent comparative research project that attempted to map and analyse the career trajectories of individuals who cross in both directions between 'third' and public sector.[1] Some of these individuals were recruited by public sector agencies from the third sector as a source of new expertise, while others sought entry to the public sector in order to try to 'make a difference' on a larger scale than they felt was possible within third sector settings. Others, moving in the opposite direction, left government or civil service positions in order to work in what they saw as a more value-driven or worthwhile organizational environment. Some were primarily motivated by the prospect of higher levels of remuneration, while others were driven by social or political goals and many by combinations of all three. Some boundary crossers effectively became 'sector switchers' and decided to remain within their new sector positions, but many others became unhappy and returned to their original settings. In some cases, the intention was always to make only a short-term transition in which a person might deliberately aim to collect and share new knowledge and expertise, sometimes with an explicit aim of taking back and applying new ideas gathered from unfamiliar sector terrains.

Using a form of the life history research method, the study aimed to document the motivations and experiences of people who crossed over, and to explore broader meanings and implications of these cross-sector shifts (Lewis, 2008a). The study collected, analysed and compared a set of narrative data generated through more than 60 detailed life-work histories that were collected across three contrasting country settings (the UK, Bangladesh and the Philippines). This chapter draws on the 20 detailed life-work history interviews from the UK portion of the data set, which contained a purposive sample of boundary crossers in both directions, covering each of the types and motivations discussed above.

The data tells us more about the ways that the boundary separating the two sectors operates, from the perspective of those moving across it; and about the ways that such acts of cross-over feed into organizational 'hybridization' processes, as new people and ideas become imported or transplanted into new sector positions. These individuals contribute to, and are in a sense 'carriers' of, hybridization. The research suggests that, while boundary crossing contributes to the erosion of third sector identities by blurring the boundaries with the public sector, leading to the importation of ideas and techniques from one sector into another, it also may also, paradoxically, maintain and solidify aspects of sector identity – as individuals either (re)identify with, revise or reject their earlier sector affiliations.

In the first section, we begin with a short conceptual discussion of the different levels at which ideas about sector operate and show the need to understand 'boundary' as a multi-level concept. In the second section, the chapter introduces the topic of sector boundary crossing, with its wide range of types, motivations and outcomes, and suggests that this can be understood as a form of work-role transition, which has potentially important consequences for both the organizations entered and those that are left behind. This idea is at the heart of the chapter's main argument that such boundary crossing contributes to the formation of hybrid organizational environments. The third section presents data that helps illustrate this point in relation to five themes: creativity; learning; identity formation; skill building; and informal linkages. A fourth section offers an analysis of the data in relation to earlier work on hybridity in public management and this is followed by the conclusion.

## Understanding sectors and boundaries

The idea of 'sector' and the nature of the boundary between different sectors both require careful unpacking. Sector is complicated in two ways: first, because sectors operate at different 'levels' and second, because it is an 'ideal type'; abstract ideas about sector are likely to contrast with people's everyday experiences and will therefore require constant mediation and adjustment. It follows from this that sector boundaries are also far from straightforward. A body of 'boundary theory' within organizational studies and geography suggests that boundaries are 'highly-charged' sites where differences meet. Exchanges between people at boundaries may generate friction, creating conditions for both conflict and creativity (Halley, 1998).

Sector boundaries are therefore rarely clear or stable, and require frequent maintenance. Sector boundaries are also permeable since they are transcended by the activities of individuals who operate across them either through professional career transitions or through informal personal relationships. The boundary between the third sector and the public sector is both 'real' in the sense that it is governed by specific rules and 'perceived' in the sense that people carry with them a set of assumptions and expectations – both accurate and imagined – about how things should operate in each sector. Even while there may be a blurring of organizations and relationships 'on the ground', many people still tend to associate specific characteristics with particular sectors, and continue to seek these out and reproduce them. This is part of the paradox of hybridization; although sector realities may become hybridized, ideas about sector continue to carry important meanings.

## Sectors

The concept of 'sector' has meaning at three different but inter-related levels. First is the ideal model of sector, used by policy makers and understood by the general public, and which is both underpinned and critiqued by academics. This level has its origins in a theoretical model which has helped to guide the work of social science researchers (Etzioni, 1973; Billis, 1993; Lewis, 2007). The ideal model has also become important as an idea that helps policy makers to develop policies in which, for example, the comparative advantages of the three different kinds of organizations can be put to work within public–private 'partnerships' (Evans, 1996; Kendall, 2003). Second, as Billis (this volume) argues, is the level at which organizations actually match to varying degrees the ideal model and the way they appeal to the core characteristics of the sector as a means of securing legitimacy. Third, the model operates at the level of the experiences of individuals who may find that the first level conflicts with the second. This is of particular relevance to the issue of sector boundary crossers, who are forced to try to deal with and manage this tension, and in doing so may contribute to shaping hybridity in organizations.

Despite evidence that the idea of the 'third sector' may be losing coherence, many of the people who choose to work in it continue to identify with it a certain set of characteristics – such as attitudes, organisational culture and values. For example, Cornforth and Hooker (1990: p. 12) have suggested that different management styles are found within each of the three sectors. They argue that a distinctive set of values which 'influence and shape how managers manage' contributes to the existence of a set of 'superordinate' goals among staff within third sector organizations. These tend to be related to underlying principles of equality and justice and may, in turn, be informed by a wide range of political or religious ideologies. These ideas help people to plan and shape their careers, including the decision to enter or to leave the sector. People try to find organizations within the third sector which allow them to put certain principles into practice and, once there, they attempt to build solidaristic working relationships with others with whom they hope to share similar ideas and approaches. They may become disappointed when those expectations are unmet, they may change organizations within the sector or they may even decide to 'cross over' into another sector. Despite hybridization, these ideas still carry important meanings at the individual level.

## Boundaries

The operation of the 'boundaries' between sectors also reflects the messiness of the fit between sector ideas and real life. They are rarely clear-cut and they are ambiguous. This ambiguity can generate anxiety about the political cooption of activists or critics, or about creeping government influence, as long-running UK public concerns about the proliferation of quasi-governmental organizations (Quangos) indicate. But ambiguous sector boundaries have sometimes also been associated with far more positive outcomes. In her influential study of development and policy change in Northeast Brazil, Tendler (1997: p. 146) observed that, while 'the assumed clear boundary between government and non-government is actually quite blurred', the shifts of key personnel between sectors were an important factor in improving health services.

From the life history data, it became clear that, for many individuals, boundary crossing is a dynamic act that may

unlock or generate change at various levels. When individuals
cross over the boundary, they are forced to engage in a process of 'sense-making' within a new work setting. Whether this
process is felt to be 'positive' or 'negative', it is likely to bring
about a change of perspective. This can be observed on one or
more of three levels. First, there may be a changed perspective
on *sector*, such as a more negative view of the third sector from
a new vantage point within government. Second, there may
be the acquisition of new learning or knowledge which can
be deployed in new *organizational* settings, such as the idea
that elements of the policy process operate in different ways
than was previously assumed. Third, there may be a changed
or reinforced *individual* work identity, as in the case of a person who crossed over and had a disappointing experience in
government, a discovery of the fact that the third sector was
where a person really 'belonged'.

For some 'successful' boundary crossers, work on the other
side of the boundary offers solutions to problems or discomfort that they might have been experiencing. For example,
the discipline and organization of the public sector is sometimes contrasted with the lack of order or consistency found
in the third sector. For less successful or unsuccessful boundary crossers, a dislike of the new organizational environment
(such as the rigid roles and rules in the public sector, or the
need to follow a political line regardless of personal values)
may simply confirm their identity as a person most comfortable with the values and organizational culture of the third
sector.

## Levels and meanings of boundary crossing

Boundary crossers provide a unique source of comparison
between the sectors, since their distinctive trajectories offer
insights into the way the sector boundary is experienced, and
into the way that hybridities are shaped. Boundary crossing can
be seen as a form of what organization theorists call 'work role
transition' (Nicholson, 1984). In such transitions, a person
must try to make sense of their new environment and adjust,
either by changing it via 'role development', or by altering their

own values and identity in order to *absorb* change as 'personal development'.

Wrzesniewski and Durron's (2001) concept of 'job crafting' is a useful way of analysing how a person actively seeks to build a new work role by drawing on previous experience and on the resources that they find in the new context. People engage in a process of 'organizational role taking', in which a previous role becomes 'unlearned' and a new one is produced by synthesising from the available palette of organizational, personal and inter-personal resources encountered within the new context (Austin, 1989). Role taking may be significant for both individuals and their organizations, and may constitute a major 'turning point' in a person's professional life.

There are usually two different *types* of cross-over roles the 'crosser' and the 'spanner'. The career of the 'crosser' involves one or more sequential sector shifts, which one can visualise as a kind of vertical zigzag pattern across the sector boundary. By contrast, the trajectory of the 'spanner' is better expressed as a horizontal 'presence' across more than one sector at any one time. Here, a person transcends a boundary by simultaneously being active in both sectors (as in the case of a person who works in the public sector but who also sits on the board of a third sector organization). In such cases, the two roles may not be entirely distinct but may reinforce each other. For example, a person may take a new job in a different sector but still interact and do business with former sector colleagues.

In the UK, there has long been some cross-over in both directions, but the movement of third sector people into government has grown more common since the New Labour government came to power in 1997. This may be part of a 'big tent' inclusive policy-making process to stimulate new thinking on key social policy issues. People may be involved initially on secondment but some of them later opt to stay on (such as Louise Casey from Shelter moving to government to work on homelessness). Alternatively, involvement may be part of a specialised recruitment of people with appropriate expertise and experience (such as the Department for International Development's [DFID] expansion of work in conflict and humanitarian zones, which has attracted people from NGOs into new DFID adviser posts).

Such people are of course still far from typical (the study has not tried to quantify cross-over trends) but it was not difficult to find people who had direct experience of cross over in both the third sector (including both its domestic and the international development sub-sectors) and in government departments such as the Home Office, the Office of the Deputy Prime Minister, the Treasury and DFID, as well as in local government.

## Importing ideas and people between the sectors

Sector boundary crossers embody, at the individual level, elements of the bigger picture of sector hybridity and blurring. A detailed analysis of key themes within their career trajectories can tell us more about the shifting landscape of the third sector in terms of the experiences they encounter; the expectations they carry; and the hybrid organizational environments which they help to create. Five such themes have been identified here from the life histories.

### Creativity

Creativity, whether in relation to improving organization performance or to everyday problem-solving, is part of the lifeblood of any organization. While it is perfectly possible for it to be fostered within 'pure' forms of organization, an important contribution can be made by boundary crossers. The data suggests that there may be a link between innovation and the collision of ideas and practices which may occur when a person carries ideas from one sector into another. Sector boundary crossing may prompt the production or application of new knowledge, such as in relation to the management of information. A common complaint among long-term third sector staff is a routine lack of efficiency in this area. This may become more visible from a vantage point outside the third sector, and a person may then attempt to remedy the problem when they eventually cross back by bringing in new more effective methods of reporting or documentation learned from inside government.

Innovation can also be explored within a third sector setting and then later transferred to the public sector. One boundary crosser had spent the first part of his life working with policy units in several local authorities from the 1970s onwards, where he had been engaged in a range of innovative projects with local community groups. When made a sector shift into a Chief Executive position in a health and disability charity during the 1990s, he was able to draw on a range of lessons and experiences from this public sector work to innovate successfully within the voluntary organization. With staff and service users in his organization, he developed new and improved approaches to take care of the more fully empowered patients. These innovative ideas also eventually began to find their way back into the public sector, and were taken up by government:

> We also developed a lot of user-led services, including a self-management programme for which the basic concept was people with [chronic conditions]...learning to manage [these] themselves through exercise and relaxation and better communication with their doctors...We got contracts with local authorities and health authorities and the whole initiative became quite influential, and then it led the Department of Health to set up something called the Expert Patients' Task Force which was based on the principle that people who've got long-term conditions like arthritis and asthma and diabetes...are in a sense the experts in the condition...So it felt like quite an achievement that something that [we] pioneered became part of NHS thinking...

Here, an idea that had been developed within the third sector had been carried over by a boundary crosser and successfully 'transplanted' within the public sector.

## Learning

Organizational learning is another process which may be stimulated by boundary crossing. It may lead to the challenging of 'normal' expectations and received wisdoms through experiencing work within unfamiliar environments. One informant was seconded from an NGO, where he had been active in policy advocacy work, into DFID. He was struck by the inaccuracy of much of the 'policy knowledge' he and his organization had previously been working with, once he had gained access to these processes 'from the inside'. For example, he found that the amount of time and effort that his and other organizations had been putting into lobbying at international trade talks now appeared disproportionate or misplaced. From a new vantage point within government, he saw more clearly that key decisions were in fact being taken earlier in the process, and that such public meetings offered little or no chance of success for third sector lobbying. Armed with this knowledge, he was able on his return to the third sector to begin a process of rethinking advocacy strategy. The shock of finding that the 'policy process' worked very differently than that assumed within the third sector was an important and ultimately creative moment both for himself and the organization that he went on to work for.

Similarly, people who cross over into the third sector from government may bring in new, or more accurate, technical knowledge about the way government works and how things can be achieved within its decision-making processes. Although many voluntary sector organizations claim to be trying to influence these processes, they are sometimes surprisingly unaware of details. A former government insider is in a good position to bring in more up-to-date or accurate knowledge. One informant, who had a long and successful career as a senior civil servant, moved into the third sector 3 years ago to run a leading UK national charity:

[From working in government]...you know how government works...my knowledge of Whitehall has allowed us to become much more influential in terms of changing government...For example, some charities get very excited about 'early day motions' [in Parliament]...I can't tell you how much they are seen as a joke in government!...I think some charities have now woken up to the fact that government is a complex place, and that you need someone with Whitehall savvy...

As Leat (1995) reported in her work on business managers working within the third sector, inaccurate or stereotyped views of sector values or practices may be common. Crossing over may usefully challenge such stereotypes (conversely, when a person has an unsatisfactory cross-over experience, it may also reinforce them).

Another interviewee had made an effort to share new knowledge in a strategic way. He had prepared a detailed set of presentation notes to educate his colleagues on returning to his old third sector organization after an 18-month (and largely unsatisfactory) period of employment in a government agency. Entitled 'Confessions of a civil servant', the presentation aimed to challenge members of the organization and their assumptions about how government worked, both in terms of accessing future funds and influencing policy. Government's emphasis on concise and effective briefings between departments and its 30 minute meeting default time were both useful disciplines which he suggests have improved the performance of the third sector organization where he works.

## Identity formation

We have already seen that the sector operates at the level of ideas and expectations as well as at the level of structures. There have traditionally been many people in the UK who characterised themselves as a 'voluntary sector person' or as 'a public servant through and through', suggesting that the idea of 'sector' is often strongly bound up with a person's personal and/or professional identity and values. These identities may be disrupted by boundary crossing, and may become altered in temporary or lasting ways.

There may be a disillusionment with, or reinforcement of, sector identities when they are viewed and reflected upon from the vantage point of another sector. Some people from the third sector may find a stronger sense of organization and purpose within government and, as a consequence, may gain a 'diminished' view of the third sector. One person found that a spell in government made him feel that many of the development NGOs where he had previously worked lacked the discipline to offer feasible alternatives to government policies:

> [It] had challenged some of my perceptions...because there didn't seem to be an understanding amongst the NGO sector that what they had to propose had to be realistic for government...I still believe that government cannot do things that are completely unrealistic just because I think they are a good idea...

There are also people, however, who do not accept sector-based identities. Instead, a 'role-based identity' is dominant, in which a person's priority is simply to follow the job, either as an activist seeking leverage to bring about change or, at the material level, seeking better pay or conditions. For these people, there is no long-term concept of a 'preferred sector' as a chosen work space or a special loyalty to the idea of 'a particular sector and its values'. One life-work history was taken from a woman, currently a chief executive in a large public sector organization, who had crossed between public and third sectors several times during her career. She described being motivated from an early age by the idea of 'trying to change the world through what you did' and had sought out organizational environments 'that have got the levers to do that at any one time'. Resisting simple generalisations about sector comparative advantage or inherent characteristics, she viewed the strengths and weaknesses of both sectors as being mainly contingent on wider politics and policy.

Finally, sector identities themselves can be highly subjective. One example of this is the case of DFID. For people in the world of development NGOs, DFID is usually (and correctly) seen as an archetypal public sector agency characterised by strict formal rules, rigid hierarchies and the need to follow hard-headed government policy priorities. Yet for civil servants in other sections of UK government such as the Foreign Office or the Treasury, there is a tradition of looking upon DFID rather differently – as an anomalous government agency, NGO-like in what many perceived as its preoccupation with what they saw (incorrectly) as charitable, 'do-gooding' work.

## Skill building

The role of the third sector as a site of skill building is increasingly recognised by government in schemes such as the Workforce Hub funded through the ChangeUp initiative (now Capacitybuilders) that seeks to strengthen human resource capacity. The third sector serves as an important training ground for work in the public sector (and vice versa). One sector creates a reservoir of skilled and motivated people who may then be recruited by organizations in another sector, in a process that contributes to the creation of hybrid organizational environments. Many of today's government and opposition politicians have the third sector as part of their life-work histories. There are an unusually large number of New Labour senior government ministers who have some kind of background in the voluntary sector (including Patricia Hewitt, Tessa Jowell and David Miliband), suggesting that an increasingly important function of the third sector is as a training space for future political leaders, particularly within social welfare. Knowledge about the third sector within government may be higher than in previous administrations because of this direct experience, although there is also plenty of evidence that lack of knowledge and distrust of the sector remain prominent among civil servants.

This increasing level of 'exchange' between the sectors has become an important part of UK public life, although it has probably not yet reached the point at which it blurs the boundaries of individual, private and public interests to such an extent that it raises concerns about 'revolving doors' – which provide privileged access to policy for individuals who operate in both sectors. Instead, it may have a positive effect in providing public sector people with more accurate knowledge about the third sector, and vice versa.

## Informal cross-boundary links

Finally, hybrid organizational environments may be maintained through sets of cross-sector personal linkages and relationships. Some of the life-work histories collected throw light on the ways in which friendships and networks formed in early career persist over time and continue to inform the relationship between third sector and government in less visible ways. One of the most interesting examples of this is the role of what one informant termed 'ex-fams'. These are people who used to work for Oxfam GB, but who now hold posts in government. Such people may play the role of 'boundary spanners', oiling the relationship between government and third sector behind the scenes. For example, when Oxfam needs information about a particular issue from within the Foreign Office or DFID (where many such people are positioned), they can sometimes secure a privileged point of access and invoke some kind of 'sector loyalty'. If they are planning a campaign and wish to explore how it may be received, or identify a possible point of potential influence in the policy process, the advice of such people can be very useful. As Howard and Taylor (Chapter 9 of this volume) report, boundary spanning can also place pressure on such individuals, since they may need to balance competing demands.

Some individuals deliberately position themselves to span boundaries through a 'straddling' strategy and this may also contribute to hybridity. One informant, who combined a very successful public sector career with voluntary work, speaks in her narrative of the value of operating 'on the cusp' of the third sector and the public sector. With extensive experience in a wide range of public sector and third sector organizations, she gained, in her words

> an enormous experience and understanding of both sectors and was therefore able to make a unique contribution...

By refusing to be limited to a single sector for any length of time, she has developed a sophisticated understanding of both sectors, and suggests that this strategy has helped her to influence policy and practice in her field. Power can be derived from operating on the boundary and from facing both ways. Boundary crossing is not therefore only a sequence of movements taking place across the boundary but can also be seen as an accumulation of positions and networks which contribute to work, career and identity.

## Boundary crossing, hybridization and accountability

Sector boundaries, once conceptualised in relatively unam-
biguous terms, are now routinely problematised. At the level
of organizational relationships, we see how there are both tensions and opportunities that open up as the sector boundary
becomes blurred as, for example, Howard and Taylor (Chapter 9 of this volume) describe in their analysis of governance
spaces within government–third sector partnerships.

Such issues need to be analysed within the wider context of
so-called 'new public management' which continues to generate anxiety about the shifting relationships between sectors,
particularly between the public and private sectors. For critics
on the political right, closer relationships across these sectors
are sometimes felt to promote collusion which can reduce efficiency and result in higher levels of public expenditure. For
critics on the left, sector blurring is seen as helping private
interests to gain control of the state and weaken its capacity
to regulate the private sector effectively. Wright (2000: 164)
suggests the following:

> The most general phrase that can be applied to the changes
> in the public sector is 'hybridization'. Rather than having
> clearly defined sectors, most public activities are now deliv-
> ered through mechanisms involving both sectors...In biology
> hybrid species are often thought to be particularly hardy. In
> public administration these species may well be excessively
> hardy, given that they are also more than a little dangerous.
> (p. 164)

What is the source of this danger? Wright argues that hybridization does not merely affect the ways that public services
are delivered, but that it also impacts strongly on the *personnel* who work for government. One major result of this
impact in many societies has been a trend towards 'the end
of public service as an exclusive career, and the increasing
recruitment of outsiders to major posts in the public sector'
(p. 166). This trend towards a movement of people in and out
of government brings certain tensions. These include differences in terms of organizational culture (around, for example,

confidentiality norms, particularly when people leave); unhappiness about internal wage differentials created by the high salaries often negotiated personally by new entrants; and problems resulting from the erosion of institutional memory and continuity by this rise in human traffic.

The other potential danger area is highlighted by boundary crossing centres on the blurring of accountabilities and, in particular, is sometimes referred to as the 'revolving door'. The formal model of sector difference suggests that there is a different principle of accountability operating between public sector bureaucracies and third sector organizations (Billis, this volume). Boundary crossers therefore need to manage their engagement with these different accountability systems and this can make for particularly difficult role transitions. This is one reason why there are often reports of disillusionment, particularly among those crossing from the third sector into government, as reported by Little and Rochester (2003) in their account of a group of mostly disappointed voluntary sector entrants into government agencies. But the possible accountability problem does not end there. Some boundary crossers leave an 'accountability trail' of informal relationships that may continue to operate and which may further blur and perhaps even compromise the lines of accountability. Potential questions of compromised accountability may arise in the case of the boundary crosser who derives power from straddling the boundary between the sectors or in the web of 'ex-fams' that stretches into many different departments of government, often at quite senior levels.

## Conclusion

In this chapter, we have explored two main issues in relation to the broader theme of hybridization in the context of the third sector. First, by studying the experiences of sector boundary crossers, we have gained insights into tensions that exist between the 'ideal model' of the sector and what actually goes on in particular organizations. These tensions are played out within the lives of these boundary crossers, whose activities and changing ideas also contribute to the shaping of hybrid organizations as they go about the task of trying to reconcile sector expectations and sector realities in their everyday lives. Second, at a macro-level, we identify a paradox; even while the hybridization process moves forward, fed in part by the growth of boundary crossing, ideas about sector and boundary continue to play important roles in the ways individuals view organizational landscapes.

Is the idea of 'sector' still a coherent one under these conditions of increasing hybridization? The data on boundary crossers lends support to those researchers who question the sector idea. For example, Evers (1995) advocates the idea of an 'intermediate area' rather than a clear-cut sector, in which hybrid roles and identities are constructed by state, market and household. Deakin (2001: p. 26) warns that an excessive emphasis on 'sector' can unhelpfully draw attention away from important issues of policy content. Yet despite, or perhaps because of, these hybridization processes, our data suggests that the sector concept, and in particular the idea of the boundary between sectors, will continue to play an important role in the ways such individuals confront and manage their work. At the macro-level, the growth of boundary crossing probably does not suggest that the third sector, or ideas about it, is/are likely to disappear. This argument reinforces Abrams' (1981) view that 'the state' – and by extension, we might say, the third sector – operates and is manifested as 'an idea' as well as a set of real-world structures and policies, and supports views of sector that refuse a rigid conception of its boundary. Perhaps paradoxically, 'ideas about sector' remain important in the way that they continue to motivate both those who move and those who stay. The data suggest that the idea of 'sector' – at the level of individuals and their work and careers – remains strong in the ways that it continues to shape people's ideas and expectations, whether these are met or unmet. The argument that 'hybridization' provides an increasingly more appropriate metaphor than 'sector' for understanding change within the third sector in the UK brings useful insights, but is perhaps ultimately contradictory, since there can be no 'hybrid' without 'sector'.

Since 1997, new forms of UK third sector career have emerged that encompass periods spent in both the third and public sectors, as job mobility has increased, and strategies of 'secondment' across different types of organization have become more common. Certain people have built distinctive careers in the fields of UK social service provision, or in international development, which have involved moving across the sector boundary from the third sector into the public sector, or vice versa, sometimes more than once. We have seen that such boundary crossing harbours both opportunities and dangers, for both organizations and for individuals. The opportunities centre on the possibility of promoting creativity, innovation and learning within organizations. At the individual level, some boundary crossers may even experience a form of epiphany that leads them to completely re-evaluate their ideas and perspectives. The dangers lie in the blurring of sector accountabilities, the unsettling of individual expectations and in the missed human resource opportunities when they fail to harness the potential of employees who make unsatisfactory 'role transitions' or fail to 'craft' their jobs successfully.

The data discussed in this chapter allows us to reflect further on the ways that some of the tensions arising from hybridization within the new public management play out at the level of these individuals who cross between the public and third sectors. This is not a subject that has so far received much attention from researchers and, as we might expect, the initial findings that are presented here raise some potentially important further questions. For example, to what extent does boundary crossing predominantly take place between already relatively hybridized organizations, within which there is already common ground? At the level of sector and organization, how far can the potential accountability challenges raised by increased boundary crossing be managed within an increasingly hybridized sector? Finally, what are the conditions under which third sector managers can ensure that boundary crossing leads to creativity rather than disillusionment?

## Note

1. The research was funded by the UK Economic and Social Research Council (ESRC) under its Non-Governmental Public

Action programme (Grant Reference RES-155-25-0064). More details of the comparative findings and the methodology used can be found in Lewis (2008b).

## References

Abrams, P. (1981) 'On the difficulty of studying the state (1977),' *Journal of Historical Sociology*, vol. 1, no. 1, pp. 58–98.

Austin, M. J. (1989) 'Executive entry: Multiple perspectives on the process of muddling through', *Administrative Leadership in the Social Sciences*, vol. 13, no. 4, pp. 55–71.

Billis, D. (1993) *Organising Public and Voluntary Agencies*, London: Routledge.

Cornforth, C. and Hooker, C. (1990) 'Conceptions of management in voluntary and nonprofit organizations: Values, structure and management style'. *Towards the 21st Century: Challenges for the Voluntary Sector. Proceedings of the 1990 Conference of the Association of Voluntary Action Scholars.* Vol. 1. London: Centre for Voluntary Organization. London School of Economics and Political Science.

Deakin, N. (2001) *In Search of Civil Society*, Basingstoke: Palgrave.

Etzioni, A. (1961) *A Comparative Analysis of Complex Organizations: On Power, Involvement and their Correlates*, New York: The Free Press of Glencoe.

Etzioni, A. (1973) 'The third sector and domestic missions', *Public Administration Review*, July/August, pp. 314–327.

Evers, A. (1995) 'Part of the welfare mix: The third sector as an intermediate area', *Voluntas*, vol. 6, no. 2, pp. 159–182.

Halley, A. A. (1998) 'Applications of boundary theory to the concept of service integration in the human services', *Administration in Social Work*, vol. 21, no. 3/4, pp. 145–168.

Hatch, M. J. (1997) *Organization Theory: Modern, Symbolic and Postmodern Perspectives*, Oxford: Oxford University Press.

Kendall, J. (2003) *The Voluntary Sector*, London: Routledge.

Leat, D. (1995) *Challenging Management: An Exploratory Study of Perceptions of Managers Who Have Moved from For-Profit to Voluntary Organizations.* Centre for Voluntary Sector and Not-for-Profit Management (VOLPROF), London: City University Business School.

Lewis, D. (2007) *The Management of Non-Governmental Development Organisations.* 2nd edition, London: Routledge.

Lewis, D. (2008a) 'Crossing the boundaries between 'third sector' and state: Life-work histories from Philippines, Bangladesh and the UK,' *Third World Quarterly*, vol. 29, no. 1, pp. 125–142.

Lewis, D. (2008b) 'Using life-work histories in social policy research: The case of third sector/public sector boundary crossing', *Journal of Social Policy*, vol. 37, no. 4, pp. 559–578.

Little, A. and Rochester, C. (2003) 'Crossing the great divide'. Paper presented at the 32nd Annual Conference of the Association for Research on the Nonprofit Organization and Voluntary Action (ARNOVA), Denver, Colorado, 20–22 November.

Nicholson, N. (1984) 'A theory of work role transitions', *Administrative Science Quarterly*, vol. 29, no. 2, pp. 172–191.

Tendler, J. (1997) *Good Governance in the Tropics*, Baltimore: Johns Hopkins University Press.

Wright, V. (2000) 'Blurring the public–private divide', in Peters, B. Guy and Donald J. Savoie (eds) *Governance in the Twenty-first Century: Revitalizing the Public Service*, Montreal: McGill-Queens University Press.

Wrzesniewski, A. and Jane E. Durron (2001) 'Crafting a job: Revisioning employees as active crafters of their work', *Academy of Management: The Academy of Management Review*, vol. 26, no. 2, pp. 179–201.

# 12 Revisiting the key challenges: Hybridity, ownership and change

## David Billis

This final chapter returns to the key challenges posed in Chapter 1 and, in particular, the issues surrounding hybridity, ownership and change. I address these questions in the light of the material presented by my colleagues in which they discuss how different kinds of TSOs have engaged with the distinctive challenges posed by hybridity. Overall, the approach is to explore what might be learnt and what remains to be learnt from these studies.

In order to achieve the objective of improving our understanding of current issues, the opening section builds a typology of categories of hybrid TSOs. This framework builds on concepts presented earlier in the book utilising case study material, and explores the challenge of mission and identity. The second section employs the typology in order to speculate about the possible implications for ownership and accountability. Both these sections discuss aspects of change in hybrid TSOs, but section three goes beyond this and looks more broadly at these aspects in relation to the sector as a whole.

The final, fourth, section is more speculative and offers my personal reflections on the implications of the study for a practice, policy and research. Although I have drawn on important elements of my colleagues' studies, I cannot fully do justice to the depth of analysis and rich agenda of potential research that flows from their detailed explorations.

## Providing a framework for understanding current issues

The studies for this book were chosen in order to provide a good range of examples for the study of the role of hybrid

TSOs and the challenges they face. At that stage, the most appropriate organizing principle was a sense that the chapters might eventually prove, in very broad terms, to move from a shallow to a more entrenched sort of hybrid.

The concepts of 'shallow' and 'entrenched', 'organic' and 'enacted' were offered in Chapter 3. In this section, I have constructed a typology of hybrid categories and examined its plausibility by utilising key findings from the studies. An important test will be whether those findings suggest that the different categories demonstrate significantly different situations with regard to the fundamental challenges of identity and mission. After all, as Minkoff and Powell remind us, mission, 'is a clarion call for nonprofit organizations and the goals or agendas attached to a mission serve to rally, engage, and enroll workers, volunteers, and donors' (Minkoff and Powell, 2006, p. 591).

The broader objective is to contribute to an improved understanding of ownership and accountability in hybrid TSOs and the alternative 'optimistic' and 'pessimistic' scenarios for change discussed in Chapter 1.

The typology is presented in Table 12.1.

## Organic forms of hybridity

### (a) The organic shallow

Most organic hybrid TSOs have small numbers of paid staff, are locally based and will have significant volunteer participation in their work. There is likely to be a high degree of overlap in the roles of governing bodies, operational

**Table 12.1**  Categories of hybrid TSOs

| State \ Type | Organic | Enacted |
|---|---|---|
| Shallow | (a) Organic Shallow | (c) Enacted Shallow |
| Entrenched | (b) Organic Entrenched | (d) Enacted Entrenched |

workers, volunteers, members and supporters of various kinds (Rochester, 1999).

The opening case studies take us into this territory of organic shallow hybridity. Thus, Angela Ellis Paine, Nick Ockenden and Joanna Stewart suggest that whereas in pure associations volunteers represent both 'the beginning and the end of the organization', in shallow hybrids they become 'both a means and an end'. They extend their analysis to demonstrate how the concepts of 'shallow' and 'entrenched' might have broader explanatory utility with respect to volunteering.

Colin Rochester and Malcolm Torry analyse three kinds of organizational arrangements arising from the contribution of congregations to social welfare. The first two describe how individuals and groups come together as a result of relationships formed within the congregation. If activities become more extensive, a third type of arrangement may be enacted as shallow hybrids that have their own separate existence and constitutional identity. The authors suggest that it is 'non-negotiable theological principles' which act as a 'significant barrier' to the hybridization of these local organizations.

The study of community anchor organizations in Chapter 7 demonstrates how some organizations working with children and young people had followed government policy and had consequently needed to employ more paid staff which, in turn, had reduced parental involvement and eroded some of the distinctive character of their informal childcare provision. More broadly, Romayne Hutchison and Ben Cairns conclude that many community anchor organizations 'are coming adrift from their moorings'. There are numerous examples of what sometimes appears (to the participants) to be an almost inevitable slide away from core mission towards public service provision.

One of the three case studies by Mike Aiken – Daily Bread – is also considered to be a shallow hybrid TSO in which high growth is not seen as a central aim. Here co-operative principles and values are seen to drive mission and action.

### (b) The organic entrenched

This type of organization is likely to have grown steadily through the infusion of resources from public contracts and commercial initiatives. It will have a multi-level hierarchy of paid staff, probably highly dependent on these external sources of revenue, with senior staff playing a significant role as principal owners.

The 'decoupled' trading subsidiaries established by charities, discussed by Chris Cornforth and Roger Spear in Chapter 4, are apparently created by the third sector and could possibly be treated as enacted hybrids. The dilemma is that these new organizations seemingly still remain owned and dominated by their parent charity. Therefore, despite their legal identity, and in the absence of the further research called for by the authors, I will temporarily park them in this category and regard them as entrenched TSOs in disguise. A key message emerging from Cornforth and Spear's exploratory research is tension between the social and business principles.

The discussion on volunteering and hybridity by Ellis Paine and colleagues warns of the complexity of the analysis but tentatively proposes that in entrenched hybrids the balance of power has shifted entirely towards paid staff. In these organizations, volunteers (except trustees) are treated as resources and as a means to an end and the move into deeper hybridity results in a situation in which volunteering feels like an instrument of delivery rather than a force for change.

In fact in the study of a broad spectrum of community-based organizations Hutchison and Cairns illustrate not only the move into shallow hybridity, but also the further step into an organic entrenched state. In their discussion section, they cover the pressures and tensions of accepting funding which is more readily available for activities which adhere to governmental priorities. They conclude that some of these organizations that are 'finding it increasingly difficult to resist pressures to be deflected away from their primary focus . . . can be described as entrenched hybrids'.

### Enacted forms of hybrids

These are established from the outset as hybrids, usually by several organizations and often with government as a sponsor or partner.

## (c) The enacted shallow

The two case studies – of the Centre and the Trust – by Joanna Howard and Marilyn Taylor provide rich data about both the tensions and the possible advantages of enacted hybrids. These may be regarded as shallow types since they were not provided with their own independent resources required to establish organizational structures that could sustain and develop future longer-term activities. Both also, as the authors suggest, may be regarded as transitional and, in the case of the Centre, ended in its demise. The studies also demonstrate that if the possible positive aspects of hybridity are to triumph, then, as they put it, 'this is likely to depend on commitment from all sides to a clear vision for the organization and a clear overall structure'. The Centre eventually 'collapsed under the weight of conflicting expectations and commitments'.

## (d) The enacted entrenched

In contrast to the shallow form, the enacted entrenched hybrid is set up with immediate substantial (usually governmental) resources and considerable (and possibly overwhelming) external influence on governance and mission.

The problems presented by enacted entrenched hybrids are first encountered by Cornforth and Spear in their discussion of public sector 'spin-offs'. They are entrenched – at least in their foundation – since the enactment is accompanied by the fundamental resources to continue running the organization and also by what are described as 'multi-stakeholder' boards. In their exploratory research they identify fundamental problems of organizational identity caused by 'delegate syndrome', where board members represent the interests of their particular stakeholder group rather than the organization as a whole.

Enacted entrenched hybrids are also encountered in Mike Aiken's studies of social enterprises. Bolton Wise, established by the local authority which seconded its staff, receives most of its resources from contracts with the public sector, has a strong public sector representation on its board and is identified as a public/third sector hybrid. Tomorrow's People was founded by a private sector company, has no volunteers, retains close connections to the private sector in its governance

DAVID BILLIS **245**

arrangements and, although a charity, is seen as having prime
accountability to the private sector with strong elements of
public and third sector hybridity. As the author notes, legal
identity, whilst important, is insufficient to define their sector
identity.

The historical and current analysis of housing associations
by David Mullins and Hal Pawson appears to cover all the
organizational types in Figure 12.1. Coming from different organizational roots, some have moved organically from
shallow to entrenched hybridity, while some, as a result of
the Housing Act of 1974, may have been shallow enacted
hybrids. Finally, there are the stock transfer housing associations with entrenched hybridity (particularly with the public
sector) firmly enacted into governance and operations. The
authors spell out the chronic and painful history of unease
about sector identity and draw on the experience of Dutch
housing associations to demonstrate that this problem of
identity is not solely an English phenomenon.

### Analysis: Mission and identity in the different categories

The preceding analysis appears to provide preliminary support
for the utility of the typology in that organizations in each of
these categories experience problems of varying severity with
respect to the critical area of mission and identity.

With regard to the *organic categories*, the main message that
emerges from the examples of shallow hybrids is the significance of the presence of a strong and pervasive mission as
a countervailing force against any possible tendency towards
dilution of core principles. There are at least hints that the
first incursions of externally funded paid staff can begin to
change the nature of original missions. When considering the
entrenched hybrids, the hints about mission drift become a
propensity, although not an inevitability. This is illustrated in
the studies in a number of ways, from the impact on volunteers
through to the pressures associated with accepting funding in
line with government policies.

With regard to the *enacted categories*, there is an overwhelming impression of much more severe problems. Indeed
the nature of these problems appears to take us much closer

to the boundary of the third sector. It is not just a question of the degree of hybridity and mission drift *within* the sector. The problem for both shallow and entrenched categories is lack of clarity about their fundamental sector identity. A tentative proposition might be that the role of individuals, particularly what Marilyn Howard and Joanna Taylor in Chapter 9 call 'boundary spanners', is critical in the clarification and development of resources and identity in the early years. For the entrenched category, it seems that confusion over identity might be a chronic fact of life.

## The challenge of ownership and accountability

This section builds on the typology of hybrid categories (Table 12.1) and, again, draws on the case studies to examine the issue of ownership and accountability raised in most of them.

According to the ideal models of the three sectors presented in Chapter 3, accountability should not be problematic. In this organizational approach, it may be seen as a chain which, in its simplest form, cascades from the owners, governing bodies (concerned with mission, legitimacy and survival) (Hager et al., 1999), and is sturdily linked to the operational chains of accountability. In fact, as a vast body of literature and our daily newspapers attest, accountability has long been the perennial problem of organizational life in the public and private sectors. And, as Chapter 4 demonstrates, 'even' developing successful governance systems (the top links in the chain) have proved far from easy. One of the main reasons for problems has been identified as the 'principal–agent' dilemma: the difficulty of getting the employees (agents) to act in the best interests of the principal (the employer).[1]

In theory, the maintenance of the accountability chain in the archetypal association should not be a significant issue since governance and operations are all 'owned' and integrated by the same mission-driven group. In practice, as David Lewis discusses in the previous chapter 'the everyday realities of life within third sector organizations are complex and messy'.

*The organic categories*

## (a) The organic shallow

The case of Daily Bread, described by Aiken, exhibits many of the archetypal characteristics since the members of the co-operative are simultaneously owners, managers and staff. Operating in the market, it is certainly a hybrid. But it attempts to ensure the maintenance of the integrated ownership role by the selection of new members on the basis of their adherence to the principle of co-operative action. Paine, Ockenden and Stuart demonstrate how with the arrival of the first paid staff, differentiation begins in the ownership role. Although the views of volunteers are generally taken seriously, they are no longer positioned as owners but as *members*, and are not the ultimate power holders.

The organizational vignettes of faith-based organizations by Rochester and Torry also point to some fragmentation of ownership in shallow hybrids. External funders can slip into the role of 'ghosts' at the ownership table, implicitly recognised as having substantial influence. However, ownership domination by congregational or other religious owners helps to ensure the seamlessness of the accountability chain upwards between owners and the need for legitimacy. The position at the shallow end was contrasted with the case of the Carr-Gomm Society which relies on government funding and has large numbers of paid staff and was seen to fit the description of an entrenched hybrid. Rochester and Torry suggest that the legal owners of the organization (the trustees) are now recruited for their expertise rather than for their Christian faith. This appears to be widespread trend in the sector (see Chapter 4) and suggests a possible further fragmentation of the previously integrated ownership role.

## (b) The organic entrenched

Here, the process of differentiation of the principal ownership role continues. Thus volunteers in service delivery roles are no longer seen as members (as in the shallow hybrid). Now, as Ellis Paine and her colleagues describe, they appear to move out of all the real decision-making categories of member/owners and become resources to serve organizational ends. Cornforth and Spear reach a similar conclusion about membership as a whole which, in these sorts of organizations, is treated as 'primarily a source of funding and support rather than a mechanism for control and accountability'. They suggest that in the smaller organizations, board members are often active in operational work and that there is a struggle to redefine the role of boards of management when a hierarchy of paid staff is established.

Community anchor organizations (Hutchison and Cairns) cover both shallow and entrenched hybrids. However, increased adherence to governmental priorities and the more ready availability of government funding is shifting the focus of accountability away from the local community. The authors conclude that the result is the expansion of the group of principal owners and the risk of 'diffusing the responsibility for the organization's strategy and sustainability'.

The study by Mullins and Pawson provides clues as to what might happen when this 'risk' of diffusion of ownership is left unattended. In their discussion on governance, they track how housing associations have become dominated by the large bureaucratic 'premier league' organizations and have in the main moved away from any traditional service sector roots in terms of philanthropy or volunteer involvement, other than on the board.

### The enacted categories (see Table 12.1)

#### (c) The enacted shallow

The two studies of enacted shallow hybrids (the Centre and Trust) by Howard and Taylor offer salutary warnings about the nature of this category of hybrid organization. The ownership of the Centre in particular appears unclear from the start, comprising a board drawn from a disparate group. First, these 'owners' come from different sectors and in both Centre and Trust there was evidence of key players continuing to operate according to the rules and operating cultures of the organizations they originally came from. Second, the chain of accountability was broken in the middle, since the management accountability of staff was never clarified, and the Director of the Centre was 'unable to act when problems arose'. The Centre of course closed.

The Trust has done rather better. Despite strained relations with the Council, the principal owners appear to have achieved agreement over the aims and objectives of the organization. A key factor here seems to have been the good relationship between the chair and the director. This relationship, certainly in nonprofits (Herman and Tulipana, 1985) and probably elsewhere, represents the essential link in the chain of account-ability, spanning the mission-shaping role of the principal owners and its transformation into operational activities.

### (d) The enacted entrenched

This category – unlike the shallow type – is established with a longer-term perspective and more substantial resources.

Both Bolton Wise and Tomorrow's People Trust discussed by Aiken were founded with substantial initial support respec-tively from local government and the private sector. As noted earlier, there were difficulties of establishing sector identity and ownership. Going one step further, we can observe that the government-sponsored organization was created with poten-tial built-in confusion. The legal board consists of represen-tatives from all three sectors accustomed to working within different rules of the game and giving rise to the sort of problems identified by Cornforth and Spear.

Problems in the chain of accountability are apparent in more chronic and large-scale fashion in the analysis of social housing by Mullins and Pawson which has grown rapidly since 1980 with the transfer to TSOs of the ownership of council-constructed homes. In common with many other government-sponsored initiatives, the legal ownership consists of boards from different constituencies. Observing the entire range of large housing associations, the authors note the large influx of paid non-executive directors and the appointment of more executive directors to the board. Both in England and the Netherlands, the principal owners are now seen as the paid staff.

*Analysis: Ownership and accountability*

### The organic categories

In the shallow hybrids it seems that the composition of the ownership group begins to change. The appointment of paid staff, particularly in operational roles, can change the principal ownership group. They may themselves be embraced as part of that group, and others, such as volunteer service workers, may drift away from the group. The first link in the accountability chain loses a certain amount of clarity which, the studies suggest, can be restored with some energetic value-driven polishing.

In entrenched organic hybrids the existence of hierarchical levels of staff appears to lead to the need to redefine the relationship between the governance/ownership role and management. The growth in scale and diversity of resources, and the rise of operational hierarchies increase the complexity of decision-making for governing bodies. Specialist skills may take precedence over deep commitment as a prerequisite for recruits to the governing body. Volunteers and members can move further away from centre stage. The principal owners can become more difficult to identify. In an extreme situation mission confusion can threaten the case for wider legitimacy. The first link in the accountability chain can look confused and tarnished. At the same time, the distance between governance and ownership bodies and paid staff increases. The potential looms, not only of confusion in the accountability chain, but also of a potential gap which is likely to be filled, as we saw in the case of housing associations, by the senior paid staff.

### The enacted categories

Turning first to the shallow category, the nature of their birth seems to present enormous difficulties. In addition to the 'liability of newness' (Stinchcombe, 1965), there is evidence of uncertainty throughout the chain of accountability. It starts at the top where, particularly if sponsored by government, it is often expected to have a multi-sector legal governing body whose participants are accustomed to working within different sector rules of the game. It can become more difficult to identify (ghostly) principal owners and the odds appear to be stacked against the possibility of developing a coherent mission. Even if the principal owners agree the general direction for the organization, they need time and resources to be perceived as 'important and relevant' and to develop their roots and legitimacy. Not surprisingly much might depend on personalities and especially the relationship between the chair and chief executive.

Entrenched enacted hybrids, if they are expected as in the case of housing transfer associations to have a multistakeholder legal governing body, have a similar problem of lack of clarity in the top link of the accountability chain. However, with their substantial resources, their problems are rather different. Some form of survival might be more guaranteed, but the absence of a clearly identifiable and explicit principal ownership group creates a long-term gap in the accountability chain which, not surprisingly, has been filled by the staff.

The unanswered questions that remain regarding the nature of the particular mission that those staff – who could 'even steer the organization in a new direction' – are the following: in whose interests and according to what principles?

We move now to a third major theme of this chapter and book. What insights have emerged with regard to the optimistic–pessimistic scenarios for the third sector?

## Understanding changes in the role of the sector

What has also become clearer from the studies is a realisation that the debate about any possible 'Faustian pact' in which the sector loses its distinctive characteristics in return for private and public sector resources is one aspect of a more complex phenomenon of the changing role of the third sector. A first attempt at examining the broad processes of change reveals a number of possibilities. In the main, I have described these from the standpoint of the third sector, although they could equally well be analysed from the perspective of the public and private sectors. Some possibilities are:

1. Erosion
2. Emigration
3. Infiltration
4. Revitalisation
5. Conception
6. Termination

*Erosion* of distinctive attributes is often seen as the essence of the third sector dilemma. The pressures towards greater hybridity have been discussed throughout the book. I do not wish to suggest in any way that there is some form of inevitable process. Nevertheless, two states of hybridity and potential erosion of distinctive characteristics (shallow and entrenched) were identified and several studies demonstrated that organizations can indeed slide from one to the other.

There is another situation when the inhabitants of the third sector have – in reality – handed in their passports and become citizens of the public or private sectors. To all intents and purposes, any original distinctive mission, to the extent that it ever existed, has been subjugated to the exigencies of government policy and/or market pressures.

*Emigration* is the reverse process. A typical example is the widespread use of many thousands of volunteers in the NHS who are essentially restricted to the supporting, non-operational tasks and have not dented the fundamental public sector nature of ownership. For the public sector, these therefore represent a modest dilution of its own distinctive sector attributes. For the third sector, on the other hand, this can be seen as a process of emigration, as a gentle bringing in of its distinctive influence, values and characteristics.

*Infiltration* is a more elusive process whereby ideas integral to the principles (the distinctive rules of the game) of other sectors are adopted by the third sector. This is tricky territory.

In the first place, concepts and systems developed in one sector may be sector-free; they may be techniques which most types of organizations could usefully adopt. They may enable the principles to be more efficiently and effectively implemented without discernible impact on them. On the other hand, some innovations proposed in the name of effectiveness, for example the payment of trustees, raise more fundamental questions about the quintessential principles of TSOs.

Secondly, whilst ideas quite evidently move across sector boundaries, we can only speculate quite how this happens and what are the most powerful mechanisms of transfer. The study by David Lewis of 'boundary crossers' provides a valuable reminder of the role of key individuals (as illustrated in the study of the Trust in Chapter 9). He demonstrates how individuals with substantial experience in one sector have made, when moving to an organization in another sector, a significant impact on its problem-solving ability to innovate. This is an important insight, since innovation has always been seen as a characteristic virtue of TSOs.

So, ideas, as it were, are in the organizational air, inhaled by stakeholders and maybe exhaled as proposals for significant change by principal owners.

*Revitalisation* is a process whereby the pool of owners (legal, active and principal) is reviewed and strengthened in the light of organizational needs and mission. Important inhabitants of the pool are those that provide the *raison d'être* of their legitimacy, for example, volunteers both at governance and operational levels (Paine, Ockenden and Stuart).

*Conception* is the process whereby new organizations arise. This may occur through the normal *organic* progression in which an individual or group decides to establish a TSO to meet their own or other people's needs. These formal organizations will usually require a legal identity and some, however modest, structure of accountable roles and some form of public presence.

There is also a process of creation of TSOs which arrives through enactment, in which new organizations are created by other organizations. Often, but not necessarily, the parent is the public sector as in the case of housing transfer associations (Mullins and Pawson). But TSOs themselves can come together, possibly influenced by government, to establish new enacted organizations (Taylor and Howard).

*Termination* sounds, but is not, straightforward as was demonstrated in the collapse of the Centre in Chapter 9. In their aptly named 'tales from the grave', Hager et al. (1999) concluded that none of the organizations they studied 'died in the same way'. Importantly, the participants in their research felt that 'organizational legitimacy was critical... being perceived as unimportant or nonessential was an important factor in their deciding to close down the operation (pp. 67–69). In associations, survival is also seen to be linked to 'the intrinsic value that members attached to the institution itself and the causes it represents' (Wollebaek, 2009, p. 279).

## Concluding thoughts

This brief discussion was not intended to cover the substantial body of literature and research on 'organizational change'. Its more modest objective was to utilise the experiences of the case studies in order to demonstrate that the debate about the future of the third sector needs to be set within a broader and more complex context of a number of processes of change.

Whilst many of them appear to be institutional and possibly susceptible to policy and planning initiatives, others take us into the broader and perhaps more speculative arena of ideas and individual behaviour and actions.

### Reflections: Implications for practice, policy and research

The search to understand the changing landscape of welfare in which third sector organizations operate has never been easy, but the current institutional landscape appears increasingly dominated by haphazard experimentation. A full understanding of welfare institutions is a pipedream, so too is the belief that we could or should fully control them. But somewhere in between the haphazard and the pipedream appears a more feasible and attractive destination for policy and practice. The ideas and studies presented in this book represent an attempt to move towards that destination.

The purpose of this final section is to offer some personal reflections on key themes of relevance for practice, policy and research.

## Practice: Implications for leadership and governance

The various chapters cover matters of strategic concern for governance and the ownership group. Chapter 3 discussed the distinctive principles and elements of the third and other sectors. It presented a model of hybridity based on the principle of prime sector accountability and defined the roles of principal, active and formal owners in TSOs. It also proposed the possible utility of differentiating shallow from entrenched states of hybridity, and organic from shallow types.

Encouraged by the evidence of the studies, this chapter developed a typology of hybrid categories. Two of its sections demonstrated the substantially different and more complex challenges of mission, ownership and accountability that are associated with each category. Together, the earlier concepts and the typology of 'categories' are intended to contribute towards a better understanding of the role of the leadership and its need to understand and control change.

The examination of change acted as a bridge between these more internally focused discussions and wider concerns about the role of the sector. Of course, organizational change and the guardianship of distinctive characteristics are of major concern for the leadership role, but that is only part of the story.

The analysis so far also leads to the possibility of more specific questions that might be raised by those responsible for the future of the individual TSO. For example,

- Who are the principal owners?[2] Are they all playing by the same sector rules of the game?
- Have we clarified what are our real roots and basis of legitimacy?
- Consequently, have we got the appropriate principal and active owners/members to ensure legitimacy, survival and prevention of the dilution of distinctive characteristics?

- If not, what action can be taken?
- Should we, for example, attempt to expand the active ownership group perhaps through the recruitment of new members and volunteers? Should we embark on a process of *revitalisation* (see previous section)?

There are also questions that arise from the relationship between the leadership and the most senior operational decision makers.

- Notwithstanding their different functions, are the most senior staff part of a much broader based mission-driven body of principal and active owners who together make the strategic decisions?
- Or, have staff become the main *de facto* principal owners? If so, in whose interests, and according to what rules of the game, is the TSO operating?

Many of these questions are relevant to both organic and enacted hybrids, although the questions for each category will need fine tuning for each category to reflect its characteristics and challenges as discussed earlier.

There are also more general implications for the governance of hybrid TSOs. Cornforth and Spear note that organizational governance operates within a broader governance framework including regulatory and other requirements. They offer three models of governance: membership association, self-selecting board and a 'mixed' type which combines participants from the membership with others selected on the basis of their expertise. Reflecting on the previous chapters, I suggest that it is this combined type which appears to offer the most promising path for an organization which requires both mission-driven leadership and the expertise required to handle the additional complexities resulting from hybridity.

As far as the broader governance regime is concerned, I can only note in passing that such evidence as we have from our studies indicates that much thought remains to be given as to how that regime, including the law, may come closer to accommodating the new era of hybrid organizations.[3]

## Implications for policy

UK public policy towards the third sector urgently requires further clarity.

First, it requires clarity in order to achieve greater confidence about the real characteristics of the organizations that are receiving public funding. Governments have their own reasons for supporting the third sector, not always without their own policy contradictions, as discussed by Margaret Harris. Undoubtedly there are implicit political considerations, but explicitly their support is usually predicated on a basket of supposed distinctive virtuous characteristics. The trends towards a more critical approach to those alleged virtues may lead to a more forensic look at the organizational characteristics of the sector's inhabitants. The prime accountability approach, the model of hybrid zones (Chapter 3) and the categorisation of hybrids facilitate a more nuanced approach when discussing governmental approaches towards the identification of 'the real third sector' and any expansion and deepening of its role.

Second, these suggestions also help with regard to the vexed and highly topical question of transparent accountability. Blurring of sector identity and the presence of organizations that exist in the shadow of government can be politically appealing. But, what has always been known, and is now painfully obvious, is that this obfuscation comes at a cost, however delayed its impact. Can government identify the accountable owners in the organizations it is supporting? When we turn to the enacted varieties, the limited evidence from our studies and other research (Chew, 2008) together suggests that the enactment of hybrid TSOs should cause alarm bells to ring throughout the offices of public (and third sector) policy makers. Potential confusion regarding ownership and accountability is often built into the foundations. Policy makers might be wise to consider the development of an organizational stress test or audit before sponsoring or enacting new hybrids. This would apply also to third sector leaders establishing trading companies or other forms of multi-level ownership structures.

## Towards a research agenda

The list of questions posed for TSO leaders and public policy represent a potential agenda for research. Certainly, qualitative studies into the nature of strategic decision-making in hybrid organizations and further testing of the robustness of the typology of hybrid categories might prove fruitful entry points into seeking answers to those questions. We might add to the list the need to revisit some of the sector's claimed advantages in the light of the typology. For example, in the previous chapter, Lewis points to the possible advantages of hybrid forms in innovation, an oft-claimed virtue of the sector. Better knowledge of possible associations between the categories of hybridity and innovation, and indeed other virtuous aspects, could make an important contribution to practice and public policy.

There are also implications for the research community itself. At this point, I feel the urgent need to reiterate the speculative nature of my comments in the light of the effervescent and ubiquitous nature of third sector research which is now both international in reach and undertaken by scholars in a growing number of academic disciplines. Even if I concentrate just on the UK during the period of the planning and production of this book, there have been two major initiatives. First, at long last, we now have a Third Sector Research Centre, established towards the end of 2008 with Pete Alcock as its Director. Second, the Voluntary Sector Studies Network (VSSN), which has steadily grown in strength, has launched a new major journal, the *Voluntary Sector Review*. So I am sure that even as I write about particular areas of lacunae, new research papers may be appearing and others in the planning stage. In view of this, I have tried to concentrate rather telegraphically on just three topics which I think are of particular importance and where the absence of systematic research is a long-standing problem. I base these comments on my own scanning of the literature and discussions with the experienced researchers in each of the following three areas.

In any discussion of change there appears to be a large gap. There is an absence of organizational research on one boundary of the third sector: the process of conception and the position of the very small 'not quite' organized groups. They remain, 'under the radar' (NCVO, 2008, 1.3). Despite the current policy and funding focus on welfare delivery, this is a fundamental aspect for the future of the broader role of the sector and deserves more serious attention.

For third sector research, the proposition that there are fundamental rules of the game – principles which draw their legitimacy from the associational model – points to the need for greater interaction between the different foci of third sector research (for example, civil society, social movements, nonprofits, grassroots organizations).

Finally, the phenomenon of organizational hybridity should encourage collaboration and integration across and within current disciplinary boundaries. Certainly third sector and public sector academics (Skelcher, 1998; Sullivan and Skelcher, 2002; Skelcher, 2005) share an interest in hybridity.

### Monstrous hybrid or the way ahead?

In these concluding sentences it seems appropriate to reflect briefly on the optimistic–pessimistic debate. The earlier analysis of change clearly indicates that if we are concerned with the broad and changing contribution of the sector to society, then the debate would need to encompass a more comprehensive range of processes. But even when narrowed down to the sector's contribution to welfare, the dichotomy between large paid staff (threatening dilution of core characteristics and mission) and the smaller, more voluntaristic organizations (preventing that dilution) indicates that the debate still remains too narrow and simplistic.

Both in the UK and the US, welfare hybrids play an increasingly dominant role. Accordingly, this study has attempted to raise the profile of hybrid organizations, and to demonstrate the importance for both policy and practice of understanding them better. Whilst we cannot answer the question posed by the title of this section, the first steps have been taken by presenting some tentative theories and asking relevant questions.

Yet, perhaps there is room for cautious optimism. There appear to be successful hybrids both in the public and private sectors that have managed to answer our question. Some have become national treasures – organizations whose life span is seen to be well beyond the life of any one government and whose contribution to the nation is seen to be uncontroversial and of deep value. Quite how they have succeeded, what if any are their common characteristics and what lessons there are for the broader family of hybrids remain to be researched.

The 'monstrous' hybrids (Fannie Mae and Freddy Mac), allegedly at the root of the current economic disaster, are hardly a good advert for the brand of hybrid organizations. Yet, the response to the disaster has been to establish yet more hybrids in the form of the partially nationalised banks. The case for understanding these forms of organization, their principal ownership, their prime accountability and the nature of their decision-making goes well beyond our study of hybrid TSOs.

## Notes

1. For a discussion of the 'principal'–'agent' gap, see Berle, A. A. and G.C, Means (1932) *Modern Corporation and Private Property*, New York and Chicago: Commerce Clearing House, loose leaf service division of the Corporation Trust Company; Demsetz, H. (1983) 'The Structure of Ownership and the Theory of the Firm', *Journal of Law and Economics*, 26 (2): pp. 375–390. The nature of ownership is discussed in the seminal work by Hansmann, H. (1996) *The Ownership of Enterprise*, Cambridge, Mass.: The Belknapp Press of Harvard University Press. See chapter 12 for an analysis of clubs and other associative organizations.

2. The existence of a group of principal owners usually emerges in change-orientated action-research projects. My own approach has its origins in the methodology developed by Elliott Jacques: see the essay on 'social analysis', in Brown, W. B., and E. Jacques (eds) (1965) *Glacier Project Papers: Some Essays on Organization and Management from the Glacier Project Research*, London: Heinemann.

3. Avner Ben-Ner argues for changes in US nonprofit law which would acknowledge a legal 'member' status in order to improve

the effective operation and governance of nonprofit organization. Ben-Ner, A. (1994) 'Who Benefits from the Nonprofit Sector? Reforming Law and Public Policy Towards Nonprofit Organizations', *The Yale Law Journal*, 104 (3): pp. 731–762.

## References

Ben-Ner, A. (1994) 'Who Benefits from the Nonprofit Sector? Reforming Law and Public Policy Towards Nonprofit Organizations', *The Yale Law Journal*, 104 (3): pp. 731–762.

Berle, A. A. and G. C. Means (1932) *Modern Corporation and Private Property*, New York, Chicago: Commerce Clearing House, Loose leaf service division of the Corporation Trust Company.

Brown, W. B. and E. Jaques (eds) (1965) *Glacier Project Papers: Some Essays on Organization and Management from the Glacier Project Research*, London: Heinemann.

Chew, C. (2008) *Social Enterprises in Disguise? Towards Hybrid Forms of Voluntary and Charitable Organizations in the UK*, 12th Annual Conference of the IRSPM, Brisbane.

Deakin, N. (2001) *In Search of Civil Society*, Basingstoke: Palgrave.

Demsetz, H. (1983) 'The Structure of Ownership and the Theory of the Firm', *Journal of Law and Economics*, 26 (2): pp. 375–390.

Edwards, M. (2004) *Civil Society*, Oxford: Polity Press.

Hager, M., J. Galaskiewicz, W. Bielefeld and J. Pins (1999) 'Tales from the Grave', in H. K. Anheier (ed.), *When Things Go Wrong: Organizational Failures and Breakdowns*, Thousand Oaks: Sage.

Hansmann, H. (1996) *The Ownership of Enterprise*, Cambridge, Mass.: The Belknapp Press of Harvard University Press.

Herman, R. D. and P. F. Tulipana (1985) 'Board-Staff Relations and Perceived Effectiveness in Nonprofit Organizations', *Nonprofit and Voluntary Sector Quarterly*, 14 (4): pp. 48–59.

Minkoff, D. C. and W. W. Powell (2006) 'Nonprofit Mission: Constancy, Responsiveness, or Deflection?', in W. W. Powell and R. Steinberg(eds), *The Nonprofit Sector: A Research Handbook* Second edition, New Haven: Yale University Press.

NCVO (2008) *The UK Civil Society Almanac 2008*, London: NCVO.

Rochester, C. (1999) *Building the Capacity of Small Voluntary Agencies*, London: Centre for Voluntary Organisation, LSE: 51.

Skelcher, C. (1998) *The Appointed State: Quasi-Governmental Organizations and Democracy*, Buckingham: Open University Press.

Skelcher, C. (2005) 'Public–Private Partnerships and Hybridity', in E. Ferlie, L. E. Lynn and C. Pollitt (eds), *The Oxford Handbook of Public Management*, Oxford: Oxford University Press, pp. 347–370.

Stinchcombe, A. L. (1965) 'Social Structure and Organizations', in J. G. March (ed.), *Handbook of Organizations*, Chicago: Rand McNally.

Sullivan, H. and C. Skelcher (2002) *Working Across Boundaries: Collaboration in Public Services*, Basingstoke: Palgrave Macmillan.

Wollebaek, D. (2009) 'Survival in Local Voluntary Associations', *Nonprofit Management and Leadership*, 19 (3): pp. 267–284.

# Index

# 270 INDEX

Southwark and London Diocesan
Housing Association, 128
Spear, R., 18, 32, 70–88, 135, 156–8,
169, 203, 243, 244, 248–9, 256
Speckbacher, G., 50
Spencer, K., 200
staff hierarchies, governance in
organizations with and without,
79–80
see also under governance of hybrid
organizations
Steele, J., 74
Steinberg, R., 21n1
Stewart, J. D., 51
Stinchcombe, A. L., 250
Stone, M. M., 71, 79
Strichman, N., 149
Stryjan, Y., 167
subsidiaries and governance, 82–3
Suchman, M. C., 48
Sullivan, H., 35, 136, 259

Taylor, M., 20, 30, 97, 149, 175–95,
233–4, 244, 246, 248, 253
tenant governorship, 200
Tendler, J., 224
Terrell, P., 6
Thake, S., 135, 154–5
Thane, P., 32
theory of hybrid organizations, 46–65
see also hybrid organization, model
development for hybrid
organizations; model
development for third sector;
ownership
third sector, see individual entries
Third Way ideas, 31
Tomorrow's People Trust Limited,
162–7
Torry, M., 19, 114–31, 242, 247
trading charities, 81–2
ancillary trading, 81
challenges for trustees, 82
non-primary purpose trading, 81
primary purpose trading, 81
Truscott, F., 26
Tschirhart, M., 53, 76
Tulipana, P. F., 249

van Bortel, G., 211
van Daalen, G., 201
Van Til, J., 8, 52

voluntary housing, 203–4
Voluntary Sector Studies Network
(VSSN), 6
volunteers in hybrid organizations,
93–110
experience of volunteering, 101–5
formalising volunteer involvement,
98–101
versus paid staff, 95–8
volunteering and degrees of
hybridity, 105–9

Wadhams, C., 210
Walker, R. M., 202
Wallis, J., 136
Walsham, M., 84
Wamsley, G. L., 48, 50
Warburton, D., 97
Warren, M., 15
Webb, A. L., 6
Weber, M., 48
Weeks, J., 97–8, 104–5
Weisbrod, B. A., 8, 50, 136
Wei-Skillern, J., 34
Wel-Care governance, 127
welfare, faith-based organizations and,
121–3
see also social policy
welfare hybrids, 3–21
Wernet, S. P., 149
Whyte, K. K., 170
Whyte, W. F., 170
Wilcox, S., 208
Wilding, K., 70, 81
Wilson, C., 109
Wistow, G., 6
Wolfenden Committee, 6, 15
Wollebaek, D., 254
Wood, M. M., 79
work integration field, social
enterprises in, 156–8
cases, 158–64
Wright, V., 234
Wrzesniewski, A., 226
Wuthnow, R., 117, 125

Young, D. R., 52
Young, P., 35

Zald, M. N., 48, 50
Zimmeck, M., 94, 99, 100